D1739759

GOLF COURSE DESIGN
-MODERN DAY ISSUES AND EXPERIENCES-

NIGEL B DOUGLAS
GOLF COURSE ARCHITECT

Visit us online at www.authorsonline.co.uk

An AuthorsOnLine Book

Copyright © Authors OnLine Ltd 2004

Text Copyright © Nigel B Douglas 2004

Cover design by Nigel B Douglas ©

All rights reserved. No part of this publication may be reproduced, stored in a
retrieval system, or transmitted in any form or by any means, electronic,
mechanical, photocopy, recording or otherwise, without prior written
permission of the copyright owner. Nor can it be circulated in any form of
binding or cover other than that in which it is published and without similar
condition including this condition being imposed on a subsequent purchaser.

ISBN 0 7552 0125 6

Authors OnLine Ltd
40 Castle Street
Hertford SG14 1HR
England

This book is also available in e-book format, details of which are available at
www.authorsonline.co.uk

Nigel B Douglas is an Internationally active Golf Course Architect with 10 years of design experience, the last 6 of these operating under his own organization. Originally from Australia, he keeps offices in Victoria, Australia and Kuala Lumpur, Malaysia.

He travels widely and is always keen to converse with others who share his design ideals. He can be contacted at www.douglasgolfdesign.com

CKNOWLEDGEMENTS

Writing a book requires sustained effort and sacrifice by many more people than the author alone. I would like to bring to light the main sources of support that I have been lucky enough to have had behind me, and without which I would not have been able to complete this book.

Thanks to Peter Clarke of Grandwinter Resources for graciously facilitating the inclusion of the roads and real estate portions of two very well planned golf/real estate layouts.

To Marcus Mortlock, for your feedback on all construction and maintenance aspects, thank you. Thanks also for providing the expert guiding hand at KGS, in constructing and creating most of the subject matter used for this book. I look forward to working with you in the future.

Thanks to all of the clubs and developers who have entrusted my team and I with the design of their golf courses. Special thanks to the management and committees, both past and present, of the Sarawak Golf Club for your support in our pursuit of a quality golf course. I am confident our goal has been achieved.

Thanks to Anita for sticking by me through thick and thin, and thanks to my parents for assisting me whenever possible, often to your own detriment. You are the epitome of decency and integrity and my greatest wish is to repay you for all you have done for me.

To my two little boys, Louis and Dylan, your smiling faces alone are motivation enough for me to push through any barriers.

Finally, to my wonderful wife Jenny, thank you for your patience as well as making me realise my potential and prompting me to get on with life. It's been a tough few years, but I've enjoyed every minute of it. We're a great team and this book is only a sample of what we can achieve together.

Nigel B Douglas, June 2004

CONTENTS

INTRODUCTION

Golf Course Architecture. For a large proportion of golfers, the mention of this design discipline conjures up many romantic notions. From those of well-schooled gentlemen, discretely and it seems at times, almost secretly working in a complicated art form, to the well-known golf professionals wearing gumboots and gesticulating seriously onsite, its proponents seem to raise as many questions as they answer. It is without doubt an area of golf surrounded by mystique, an area that captures the imagination of a great many people who have an interest in the game.

How do these people come to be? On what basis do they make their design decisions? Can they really visualise all they create? Do they love the game as they publicly state, or do they secretly hate it? Are they sadists who enjoy watching others struggling in the hazards they create? From where do they get their design ideas? What is a good design? Why do we like the design of some courses and dislike others without being able to explain the reason?

Questions such as these, which seem to be asked by a large proportion of golfers, club managers and golf course developers alike, have over a long period of time raised the profile of Golf Course Design and its proponents.

Golf Course Design is a discipline that in many ways has no rules and does not fit well with the mental standards of categorisation by which, in modern day society we must live. There are construction techniques that at best can be called generally accepted guidelines, but as far as design is concerned, there is in effect, no right or wrong.

This does not mean that an 'anything will do' attitude prevails in the design and construction of Golf Courses. On the contrary a good designer will have a very specific set of design ideals that he wishes to set in place on every golf hole, which can be very difficult to convey and achieve against a seemingly vague backdrop of romance and mystique.

Consequently, the possession of a strong set of design ideals alone is not enough. One cannot do everything oneself when it comes to creating or realising such Golf Course Design ideals, however strong they may be. And therefore communication is the key to realising great Golf Course Designs. The great Golf Course Architects of the past were not only creative geniuses, but they all had an ability to communicate their ideals in a way which empowered others to go forth to create & care for the designs that had sprung forth from their mind's eye.

Communication of course takes many forms, from sketches, to plans, to photographs and of course speech and discussion. The best form of communication in this context comes by actually constructing and completing a portion of a golf course, whilst engaging those involved with discussion to clarify the pertinent design issues as they arise. Most of the great designers of yesteryear employed this method, spending extended periods of weeks or even months onsite to set a course of action, leaving only when their proteges were producing what was required.

Nowadays we rarely have the time to do this. We have the benefit of high-speed travel and communication and our input is quite frequent, but rarely for longer than a day or two at a time. In any case, constant and extended periods of onsite input by an Architect, which was common in yesteryear, often does not sit well with modern day construction methodology. We therefore cannot readily employ the benefits of extended, hands-on input and must rely on other methods of communication to achieve the product, which is not always ideal.

As a Golf Course Architect, I personally find I can talk continuously, for hours about any aspect of my design philosophies, to the point where I often come away from an onsite discussion wondering and hoping that my words provided more clarification than confusion regarding the pertinent points relative to any particular design issue.

On occasion, I return to a golf course construction site with my previous visit's discussion and design images still fresh in my mind, only to find that the information I thought was clear had been somewhat misinterpreted. This happens quite regularly in untested construction scenarios. In fact, it happens to some degree every time when dealing with supervisors with whom one does not share a reasonably long working history.

A very detailed set of plans, and adherence to some simple surveying techniques allows us to minimise this effect in most cases. However in order to go to the next level; to turn a good design into a great one, a certain synergy is needed onsite between the designer, the construction manager and the machine operators. In an offsite capacity, the client must also share the same pursuit for quality.

As the old saying goes, 2 heads are better than one, and 3, 4, 5 or more are better than that, providing they are all working in support of one another, pushing each concept and idea to its point of optimum improvement.

The key then, is to instil the relevant background information into the construction personnel, as well as the client and any interested onlookers, be they club committee members, board members, or prospective golfers. The more people are aware of the design ideals and the processes that have been undertaken to achieve them, the easier it becomes for them to be realised. If an ever increasing wave of enthusiasm can be made to encapsulate a golf design and construction project, in an environment without egos and personal issues, where everyone is focused on the best interests of the game of golf and the piece of land which will be borrowed for its playing, then a truly great design will be free to evolve.

The question then, is how to create such an environment, where all involved feel absolute pleasure and humble privilege just to be a part of the process? The key has to be in education, and then more specifically, gathering a group of people who share the same, pure ideals for the game, and for life itself.

Most people have the best intentions in this regard. Indeed, passion is never in short supply in the Committee & Membership of a Golf Club. Unfortunately however, this passion is rarely all encompassing, and usually does not extend to every small facet of the design, construction and upkeep of a golf course. This can invariably cause much in-fighting at Golf Clubs, which inevitably leads to division, with everybody's action becoming diluted, and ultimately ineffective. This can be likened to a medieval witch-hunt, where temporary heroes, villains, scapegoats, and internal factions cause all manner of strife, which ultimately benefits no person, and definitely has a negative impact on the game and its playing fields.

What is required is a bridge, creating an ability, a reason or a way for everybody to appreciate their small differences and use them for the *benefit* of their Golf Course, such as the best designers employ a multitude of subtle variations to make each design solution unique.

Differences of opinion are to be treasured. In Golf Course Design there is no right or wrong, only differences in treatment of any given problem. A good designer is forever in search of new ideas, images and experiences, which he can tuck away for future use whenever suitable situations arise. In this way, he can prevent himself from designing the same type of solutions for each situation, which will soon become predictable and in the extreme, boring. Repetitive design solutions will not be seen as eternal design treasures like the precious few golf courses that always spring to mind when the term "great" is used.

The challenge therefore, in a similar analogy to religion, is for all lovers of the game of Golf and those who are interested in Golf Course Design, to remember that our basic ideals are essentially the same. The basic tenets of all the major religions are almost identical, so why do they fight? In the golf world, there is a fairly general agreement about which courses are the best, so why do we not gather our energies and in the best traditions of the game and the great golf courses, collectively proceed to aspire to them?

Why indeed. The unfortunate answer to this question is I believe there is a void; a lack of pertinent modern day, up to date information to address this issue. There are very few books, magazines or publications of any description that adequately portray the design ideals that are needed as basic background information for anybody to competently express their passion for good golf course design.

Put simply, in today's marketing driven golf world, many people find it hard to define what it is they love about the great Golf Courses, and as such, they are often confused or misguided about what to believe in. In many cases, this effect is quite extreme to the point where the best intentions of a great many good and well-meaning people are so far-off on tangential issues that the situation seems hopeless.

In today's complicated world there is a plethora of books giving mountains of technical data on how to grow grass, drain and irrigate every square inch of any piece of land you can think of. At the other end of the spectrum are the coffee table publications with glossy pictures of golfing greats playing impossible shots on courses that are unbelievably well manicured, and there are even those with glossy photographs of the machines used to prepare the courses on which the shots are played!

Along with this are the articles, magazines, books & films which illustrate the widely marketed face of the modern golf course design industry, being the all-conquering professional golfer-designers. This often has the effect of presenting the Golf Course Design business in a manner that promotes the personalities involved rather than the virtues of good Golf Course Design.

The typical images of the famous Pro-Golfer wearing gum boots, holding a plan and pointing to something on a construction site is not an accurate reflection of what Golf Course Design really is. Likewise, one or two site visits by a high profile golfer during the course of a project is unlikely to make any noticeable difference to the outcome of any well-designed golf course project, except for its initial marketing.

Indeed, the only style of marketing mentioned in this book is the old fashioned type, and a type which is still the fastest to travel and the most effective, being word of mouth. Word of mouth marketing negates all peripheries; it deals with the truth in one-on-one, face-to-face situations between people who do not want to be seen as liars. Without reason to mislead, a golfer tells his friends which Golf Course is the best.

A slick marketing campaign cannot create this type of promotion when applied to Golf Courses; it can only be achieved at the source, in design. It requires synergy, generated in liberal doses from the very early concept stages of a project. Synergy is like a magic fertilizer, which makes only good ideas grow. It is devoid of egotism, the number one killer of harmonious design processes, and the scourge of the modern day version of the gentlemanly endeavour, which is Golf Course Architecture

Egotism, an indicator of insecurity breeds a need to impose one's will upon people and the land, which shows in Golf Course Design. Distinctive, often repeated features in an organisation's designs, often sold as "signature" design elements are nothing more than an illustration that somebody believes they are either bigger than the game, or they lack creativity.

Time will ultimately belittle these design decisions and achieve the opposite of the immortality that they are supposed to buy.

Conversely, talented designers and their teams will ultimately be connected to more golf courses than they ever designed, regardless of short-term credits.

With all of these issues clouding the scenery, as well as the short term wonders that marketing dollars can do for any substandard product, is it any wonder that there is widespread confusion? The many onlookers, who seem to be so easily affected by seasonal trends and the whimsical comments of the relatively few and often uneducated, are not being adequately informed of the core facts in an industry that aims to uphold timeless qualities.

This book discards the disposable clutter of modern day golf, whilst - audaciously perhaps - attempts to fill the void of basic modern day design based information to help facilitate a healthy transformation back to the best traditional values of the game of golf.

The subject of modern Golf Course Design is a very difficult one for which to provide definitive, all-encompassing examples that explain all issues with absolute clarity, beyond dispute. For this reason, many publications on Golf Course Design shy away from the pertinent issues and stop short of saying what is required; however right, wrong or controversial it might be seen to be. Indeed, the very nature and diversity of the game makes it virtually impossible for one to provide definitive reasoning for all pertinent issues.

For the purpose off addressing this issue, and in an attempt to give a greater worth to all the issues covered, this book is structured rather differently. Rather than attempting to provide evidence and backup information for each issue, the text merely presents the issues and gives a unique personal view of how such issues can be processed in light of the host of modern day issues and constraints.

We are not for a minute contending that every issue and view raised is "right" or "correct." Indeed, some points will no doubt be proven somewhat inaccurate, and in most cases it will be impossible to prove otherwise. This however is not the issue. Rather, the text is intended to serve as an insight illustrating how a practising, modern day career Golf Course Architect processes issues pertinent to design, right or wrong.

The photographs and examples show how the essence of many of these points of view has been put into practice. The success and therefore validity of such viewpoints can only, ultimately be decided by the level of satisfaction of the golfers who play on these final, finished products.

We trust that under this free, honest and unrestrained structure, the whole cross section of modern day golf enthusiasts, from developers, to club committee members, to everyday club members and casual golfers, will be able to draw some thought provoking ideas and hopefully a little clarity, from the following text.

1

Selecting A Designer

The common strategy often used in selecting a designer is similar to that used to select other key consultants in other fields, being to conduct a background check.

Golf course design is very much a creative form of engineering, in a very nature based setting. Consequently, it is my belief that the standard background checks that one might undertake on an Engineering or building Architectural Company will generally not show up the key issues required to be put in place to ensure the work will be of a *great* standard, as opposed to merely serviceable.

Golf Course Architects tread a thin line. They need to promote themselves to such a degree that they can win enough work to be able to survive and prosper, and the best form of promotion is previously completed projects. For emerging Golf Course Architects, it is likely there won't be a lot of previously completed work, which makes winning new projects difficult. A Golf Course Architect must also be working fairly continuously, without being overworked, for a reasonable period in order to learn and refine his skills to a point where he could be considered experienced enough to be able to competently conduct a full golf course design exercise.

A fact often overlooked is that Golf Course Architects are not simply born with all the skills required to create great designs. This is impossible, regardless of the level of creativity and raw skill that they may have been blessed with at birth.

As with most things, trial and error is the best way to learn, with the obvious problems being firstly securing clients willing to put up with any kind of possible "error" on their Golf Courses and secondly, making sure these errors are repairable within the framework of the construction contract with which one is working. (It is not easy to work any major kind of flexibility – and therefore possible extra cost – into a construction contract). Emerging Golf Course Architects are therefore invariably caught in a catch 22 situation and it is for this reason that new entrants into this area of the market (career designers) usually begin by working for another recognised designer.

This, no doubt is a good way of getting a start in the industry but it too has its drawbacks. I personally made the journey via this route and I will take the opportunity to expand on some of my experiences, as an example of what might constitute valuable background experience gained along the road to competence.

In my time working under a recognised designer, I took in large amounts of basic background information about design related issues and approaches, as well as learning how to deal with clients, and generally how to administer a design company. This information was gathered more so by closely observing and questioning every aspect of the operations of a functioning design company, rather than by direct and formal instruction. Initially my involvement was something similar to that of an office boy, kind of a helpful observer.

For the first couple of years, my actual design input was virtually nil. Whilst I was gradually learning the true meaning of contours, it took time before that understanding reached a level where it could readily translate creative thought into useable designs at a standard comparable to the designs that were already being produced at the office in which I worked. I was at this stage, unable to give any useful design contribution and as such, I found myself being given more responsibility in other areas. I spent several years observing the design process, whilst undertaking project management and administration of design contracts, drafting of others designs, concept compilation and presentation, and later, actual General Management of the company.

Whilst these items are all essential to the running of any design company, and every Golf Course Architect needs to be competent at them, no aspiring designer wishes to concentrate solely on them, seemingly at the expense of the core of the profession, being actual design.

Gradually, I felt my design proficiency increase and I began to get more actively involved in design formulation; and after three or four years actually contributing some useable contour design. Initially this took the form of amending others designs to achieve localised earthworks balances and doing very broad scale earthworks balancing contour exercises.

As I became more proactive in design, I found myself becoming progressively more frustrated that I never really got to *test* my designs. My superiors would always amend my designs before they ever made it to the field. As such, I was never able to see the results of my errors, which removed the benefit of any real feedback.

After 5 or so years, a period which I would consider the minimum for such an "apprenticeship" I still found myself wondering if I was going to be capable of "great" designs, or was I destined to remain serviceable at best and possibly struggle to build any kind of reasonable personal design record.

I knew that all my designs were technically very much acceptable, but I was never really completely satisfied with my designs, and I couldn't seem to improve them.

The final stages of my development to a fully competent designer slowed considerably and did not completely occur until I eventually (after 8 years) broke out of that structure and took a chance on my own ability. As it turned out, my designs almost immediately went to the next level, because my design errors were by this stage small enough to be easily amendable onsite within the contract structures under which I was working. I quickly learnt the extra 10-20% that I felt I needed to be able to compete with the best and although I will forever continue to learn more, I know a level of competence has been reached that will facilitates the production of "great" designs.

My formal apprenticeship therefore took about 8 years. Prior to that I had spent 4 years as a ski guide/mountain rescue enthusiast where everyday, unbeknownst to me at the time, I was continually studying and evaluating terrain, weather (particularly wind) and snow (which behaves somewhat like sand) conditions.

Prior to that, I studied building architecture. Interspersed throughout the period I spent as much time as possible with my father (an architectural designer) and worked on the family farm, both activities requiring lateral thinking and a practical work ethic.

No doubt, I consider myself very lucky, as most decisions I made, over some 16 years were unwittingly preparing me; filling in the gaps of knowledge required to become a competent golf course architect.

I always had an interest in design, but only studied Architecture because I could think of nothing better to study. After achieving a degree, I discovered that the regulations & red tape of building design was not my cup of tea but if nothing else, I achieved an appreciation for building design and a basic knowledge of surveying. Both experiences continue to serve me well in liaisons with planners, clubhouse architects and the needs of residential developments, which regularly must be made to co-habitate with golf.

My mountain experience was borne out of a penchant for travel, skiing and unusual landscapes (which at the time seemed strange even to me). Studying avalanche phenomena, weather and the best way to traverse all types of terrain on skis gave me an intimate understanding of contour maps and the relation of the weather on what they represent. I recall thinking this interesting information was leading me nowhere, but looking back it was invaluable.

My assistance in my father's design office obviously taught me the importance in design, of reputation and integrity as well as the standards applicable to the operation of any design company.

My farm work taught me the basics of drainage, geology, agronomy and the importance of fully thinking through and planning the implementation of any idea to ensure it can be achieved without undue cost in time and expense. (Hands-on practicality).

The multi-faceted nature of the Golf Architecture Profession is to many people, a strange combination. It is not at all common that one would happen to posses the basic practical nature and aptitude for technical information *as well as* a reasonable amount of free-form, creative design flair (people are usually one or the other). It is even more unusual that an individual would, through his normal activities, gain relevant experience in all or most of these areas, especially considering modern day tendencies for people to specialise in order to become successful.

The Great Scottish Designer Alister MacKenzie, for example was a Doctor of Medicine (Technical) who had an interest and a gift in military camouflage (natural/creative). This is a very odd accompaniment of interests by anyone's standard, and it gave him the basis of a great Golf Design Mentality.

I personally was just lucky to have differing types of experiences, and I would not trade any of them as they all gave me something of use, although I did not know it at the time. My 16-year preparatory period to what I call full competence could in theory perhaps, have been shorter in terms of focusing on the formal study of each of the many different disciplines. However, I am of the belief that nothing can replace living and experience, and for that reason I do not believe I could have done it any quicker.

For example, there is no better way to gain an understanding of the potential of wind and weather on terrain than to spend 4 years travelling the world, standing on every weather prone area you can find, with a map and a camera in your hand. Likewise, Dr. McKenzie no doubt quickly found out whether his camouflage skills were successful or not. Obviously they were, nobody killed him in the process!

It is these sorts of extreme experiences which not only enable one to set the parameters for design, but which evoke strong feelings of respect and in the absence of a better word, love; for natural terrain. To be a great designer one must possess a long cultivated connection with the land. It must be felt to be an honour and a privilege to be entrusted with the formation or transformation of a piece of land. This almost sacred connection must be in place in the designer for his designs to evolve to a level of true harmony and therefore greatness.

With all this in mind, and with my situation as an example, I am suggesting that in selecting an architect, one should endeavour to not only check the previous works of a company, but - at least as importantly - ensure that the person who is finally responsible for the crucial design decisions has all the necessary experiences and the right attitudes, which will enable the design to evolve to a level of greatness. There is obviously quite an amount of investigative work that needs to be done to ensure these issues are in order. One might ask the following questions of a prospective Design Company.

Who is the designer?

The designer may have assistants and so forth, but one needs to know who, at the end of the day, is taking responsibility. It is easy to make design decisions on behalf of a company that one works for, which is controlled by others. In this situation, as hard as one might try to consider all the issues, one's design decisions will not be the same or quite as seriously considered, if one is not ultimately responsible for their outcome. If one's senior is taking full credit for one's designs or conversely if one knows he or she will take on the responsibility for one's failures the odds are, one *will not be* quite as attentive. Human nature makes it almost impossible.

In following with that, the actual designer and person through which all decisions must go - both in the design office and onsite - should have at least some and preferably a substantial equity in the design company.

Background of the principle designer

The principle designer should have taken the time to educate himself, in practical terms and beyond basic textbook stage in the relevant important fields of knowledge, such as :- Geology, Agronomy, Maintenance, Weather, Drainage, Irrigation, Landscape, Civil Engineering, Surveying, QS & Contractual matters, Map Reading, Real Estate subdivision and planning, Building Architectural needs, as well as the specific golf design elements as detailed in subsequent chapters.

What is the designer's long-term personal background? Does the designer display a real sympathy, appreciation and spiritual connection with the land and natural landform, and this leads to the next question, namely:

What is the designer's relationship and involvement in the game of golf?

Put specifically, is the designer a golfer? It may come as a shock, but many of the designers in todays relatively well known design companies are relatively poor golfers at best. How this actually effects the design outcome is difficult for me to say, and obviously varies from company to company, but quite often it seems, the design focus is not so much on the golf, the playing hazards and an optimal line of play, but more on any number of other things. One often gets the feeling that the golf holes are routed with a priority on perhaps landscape imagery, or distant views, or engineering solutions, or other tangential issues.

I subscribe to the point of view that the principle designer must be or have been a golfer of reasonable standard, say below a 13-15 handicap, just to be able to reasonably appreciate what all levels of golfers, from beginners to mid and low handicappers through to professional golfers can or cannot do, in terms of shot making.

As well as this, there is a certain mentality that a keen golfer possesses which I do not believe can be truly comprehended unless one is a keen golfer himself. I believe many "golfing widows" would attest to this. As designers, we strive to create golf courses that golfers cannot wait to play again. If one has never felt like that, how can he or she hope to create such facilities?

Another key issue is the designer's level of enthusiasm for the history and traditions of the game. One of the biggest challenges in Golf Course Design is creating playing fields which are enjoyable for the masses whilst remaining challenging to the pros, and which will not become outdated in the near future.

Knowledge of the history and traditions of the game, the ongoing procession to the present in regard to ability of golfers and improvements to equipment, enable the designer - to some degree - to forecast the future and allow for the next generation in their present day designs.

This knowledge should also extend to information on the old scoring systems and the ways that the game was played in days gone by. More specifically, it should include an understanding of what it was that gave golf such on incredible level of widespread appeal, which has subsequently enabled it to become one of, if not *the* dominant participation sport of today.

This is not an easy concept to understand, as it is very much multi faceted. In any case, one has no hope of grasping such concepts if there is not a reasonable level of studious inquiry into the pages of a sometimes-distant past.

Persistence

The fact that we are not surrounded by great golf courses indicates it is not a normal practice to create one. The practices required to be employed by one who endeavours to do just this will therefore be viewed by many as unorthodox or unusual and will potentially not gain widespread support, at least at the outset.

As well as this, a competent Golf Course Architect, in relentless pursuit of the ultimate design solution for any given situation must be prepared to amend and sometimes completely change elements of his designs in favour of a better solution, regardless of where or from whom the idea for that solution may have come.

The pursuit of such levels of excellence requires, at most times almost boundless levels of passionate enthusiasm that regularly has to be professionally displayed to many stakeholders throughout the length of a design and construction process.

This is not an easy mindset to sustain, and requires huge amounts of patience, and measured diplomacy, as one endeavours to resist embarrassing a well meaning client, whilst hearing out the often unfounded concerns that surround anything to do with change. One must be firm, forthright and open in one's demeanour, maintaining an environment that is conducive to continual communication, lest he cut off opportunities for the collection of further design ideas and risk creating an environment in which divisive misinformation can fester.

On a broader and more general level, self-confidence, patience and perseverance are also required. When a designer reaches a level of competence, there will invariably be a lag period, before the market accepts this level of competence. During this period, promotion of one's own recently and completely acquired set of skills can be difficult and one will come up against all manner of obstacles and reasons why one might not become successful. Depending on where the "new Architect" is practicing their skills and qualities, he will most likely be taken advantage of at some stage, and used by other more established, but possibly less scrupulous clients and designers to further their own cause.

On several occasions I have seen my own work, or substantial portions of it appear as part of somebody else's successful submission for a project. In times like these, especially prior to any substantial personal design success, an undying optimism is required to simply continue.

No doubt, persistence and refined natural talent (design skill) are the two most important ingredients for success.

I have touched on several attributes, which I consider to be important, but I would like to stress the following: -

a) I am not suggesting the attributes listed are in any way exhaustive. For sure there are others. It should be remembered that these are my personal perceptions which are tempered to a degree by my own experiences

b) More so than merely holding these attributes, it is the innate knowledge or sense of the balance of their relevance in any given situation that is just as important. Any studious historian-type of personality can obtain this information, but without knowing how to use and communicate it, he exists as nothing more than a human library.

We've spoken of persistence, design background, but what of design skill? How can we define that?

2

The Layout

Introduction - Design Skill

The proceeding chapters, which consist of the main body of this book, deal with Design Skill.

For the purposes of explanation, I will define Design Skill as *"The selective implementation of what might be considered as a refined set of design techniques"*

These techniques and principles are represented here by my own very much-personalised methods of compiling a set of design plans and thereafter overseeing their onsite use. These techniques or principles, whilst varying somewhat from designer to designer – especially in the way they are represented and compiled, are fairly common in that they are all designed to produce quality golf facilities.

Following on from the final points of the preceding chapter, I must stress that these are my own generalised principles and the real skill in implementing is *knowing when to adhere to them and when to alter or discard them.*

In today's legally oriented society the concept of a professional breaking his own rules at times of his choosing seems unethical and is difficult for many professional people to grasp. However, once one has undertaken the appropriate checks and selected a competent designer, one will be best served by not confronting him on breaking one of his own rules, because it is he alone who can be the judge of when that is appropriate.

Another point to remember is that a great designer is one who continues to learn and is forever in the pursuit of more information. As a designer, I question every day, most every thing I do. This quite often has the effect of appearing vague, or being off in another place mentally, but it enables me to get the most out of my design skills, and continually form new ones. As a designer I am ready to discard, or turn upside-down a design tenet that I have long operated by, if I am sure it will yield better results. In any case, one or several of these design tenets will be turned on its head for the purpose of any particular project, depending on its specific site attributes and project needs.

The Layout

Anyone who has seen a Golf Course layout plan, prepared by a reputable Golf Course Architect, this is, a plan showing all the fairways, greens, tees & bunkers will note that there is usually a centre line drawn down each hole. This line generally extends from a point on the tee to the landing zone, where there is a point, or bend, then the line continues to the centre of the green, for par 4's. On par 5's there are usually two fairway bend points and on par 3's there are none.

Why are these lines shown, and what do they represent? Of course, these lines show the general direction of play, and if you hit your ball theoretically from the start of each line, with each progressive shot finishing at each node, with 2 putts on each green, you would par the course.

The centre lines also show the means by which the average length of a course can be measured. Obviously if you cut every dogleg the course will be shorter and if you go wide around every dogleg, the course will be longer.

Beyond simple representation of a previously completed layout design solution, these centre lines actually serve as a very important design tool, possibly an indispensable design tool in today's space conscious planning environment.

In yesteryear, the old time golf designers did not have detailed contour surveys or aerial photographs, but they did have, in most cases, much more land to play with. Many of the great old designers had little use for drawing centre lines on paper. The only means they had for figuring out the optimum layout balance was to go onsite and physically check every square inch of the site, progressively marking potential green & tee sites as they went.

Although I personally have never had cause to lay out a course in this manner, I can imagine that after a week or so, a high quality layout would usually be the result. Conversely, I can also imagine it would, at times be difficult to come to terms with an appreciation of the whole site, especially should dense vegetation be present on large portions of it.

But in any case, with land not of a premium, it must have been a pleasure to roam a site, looking for the best natural golf shot opportunities, without having to worry too much about how much land area one is consuming. The down side would have been not having the means to improve elements of the site that are not quite as one would prefer them.

This issue, I think, is some of the cause of confusion for many as they try to evaluate old Golf Courses. A great Architect of yesteryear, given a great site of ample acreage, would no doubt, have created a truly great Golf Course. And they did. All of the great Architects got their hands on at least a few great sites each. Henceforth came Royal Melbourne, Cypress Point, Pine Valley, Pinehurst No2. etc, etc.

What many people fail to take into account is that not every site those great Architects worked on had those great qualities. Because, however the great Architects have their names associated with those few great old courses that did possess the near perfect set of natural attributes, many modern day critics take the issue a step further and assume that *every* course that bears the name of a MacKenzie, Colt, Ross, or Tillinghast is therefore great.

It must be remembered that most of these designers had nothing more than a horse and scoop with which to bring forth their designs, and when confronted with solid rock, a huge sink-hole, or some other such insurmountable problem, they had no choice but to go for an option that was less than ideal. Let's face it, there are maybe only a handful of sites on earth that do not require at least some small pockets of earthworks to create the optimum design solution.

On this basis I contend there are many old golf courses that are wrongly considered great in comparison to some of the newer ones because of little more than name association. I contend that if you could go back and ask the designer if he would like to change anything, he would. Most old writings by such designers on issues such as blind play and other less than ideal playing conditions attest to this.

In any case, modern day designers have no excuses. With modern technology and equipment the only reason any design might not end up great is lack of design skill, lack of communication, or lack of integrity by the designer.

Using Centre Lines To Lay Out A Golf Course

After diligently collecting and mapping all site constraints, the Architect will have a generalised land use concept in his mind's eye, before putting pen to paper. It is often a good practice to illustrate, for the benefit of a client or committee, the reasoning behind this. In addition, if this exercise is actually carried out together with a client consultant team or club development committee, snippets of extra, localised information are likely to be brought

11

forth by those sitting around the table, that might otherwise never see the light of day. Stories of "that big flood back in '64" or "an old mineshaft" and so-on are examples of useful information that may not be on any record, but which will have an effect on the layout design.

Indeed, a detailed Site Analysis Plan, illustrating all constraints, be they buffer zones, existing services, prevailing winds, etc as well as client preferences, will quite often clearly illustrate the obvious best land allocation solution. If it isn't obvious, the luck is on the side of the designer, as there is more space for uninhibited design decisions.

Following is an example of a typical site analysis plan. It was compiled at the commencement of the design process for an existing Golf Club, which plans to acquire additional land to redevelop their Golf Course with added real estate.

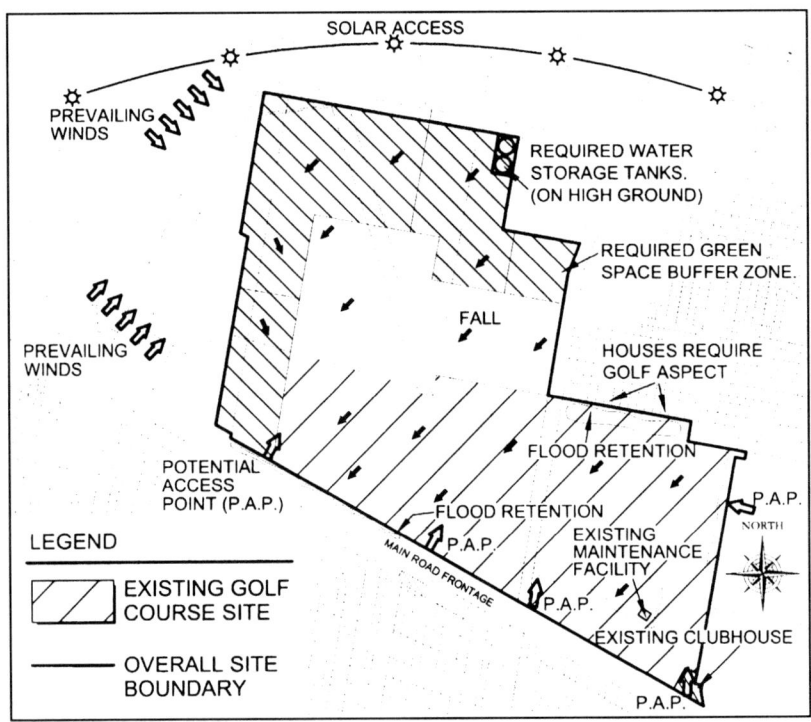

Diagram 1. Typical Site Analysis Plan.

With this information tucked away, an accurate contour survey, clear definition of the site boundaries and a recent site inspection still large in the memory, the architect is ready to make a start.

Positioning centre lines on a survey is a great way of making preliminary design decisions on each golf hole, whilst keeping the impact on the whole site in perspective at all times. By today's standards it seems one cannot have a golf course with a number of holes that is not a factor of 9 regardless of how great the holes are. Likewise it is pointless to have 15 great holes and 3 bad ones, or 18 great holes that require climbing gear and a safety harness to get from each green to the next tee, or a nice layout that has golfers finishing with a half-mile walk back to the clubhouse.

So in putting down centre lines, one does it in such a way that one knows that each golf hole will relate well to what is around it, and with some modification to the survey contours, each hole can be made to be great. And how does one know that? By having a complete knowledge of the issues touched upon in this book plus a large amount of experience stored in the subconscious, as direction.

Not only must each hole be great, but the layout should also generally conform to the following guidelines:

-There generally should not be too far between each green and the next tee.
-The layout must be relatively safe without wasting land.
-There must be adequate space for other important land uses such as practice range, car park, clubhouse and maintenance facility.
-It must preferably have returning nines.
-It must be mindful of East-West Sun in the starting and finishing holes respectively.
-It must create the optimum relationships with the adjacent land uses.
-It must incorporate or at least allow for adequate irrigation water storage, generalised site drainage strategies and access routes for construction.
-It must be mindful of any number of environmental issues.
-It should minimise the incidences of blind play.
-It must have the right mix of golf holes.

The Right Mix Of Golf Holes

Most Architects would agree that a great course is one that tests as many facets of the players' game as possible. In layout design this variation can be allowed for by including golf holes of different lengths, directions, uphill, downhill, doglegging left, and right, and maybe one or two double dog legs on par 5's.

The holes should be combined in ways that give maximum opportunity for interest & strategic value that can be brought out fully in the detailed design.

The average optimum par 72, 18 hole members layout might be described as follows:-

Hole No.	Par	Length(M)	General direction	Dogleg direction	Uphill or Downhill
1	4	370	N	Right	D
2	5	490	S	L/R	U
3	4	390	W	Left	D
4	3	160	SE		U
5	4	330	S	R	D
6	5	470	W	L	D
7	4	350	E	R	U
8	3	180	NW		D
9	4	410	N	L	U
	36	*3150*			
10	4	380	S	R	D
11	5	480	N	R	U
12	4	360	W	L	D
13	3	140	SW		D
14	4	340	NW	R	U
15	3	200	NE		U
16	4	320	N	L	D
17	5	500	E	R/L	D
18	4	400	S	R	U
	36	*3120*			
TOTAL	*72*	*6270*			

It should be noted that this example is not meant to portray the perfect mix, but is intended to illustrate the following;-

a) The four par threes and four par fives all play in different directions

b) The par threes play at differing lengths, from 140m up to 200m, and with an uphill/downhill mix, a wide array of iron, and sometimes wood play will be required to approach them.

c) There is roughly an even mix of short and long par fours on each nine, ranging from 320m up to 410m.(although 410m is not necessarily considered long any more)

d) There is roughly an even mix of par 4's that dogleg in opposite directions and they usually occur in a manner in which no two similar hole shapes (either left or right) occur one after another.

14

e) There is scope for good design for the starting holes, with no par threes early in the round (which can slow up play), and no early holes hitting into the rising sun.

f) There is scope for the design of an exciting finishing stretch, where nerves will be tested, and a lot of shots could be made up or given away. Ie. 15 is a long, tough par three, 16 is a short, tempting downhill par four, 17 is a long, but downhill par 5, and 18 is a relatively long, uphill, testing par 4.

g) Starting holes are medium length, downhill par fours, to get the field away quickly. Finishing holes are fairly long, uphill par fours that can be made to be exacting tests of golf, and in playing uphill, it assumes the clubhouse will be situated on a reasonably high piece of land where patrons can view the course, especially the starting and finishing holes. This is not to say that I only advocate par fours as starting and finishing holes; par fives also can be used, but generally par threes are not seen as good starting and finishing holes.

Again, bear in mind that this does not apply to all sites. Indeed, it will not apply exactly to any, but is a theoretical take on a typical mildly undulating parkland site, which nowadays is possibly the most common type of site. Extremely flat, or links style sites are a little different, and these will be addressed in later sections.

Diagram 2) shows the layout resultant from the site analysis plan illustrated in diagram no.1) Note the variation in hole lengths and directions is not exactly as per that described above. However, according to modern day standards such as the need to keep the course relatively compact, without compromising safety or playability, we would consider this layout as achieving a relatively high level of variation.

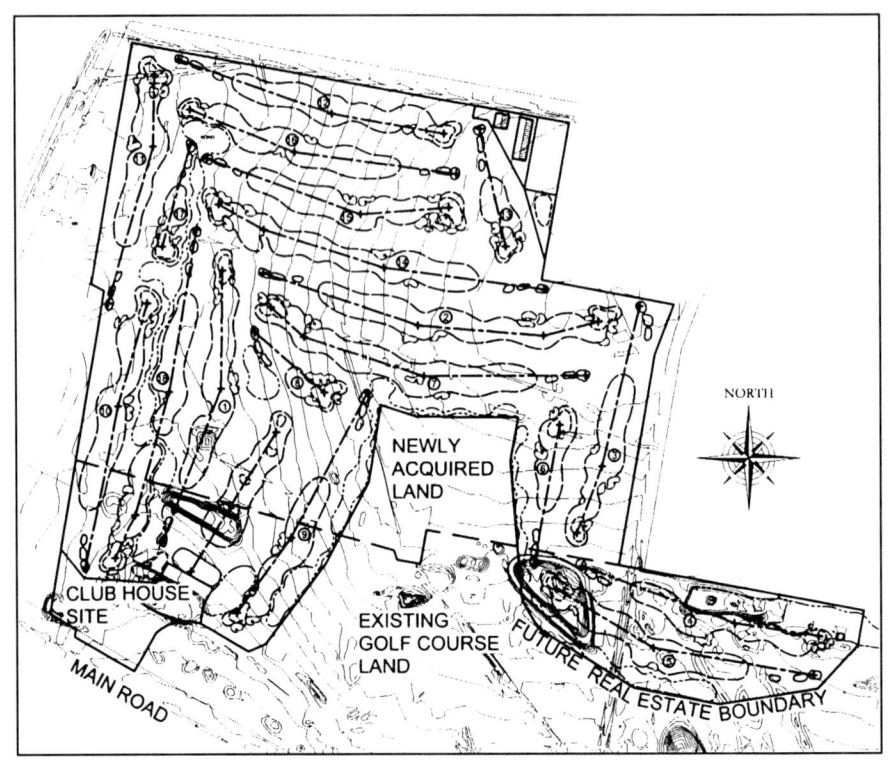

Diagram 2. Sample Layout Plan.

Laying Down Of The Centre Lines

As previously mentioned, knowledge and experience will direct one's approach, when actually commencing this process. Beyond the constraints as illustrated in the site analysis plan and allowing for the incorporation of exciting golf holes, the main initial consideration is usually to minimise the amount of disturbance to the site, and thereby maximise the existing site attributes.

For example, if the site analysis gives a very fixed land use area and the land space is too hilly, flat or limited in other ways one may have to allow more disturbance and earthworks to construct the features that will enable technical, as well as pure golfing function. If, for instance there is not at least a 2% gradient on all turf areas, they won't drain adequately. If the fall is not naturally there, one has to allow for the creation of it.

This should be ascertained at the outset, as a good designer will generally look to minimise items such as earthworks, in creating optimum solutions.

Other issues which are at the forefront during this process are:-

Gradient On The Line Of Play

Uphill along the length of a hole, greater than 6 or 7% will generally be too tough for most people to walk and play, and in any case will be more prone to produce blind shots, which are generally to be avoided if at all possible. Like wise, drop shots can be fun, but large downhill level changes make club selection a guessing game and removes the skill factor – to be avoided in its extreme form.

Doglegs

Doglegs of a greater angle than about 45 degrees risk becoming gimmicky. Take, for example, a 350-metre long golf hole with 45-degree dogleg at the 230-metre mark. Upon hitting a 220-metre tee shot down the left side edge of a 40-metre wide fairway, one will be left with approximately 116 metres to the centre of the green. A 220-metre drive down the right edge of this 40 metre wide fairway will leave an approach of approximately 140 metres. This 24 or so metre difference in approach length equates to between 2-3 clubs to the average player, which under most circumstances is adequate reward or penalty for hitting down either side of the fairway. In addition, earth shaping and fairway profiling (detailed design) can further moderate or accentuate this effect as desired.

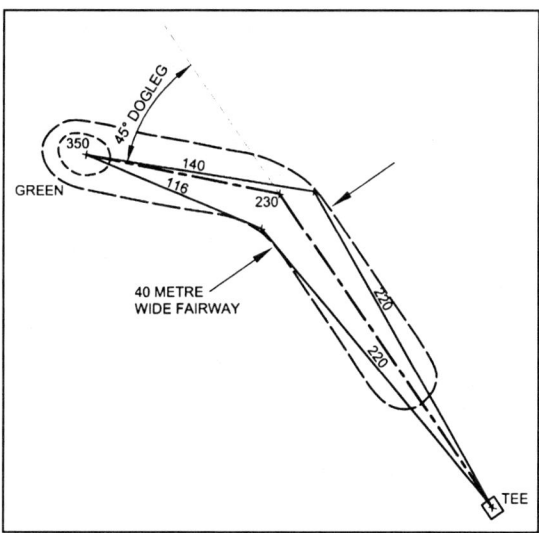

Diagram 3. 45° Dogleg and its general effect on the play of a schematic par 4.

As well as this, overly sharp doglegs can have the following negative effects:

- The inside of a sharp dogleg will generally require extensive protection in the form of hazards/trees, etc to stop golfers from trying to cut the corner without due consideration. Even with this in place, many will still try, and although there is nothing wrong with that in itself, there are issues such as:

- Slow play/unsighted golfers who might be endangered if they are near the green. A wider area of land is required adjacent to this inside of this dogleg to safely allow for wayward corner-cutting balls, which hook or slice further away from the fairway.

- Shorter hitters who cannot make the corner of the dogleg on their tee shot will not get a view of the green. They may therefore be forced to hit a short iron lay up second shot to a position somewhere near the apex of the dogleg just to get a view of the green for their third shot. This is especially demoralising, and even more so if that short hitter has just witnessed his playing partner put his ball on the green off the tee, using nothing more than brute force, without thought.

Length of Line from Tee to Dogleg Node.

We generally make these 230 metres, as it is what we consider to be quite a reasonable tee shot length for a good player, but not so long that it still enables us to avoid the scenario described directly above. This is a very important point.

In golf course design, a product that will gain widespread approval is one that narrows the gap between professionals and amateurs.

We must do what we can to challenge the pros, while simultaneously encouraging the beginners. We must make everyone feel that they have a chance to score better, without making it easy to do so. With a 230 metre dogleg node, the shorter hitters will generally still get a view of the green for their second shots, while the very long hitters will need to be very accurate it they wish to hit the ball around the dogleg, off the tee.

Siting Of Tees, Greens and Landing Zones

In endeavouring to create golf courses that appear naturally occurring, and to reduce construction costs, good designers take advantage of the existing site attributes wherever possible. Sometimes, however it should be said that there is a need to make substantial changes to the site *in order* to make it look natural.

In our experience it is generally best to locate holes such that they play in sympathy with the lie of the land. By that, I mean if the terrain on a par 4, for example, pushes most bouncing and rolling balls to the left, it is usually best to make the hole dogleg to the left.

The diagram below deals with a theoretical piece of land shown in 2m survey contours on which we have decided we want to position a par 4, with the tee somewhere at the bottom of the page, and the green somewhere near the top.

Each of the 5 sketches contains a different centreline position, and therefore a different design approach, used to create golf holes of about 350 metres in length..

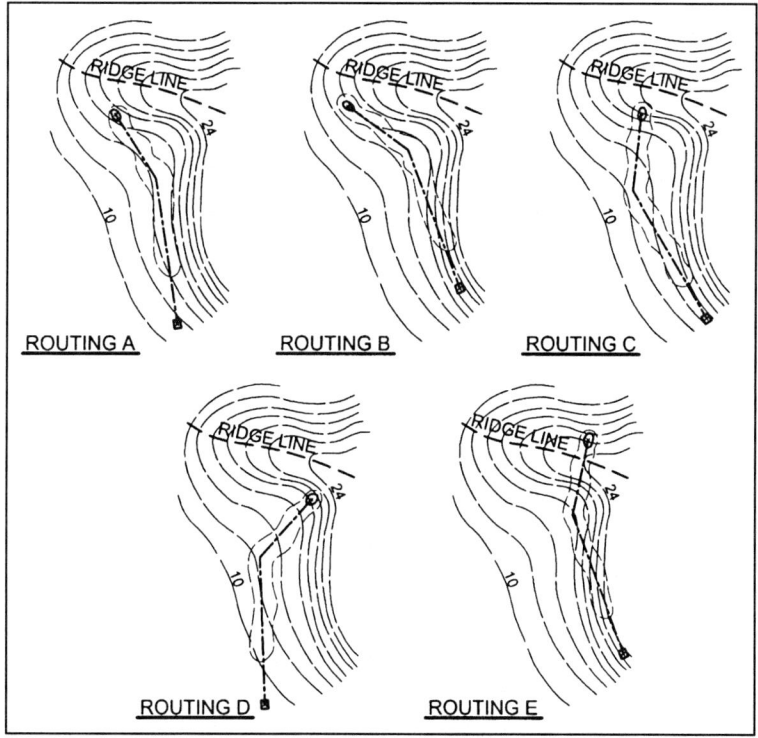

Diagram 4. Centrelines of a theoretical par 4 of 350 metres in length, showing five different routing approaches.

Removing all peripheral issues, such as the routing of the holes that fall before and after this par 4, (which under normal circumstances would have a large

19

bearing on the character and positioning of this hole) one can dissect the virtues of each of the 5 routings shown.

Routing A), - Shows the tee situated just lower than the RL (reduced level) 12metre contour, with the landing area at about RL 15, and the green at about RL17. Key aspects of this design option are:

i) The land falls from right to left, pushing bouncing balls left, and towards the green, if positioned correctly off the tee shot.

ii) The fairway is situated at the base of the steep part of the hill, meaning it will require little, if any earthworks to make it receptive to strategy & drainage.

iii) The green is sited some 3-4 metres below the adjacent ridgeline. This is an important point, as it is generally easier to make greens & bunkers appear more naturally occurring if they have some kind of backdrop. Nestling green sites into or just under the brow of a hill is a practice used quite regularly to achieve this natural look.

iv) The tee location is probably the least receptive in terms of work needed to position it acceptably so the hole will play well. The biggest issue with the tee location is that it is slightly behind the curve of the hillside contour, which means that when combined with the fact that it is some 3-3.5 metres below the level of the fairway, areas of the landing zone are likely to be invisible from the tee, unless changes are made.

The result is, while I consider solution A to be quite acceptable, I would allow for some minor earthworks to raise the tee level by 1.0 metre or so. The normal amount of shaping would be required on the landing zone for strategy (positioning of bunkers, etc) and drainage and I would allow cut to fill of about 0.5 to 1.0m in depth around the green to position it well. In normal circumstances, this type of work is minimum, considering that:

a) With modern irrigation, all play zones must be well drained and therefore well shaped to a nominal grade of at least 2% to direct water to field inlets.
b) Greens should be constructed to ensure they can be easily maintained and last a reasonable time, at least 15-20 years in most cases. This dictates excavation & import of drainage and sand layers.
c) Bunkers need to be shaped, excavated, drained & sanded.
d) Tees need to be, as a minimum, levelled and prepared with a suitable turf-growing medium.
e) All play zones must be prepared for turf grass planting.

As can be seen, with all this work needed as an absolute minimum, items such as raising the tee level and doing some cut to fill at the green site can be undertaken in conjunction and constitute hardly any extra work.

As a result, I contend that routing A) is a perfectly acceptable solution under almost all circumstances and can yield a naturally appearing golf hole, playing gradually uphill by about 5 metres along its length.

Routing B) – This solution is the downhill equivalent of A) above and will require approximately the same amount of work. This time the tee is situated higher, (at RL 20) on the steep hillside and again will require some work to form a level teeing site.

The landing zone is very receptive and at RL 15, gives a good 5m downhill tee shot. This combination will be very good for vision, although depending on strategy, there may be a need for some cutting of the slope some 80-100 metres front right of the tee to ensure complete vision of the landing zone, if desired. The landing zone is positioned on the flattest part of the area in question and like A) above will require only minimal disturbance for drainage & strategy.

The green site, like A) above is nestled under the brow of the ridge and will require minimal earthworks to make it acceptable.

From the viewpoint of strategic value & ease of construction, I would put solution B) on a par with A), although B) is likely to be better liked as a golf hole than A). This is because when playing from a naturally elevated tee it is easier to make the hole appear more spectacular.

This is a general concept – The vertical field of vision is much greater on a downhill hole with an elevated tee than it is on an uphill hole where it might be more difficult to elevate the tee in a naturally appearing manner. It is therefore usually easier to design downhill holes than uphill ones, because with the latter, one must be very careful with the design levels to ensure the golfer sees enough of what the designer wishes him or her to see. A narrowed vertical field such as on this uphill hole is a more exacting design proposition. It does however give more options with regard to "dead ground" or purposely hiding sections of the hole to affect depth perception, as well as the incorporation of other design subtleties.

Downhill holes are also universally more liked because everybody feels like they hit the ball longer, and on average they do, through increased airtime, and improved bounce & roll. A good Golf Course layout is however, a balance of all golf hole types and there must be a good sprinkling of both uphill and downhill holes on any good undulating Golf Course.

That is why I rate solution A) as good as B) – Because it is an opportunity to design a good version of the more difficult uphill hole. In addition, design techniques can be used like raising the tee by a metre or so. This helps to widen the vertical field of vision, as well as helping to increasing the feeling of confidence that a golfer feels when hitting from a raised area, even though he is still hitting to an uphill target.

Solution C) - Sees a centre line that doglegs to the right, and goes in this case, what I call against the lie of the land. That is, the natural lie of the land pushes running balls from right to left, but in this case the golf hole doglegs left to right. Bearing in mind that our basic design tenet is to encourage the poorer golfers whilst challenging the good players, the effects of this type of routing can be quite negative.

A good player will more than likely position his or her tee shot down near the landing zone node and the hole will for him be, in effect no more challenging than solution A), where he is also left with an uphill approach. But for the lesser golfer who is more likely to hit his or her drive off line, the lie of the land will more than likely push the ball toward the outside of the dogleg, further away from the green. (Refer the section on doglegs under 'laying down of the centre lines.') This thereby leaves a longer approach shot, which is more likely to be played from the rough.

You often hear people say "you hit it in the rough, you pay the price." That idea can be employed for good golfers, playing on lush 'target golf' courses where the ball does not roll much. I contend, however, that for average players, it is demoralising to be always in that situation and we need to encourage lesser golfers by keeping them in the game as much as possible. We therefore like to give lesser golfers a chance to recover after a bad shot, with more of a half-shot penalty for this type of deviation as apposed to a full shot or greater, that such a routing decision will often generate.

In the case of scenario C), this is probably not so well illustrated. A bad shot here is likely to be a slice from a right-hander, which in this case might get a kick forward, and to the left, back onto the fairway. But this also is not a good solution, as it will encourage golfers to 'blaze away' without worry of a slice, thereby disadvantaging older & shorter hitters who have no option to do such mindless long hitting.

In spite of these issues, layout C) is not a lost cause and in the balance of a full layout, might be used. The hole would look quite spectacular off the tee, and the downhill tee shot followed by an uphill approach arrangement is quite acceptable.

Like A) & B). A similar amount of work will be needed at the tee and green sites, but a substantial amount more would be required at the landing zone. I would advocate that on a hole playing against the terrain such as this, the landing zone should generally be earth worked and probably filled mostly on the left side. This would at least give the landing zone a neutral slope effect, as it would generally appear unnatural to bank up the left side so much as to turn wide balls back onto the fairway from the left side rough.

It is also more difficult to position fairway bunkers or other design hazards in the vicinity of the landing zone. For example, to put bunkers on the left side could tend to accentuate the negative aspect described above. Positioning bunkers on the right would generally be more strategically valuable, however it would be difficult to make them fit, or make them visible from the tee.

A more costly and awkward design solution, scenario C) would be unlikely to be regarded as a great hole, in front of others on any reasonable golf course but it could be made to be acceptable if need be.

From the scenario explained here, it can be seen that simple routing decisions, if done poorly will either create a negative playing experience, or a very much more costly and still far from ideal result. Even if extra earthworks are to be used to minimise the effects of the routing decision, the result is still not as great as the much cheaper and easier to achieve scenario A) or B).

It is situations like this that see poor designs cost much more to implement, and in most cases, for no real benefit. Viewed in this light, the value of good design is obvious.

Scenario D) - Is also a dogleg right going against the lie of the land, however it has a few more strategically redeeming features than C).

The tee site, on relatively flat lowland is acceptable, as is the landing zone, which is located on a fairly gentle side slope, at the base of the gentle gully. While the dogleg arrangement is negative in so far as the land moves running balls away from the green direction, there is a little more scope for treatment of this landing area.

With the tee site slightly elevated, Most of this fairway-landing zone will be visible, including the central and higher right side. These areas would easily accommodate bunkers or humps and hollows, which not only would be visible but which could be made to have quite a positive strategic effect. While the landing zone will need a little bit of shaping work to improve its receptiveness, it would be no more than that required under C) above and in comparison, the work would yield much more positive strategic results.

Thereafter, the green site is in a perfectly natural amphitheatre arrangement which, for the approach shot will work well to give the positive impression that wayward balls will be likely to bounce back towards the green, from both sides.

Scenario D) is still a tough hole for the lesser players, especially on the tee shot, but is strategically much more acceptable than C), although it may not appear as spectacular.

Scenario E) – Illustrates possibly the last resort for this piece of land. According to our basic design tenets, it does almost everything wrong. The tee location is sufficiently behind the rounded slope contour to render almost the entire landing zone invisible off the tee.

Being positioned high up on the slope of our mythical site, the negative effect of the natural contours carrying wayward balls away from the preferred line of play is accentuated.

The location of the green is over the back of the crest of the ridge meaning that like the tee shot, the green approach is totally blind.

It is quite probable that you could stand on the tee of this hole, should it be built without being substantially earth worked, and have no idea of which direction the hole plays.

If, for some terrible reason this hole had to be built in this configuration, it would need to be extensively earth worked, just to bring it to what I feel is an acceptable level. On this hole, that would constitute cut to fill on about two thirds of the area at depths of about 2-4 metres.

Should these earthworks be done, there is no doubt the hole would play acceptably well and would appear quite spectacular. It is worth noting that the landforms would look virtually nothing like they do now, and strategically, at least on the drive one will still be fighting the land somewhat. It would still be not so receptive and playable for the lesser golfers, and in any case, it would be difficult to shape and place bunkers and other strategic elements inside a naturally appearing framework.

It should be noted here, that what I am describing assumes the production of a new course, in which case it is much easier to avoid the relatively negative situations described under scenarios C), D) & E). However, a high percentage of our work nowadays is re-planning of existing courses, the guardians of which might wish to update their layout in conjunction with a greens replacement program, or because of litigation pressures due to safety and errant balls.

Under this scenario, Golf Clubs often have limited resources and it is a matter of staging various upgrading works to cater for a limited spending ability and a need to keep most, if not all 18 holes in play, whilst any upgrading work proceeds.

Under this scenario, every potential change has to be weighed up for worth and value in terms of safety, cost, playing strategy and staging, usually in that order. Quite often one comes across golf holes that fit into the category of C) or D) which, because they have been there for a long time and have mature landscape or other virtues, are best left alone until very late in the upgrading process. In many cases, if it were to force the change of several other golf holes or other such major discomfort, they may be better left as permanent fixtures, providing a sufficiently adequate comfort and playability factor can be achieved by other less obtrusive micro-design means.

This brings me to the next point, being what I call the "Comfort Factor".

Routing of Golf Holes and 'The Comfort Factor'

The minimum amount of work required on each of the design scenarios referred to above, is advocated in reference to creating golf holes which possess a certain comfort factor that one experiences when one stands on the tee and prepares to negotiate the hole.

This is difficult to explain, but it is a quite definite semi-subconscious feeling. It is not a feeling of confidence in being able to have a good score on a hole, but rather a feeling that you know enough about the hole to understand how you might best attempt to play it.

In addition, it includes a sense or a feeling that it is actually possible to play the golf hole, however tough the hole might be. As well as that, it is a sense that the hole is worthwhile playing, and not gimmicky or an insult to a golfer who might have gone out of his way or paid good money to play on the golf course.

As well as this, there are other shape-related factors, which contribute to the comfort factor; these will be covered in later chapters.

This sense of comfort and worth of each and every golf hole must be present for the golfer to be able to feel that he is playing on a course that is at least very good, and possibly great.

It is worth noting the relevance of this fact in researching many of the old golf courses. Take for example the Scottish Links Courses. Whilst the design issues are vastly different to parkland golf there are a multitude of design elements present on most holes that can be tucked away by designers for future reference.

But on a tour of Scotland, playing golf at all the little known links courses, there are relatively few courses when compared to the total number of courses, that can be termed great by modern day standards, and it is due to the above-mentioned factor. Playing on most of the lesser known links courses there is a vast mixture of golf holes with incredibly variable playing strategies, but more often than not, there are a few holes in there somewhere which do not give that same feeling of worth. While most of the holes are good, one can still come away feeling a little disappointed with the overall experience, if a nicely balanced layout is what you're looking for.

Personally, when I visit such places I rarely look at the layouts in detail, for many are outdated or put together many years prior to the formation of modern day expectations. I find one is best to look at the attributes of each individual golf hole that one experiences, thereby coming away with a wonderful sense of discovery after each course.

As referred to above, there is more to this comfort factor than this fairly vague explanation. The other factors depend more on micro design elements, mainly to do with strategy and shaping, which will be covered in later chapters.

Siting Of Par Fives and Par Threes

The basic ideals put forth in the above section pertaining to the mythical par 4 examples generally hold true for par fives by adding another interim node. I usually add another node denoting the second landing zone at the 400-430 metre mark measured along the centre line.

Similar theories are applied, as is my general rule regarding angles of doglegs and other such issues as mentioned above, although options do exist for the inclusion of double dogleg par five holes, should the terrain permit. By this I mean the first part of the hole doglegs the opposite to the 2nd part of the hole, as opposed to both nodes directing the centre line either left or right. These can be made into interesting and high quality golf holes.

Par threes offer more flexibility with their siting in that they can be used as "linkage" holes between one land feature and the next. This facilitates the holes before and after to fit together nicely whilst producing spectacular and variable conditions in which to test the mid to shorter clubs. Like the longer holes however, we are always looking for a spectacular "tiger-line" shot for the low handicapper, whilst giving an ample bail-out area for these who are not so confident in taking on big risks.

Spacing Between Golf Holes

This can prove to be a very contentious issue, because unlike codes of regulations that apply to buildings, there are no fixed legal widths for things such distance from one centre line to the next, or from a golf hole centre line to an adjacent boundary.

The nature of golf is that of a sport where basically there are no real standards for design. The game is played on natural, evolving playing fields, where things like the blooming of a tree can have an effect on the way a match is played, i.e. more leaves may make it harder for a ball to go through, should a ball need to be played from underneath such a tree. This analogy applies for almost all aspects of the game. How then does one reduce the blooming of a tree to a set of regulations that are sensibly applicable to all golf courses, old and new? It's virtually impossible and it is this natural mystique, which I think is part of the reason the game is so popular.

In golf course design, one cannot generalise, and simply apply an all-encompassing concept to any design problem. Every decision made in design has to be taken in consideration of the *actual*, specific conditions & constraints that one finds on any golf hole, or even any small part of any golf hole. In fact, the generalisations made by me in this book will no doubt be viewed as being very contentious, because they do appear to be all encompassing, and in real life design situations, no doubt they are over simplified and could not apply in the exact same form as shown herein.

The result of this is quite an amount of design flexibility. This is wonderful if competent designers are in change, but unfortunately this 'no rules' framework under which we work, attracts many unscrupulous types, who, with little more than coercive communication skills, can justify poor design decisions to their unsuspecting clients. It is that scenario which this book attempts to negate.

With regard to standards for hole spacings, in short, there are none that are widely recognised, because apart from the above mentioned design reasoning, it must be remembered that it is practically impossible to totally guard against errant golf balls leaving a site or straying onto other internal play zones. We can only hope to minimise it to a reasonable degree, unless all centre lines are located 300 odd metres from adjacent boundaries and fairways. Obviously that is not practical and with this in mind, who would want to take on the legal responsibility of deciding what is a "reasonable" amount of risk, when one errant ball alone has the capability of causing quite severe damage to property and person?

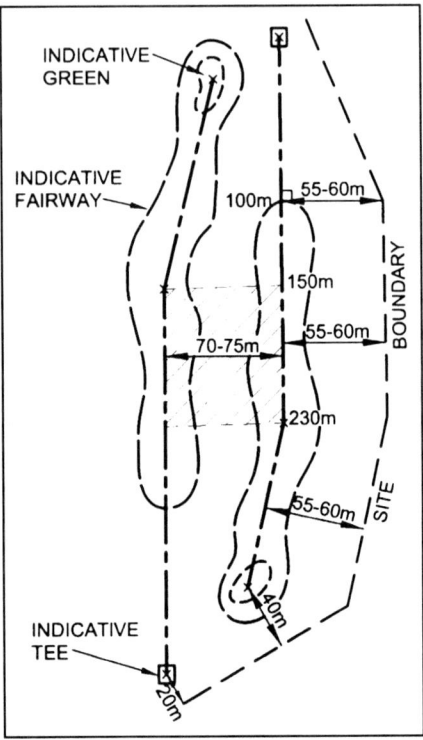

Diagram 5. Estimations of acceptable golf hole centreline and golf course boundary line spacings, according to present day ball flight characteristics.

Diagram 5 gives an indication of what the golf/real estate market seems to find acceptable in today's environment, assuming a new golf course, real estate on the boundary (with some 10-15m setback to buildings) and flat, raw land with little initial tree cover. Note the following with regard to this schematic: -

a)   The property boundary is on the left side of the golf hole, which minimises stray balls in this area since 90% of golfers are right-handed slicers.

b)   Note the maximum width between holes, shown here at 70-75 metres is at the 150-230 metre marks, where the majority of errant balls hit with woods and long irons are likely to finish.

c)   Note there is some scope for the golf hole separation to be narrowed a little between holes near the tees & greens, and also from the tee up to about the 100m mark on the site boundary side.

d)   Note the buffers of 40m at the back of the greens, and 20m at the tees, which give space for loud and invasive voices to be less pronounced and landscape buffer planting of reasonable size to be included.

Use Of Centre Lines In Evaluating And Adjusting Existing Courses

As per on a new course design, the Golf Course Architect's evaluation of an existing course generally begins with the acquisition of a scale aerial photograph, and a detailed contour survey map showing locations of all existing features such as greens, tees, bunkers, ponds, trees, boundaries, etc.

From here we proceed to draw the centre lines on a copy of this survey, with tee nodes, 230m fairway-landing nodes in the centre of the existing fairways and green nodes in the centre of existing greens. This, I regard as an extremely beneficial exercise, because in most cases, any bottlenecks, under-utilised areas or dangerously directed golf holes will show up very clearly.

This exercise does not necessarily show how golfers presently play the golf holes, as there are many other mitigating circumstances. It does, however show how the average golfer of reasonable standard would *like* to play the course, as it stands, and therefore indicates in a very general manner, where layout changes might be necessary in order for the course to meet modern play standards.

The picture shown below is a survey plan of an existing golf course, many of the golf holes of which are in the same locations as they were 110 years ago. As can be seen by the plan, several bottlenecks, or crowded areas are present. Centre lines that start and finish very close together indicate this.

Several pockets of under utilised space also exist onsite, indicated by large areas with no centre lines crossing them. The only holes that roughly correspond to the generalised layout principle for golf hole separation outlined above are holes 4 and 6. These holes run parallel to each other with some 70-75 metres between centre lines at the critical landing zones.

There are several golf holes that play close to boundaries with the out of bounds on the right side. In addition, there are several tees and greens that are becoming increasingly unsafe with the progressive advent of new balls & clubs that see greater distances hit by more golfers, not necessarily with greater accuracy.

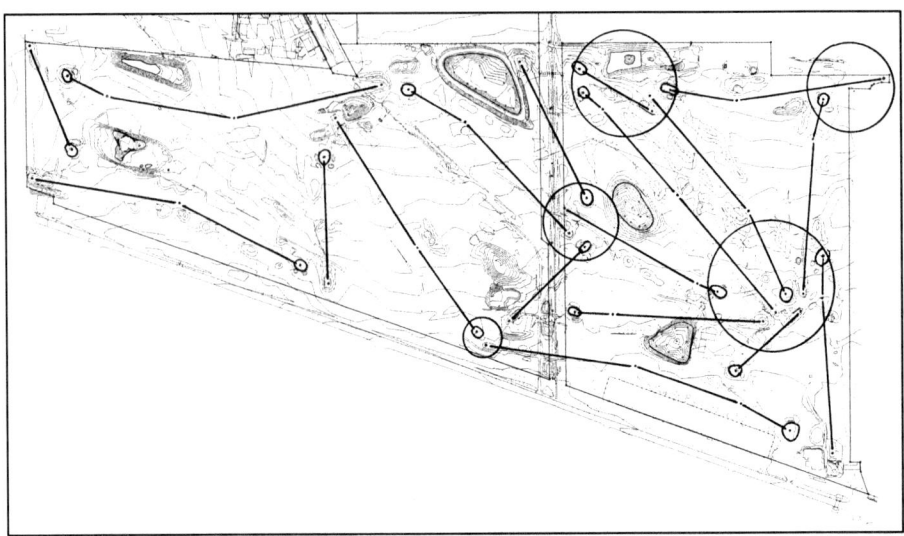

Diagram 6. Survey of typically outdated Golf Course Layout, with centrelines illuminating potential safety problem areas (circled).

The saving grace for this club at this time are the big old trees which line the edges of each hole as well as the lack of close residential development which frequently puts pressure on golf boundaries. The trees however, are nearing the end of their lifespan, and aside from the prohibitive cost of removing them; their absence would see the course fully exposed to many of the negative aspects of the modern game.

A new layout has therefore been proposed which will see extra adjoining land acquired on which a developer will proceed to build what amounts to a new Golf Course in return for a portion of the main road frontage land on which the Golf Club is presently located. (Refer diagram 2. on page 16)

Note the following elements:

a) Correlation of the proposed layout to the site Analysis plan prepared for this project (diagram 1. on page 12).
b) Relatively even and efficient spacing of proposed golf hole centre lines, according to diagram 5. on page 28.
c) Use of waterways to augment safety buffers between golf and real estate areas.
d) North-south orientation of practice range, opening & finishing holes.

e) Inclusion of pond system for irrigation water storage, sources of fill, strategic golf use as well as beautification for both golf and real estate outlooks.

This plan represents the extreme approach to an existing golf course, namely replacement, and is not typical of the approach usually taken in evaluating and selectively upgrading an existing layout.

In generating a new layout as has been done here, the process of laying out centre lines to create the best mix of golf holes is a proactive, positive type of process due to the absence of any previous improvements to the site (in golf terms).

Usually, the best mix of golf holes is also the most natural hole routing, which maximises the value of existing land features. This usually minimises the amount of artificial type work that is required to be done, resulting in the best golf course for the minimum amount of work and consequently, the cheapest price. (Contrary to popular opinion, which says that more money simply equals a better product).

In reviewing the planning and design of an existing golf course, several factors contributing to the present condition of that course & the club that uses it, means in most cases the approach has to be a little different. These factors might be as follows:-

a) The Club may or may not have the resources, such as land, capital and management that a developer usually has at their disposal when building a new golf course.

b) The main asset of most Golf Clubs is their existing golf course that, good or bad, is what brings patrons to the club, which in turn keeps it running.

c) Golfers want to play golf at any time and use the facilities regardless of whether upgrading work needs to be done or not. The club in question usually has an interest in seeing this happen also.

d) The Golf Course obviously needs improvement (otherwise there would be no need to consider re-planning). Which indicates that one or some of the following issues has occurred or become urgently in need of attention

  i) Bad design decisions have been made in the past.

  ii) The existing design has been made obsolete by modern club and ball technology.

  iii) The Golf Course has been encroached upon by adjacent land uses.

  iv) The Golf Course is worn out and play zones need to be replaced or upgraded.

In the majority of cases, upgrading of an existing play-zone will be vastly more efficient in terms of cost, time, landscape and re-instatement of turf, than building a totally new play-zone on virgin land. This may take the form of a whole or part of a golf hole, and might mean that golf hole is played in the opposite direction, or with some relatively minor correction to its alignment.

From these factors it is easy to see that it is usually in the best interests of the club if design problems can be solved with a minimum of change to the existing layout. That may seen like a contradiction in terms – improvement without change – but this, in most cases is the best starting point of reference for the planning and upgrading of existing Golf Courses.

In planning a new Golf Course we are asking ourselves "where will be put *new* golf holes?" which is very much a proactive design approach.

In planning for upgrading of existing golf courses we are asking ourselves – "what can we leave as *old* golf holes?" (Or part thereof) which is, in effect a much more defensive or conservative approach.

In both cases, it is all about maximising the existing site features, and with existing courses, that requires almost the opposite initial approach to achieve the same end result as a new course, which is – *a great golf course.*

Existing Golf Courses – The General Approach

The initial marking-on of modern day centre lines on the existing survey will quickly illustrate where golfers *want* to hit their shots. (Whether they can or not will depend on the present site constraints) This will also show, in a generalised and simplistic format, where many of the potential trouble spots lie. A site visit will confirm these, and probably bring to light other issues that a survey won't pick up. Issues as soil condition – drainage and other soil related problems, vegetation related issues, maintenance related issues, circulation, golf hole strategies and a general feel for the course that the members & guests are used to playing on, can only be gained from site inspection.

Obvious routing issues will be clear, at this stage. How to correct them may not yet be so clear. The Golf Course Architect must undertake reasonable amounts of detailed on-site research over the course of several days, where he will evaluate each golf hole, and note the general good aspects of it. (Those that don't need infrastructural change such as earthworks, major shaping, etc.) He will also isolate the aspects and areas which must be changed, be that by earthworks, sub-surface drainage, shaping, or by simply playing the hole in a different direction or manner.

One can imagine that this process is a very complicated balancing act. Every small change usually has an effect on another golf hole or part thereof, in terms of the balance of the overall playing experience, and often physically, in terms of encroachment. One must be careful in making changes to solve a problem in one area, that the problem is not simply being moved to another area, in the same or different form.

The exercise attempts to come up with the optimum solution on an existing golf course with the normal cross section of issues such as:

a) Boundary encroachment.
b) Internal bottlenecks.
c) Existing clubhouse and maintenance facilities in less then ideal positions.
d) Allowance for future, extra facilities or extensions, which the club may want.
e) Areas of less than ideal sub surface conditions, which must be extensively drained, for example or avoided if possible.
f) The unnatural appearance of the existing man-made features.

And the list could go on indefinitely.

The process required is to mentally marry these technical and creative issues, turning each negative into a positive, and creating something that not only is fun and challenging to play, but looks as if it evolved naturally. The demanding nature of this procedure is, I believe, an indication of the high level of skill required to be able to competently undertake the design of an internal golf course remodel project on cramped sites with predetermined boundaries.

But how is such a multi faceted design process undertaken? It is a little difficult to describe the process that I personally go through in compiling an optimum layout. I think the best analogy would be that of a car, that still runs, but is brought to a mechanic to be thoroughly checked over, repaired and improved upon to ensure it will not need major works again for a long time into the future.

Like a car, a golf course is made up of thousands of small components, which are the onsite features, most of which rely on each other to form a well functioning unit. Like an engine, some major components are essential, but some smaller ones can be added or removed depending on whether you want a high performance, finely tuned top-end model or an easy to maintain, reliable, long lasting version.

Like a mechanic we first begin with an investigation of the car (golf course) to find what the problems with it might be.

Firstly, we apply spectacles (existing centre lines) that enable us to quickly see any glaring corrections that might need to be made.

Next, we proceed to conduct a further preliminary exploration of the golf course, on a hole-by-hole basis, as a mechanic would start the engine up and take the car for a drive.

Next we refer to the client, provoking lateral thought and ask them what they perceive the issues are, and what should be included in the solution (often known as a wish list). The mechanic would, in equivalent terms, question his client about the desired performance, comfort and appearance characteristics they would like to see in their renovated vehicle.

Next we proceed to systematically check every small component, noting the suitability, and potential to be included in the updated version. This is the equivalent of a mechanic pulling the car to pieces, checking each component and noting if it should be included in its present form, upgraded, replaced with a better version or discarded altogether.

Next, after the completion of a couple of progressively refined draft plans, a final master plan is presented to The Golf Club, which shows the original layout in faint lines with a coloured version of the proposed new layout superimposed over the top. This enables all proposed changes to be easily seen in schematic form by anyone who knows the golf course. In conjunction with this, a planning document will be provided which gives a written explanation of the rationale of the changes, a hole by hole playing description, an estimate of the extent of the changes, and a cost and scheduling arrangement which illustrates how the plan can be implemented according to the means available to the club.

This is the equivalent of an extremely detailed quotation from a mechanic to complete the works as agreed with the client in the initial stages.

Thereafter, the works will be systematically undertaken (designed in detail, and constructed) usually in stages in accordance with the respective urgency with which change must be made (correction of safety or litigation issues are usually most urgent).

After the initial works, the less urgent but no less important issues concerning works that portray the desired overall feeling of quality can be undertaken as funds permit.

The equivalent here in our car analogy is to fix the engine, steering and suspension immediately, while scheduling other upgrades for the future, such as the paint job, interior, etc.

We will leave the car analogy there, except for a couple of notable differences:

a) The client of the mechanic does not usually represent hundreds or possibly thousands of people (club members), most of which are concerned about change to their car (club) and who like to have their personal issues well heard, if not addressed.

b) The mechanic can usually describe or portray what his client will be receiving by making comparisons to other components or products. This is difficult for the Golf Course Architect to do when he is endeavouring to create unique solutions every step of the way.

c) The mechanic does not have to deal with people driving the car while he is working on it. In comparison, rarely does play totally stop on a golf course due to upgrading works.

d) The car will usually be at its peak of performance as soon as the works are complete, while the golf course, if kept well, will continue to improve for many years after the works are complete. Conversely, a great design under the responsibility of someone who does not share the vision will quickly appear substandard, which is the same for most endeavours.

Difficult Planning Decisions

Quite often, in today's environment where land for golf is becoming increasingly scarce, a Golf Course Architect will be faced with situations that on the surface appear impossible to solve.

Take for example the inner city golf course. In most cities of the world the golf courses that are closest to the centre of town are the oldest, being originally built on what was the outskirts of the town of the day. On average, it is fair to say that most of these courses were originally laid out in ways considered obsolete by today's standards of length, safety clearances and other such relevant issues. In fact, it is quite amazing how many of the courses I have come across that are older than say 35 years in which the site boundaries lie to the right side of many of the golf holes, being the slice side for the right hander. This is the most dangerous arrangement, because this is

35

where the errant shots go for vast majority of all golfers. It appears that many who laid out courses during those times shared a common ideal that it was very much acceptable to use the right side out-of-bounds line as a buffer to catch errant balls. I suppose there was no way of knowing at the time that space might become so precious people would actually want to live in these buffer areas. It was probably thought better to let people slice balls into vacant land than where other golfers might be.

Moving to the present, the type of issues these clubs now face is fairly obvious. Totally built out-boundaries and the progress of modern equipment technology means that technically, there is often not enough land space to be able to re-align golf holes without, as referred to earlier – simply moving the problem to another area of the site.

In many places, as at the present time, it is the legal responsibility of golf clubs to show, regardless of whether the club or adjacent land holder was there first, that all due efforts have be made to minimise the occurrence of stray balls. As we have stated earlier, it is virtually impossible to guarantee that there will be no stray balls, but a marked improvement to any situation as it stands is likely to gain a favourable response from all concerned.

Solutions to such situations are likely to involve a revised layout with the following allowances:-

a) Changing or reversing the direction of play on holes that play with the right-hander's slice directly adjacent to a boundary.
b) Angling the preferred line of play away from the boundary. Ie. Positioning the tee closer to the boundary than the landing zone for holes that play along boundaries.
c) Locating landing zones of such holes adjacent to thick trees on the boundary, and augmenting this with thick landscape planting in such areas as well as just in front of the tees on the boundary side, to "smother" most wayward shots before they cause trouble.
d) Including hazards such as water, mounds or other obstacles between these holes and the boundaries, which have the effect of encouraging the golfers to take particularly careful aim or which accentuate the division between the golf hole and the boundary, and preferably both.

Should this still not create an adequate improvement, the Architect would be well advised to shorten some of the golf holes and/or drop at least one shot from the par of the course, in order to make a difference.

This brings forth a very pertinent point regarding the responsibility of the designer as a guardian of the land, and its use. A responsible Golf Course

Architect is obliged to inform the client when the limit has been reached in so far as endeavouring to squeeze as much out of a precious piece of land as possible. However badly the client may not want to hear it, an Architect should be the first to advocate a shorter course or less than par 72 if that is all the land can comfortably sustain.

Other important responsibilities with regard to Master Planning are as follows:-

The Golf Course Layout Should Be Considered As A Whole

This consideration should be made at least in preliminary form, prior to undertaking planning for an upgrade of any small part of a Golf Course, such as a green. Often, club management and committee will not hear of doing a costly and lengthy Master Planning exercise just because they want to fix one problem green.

The Architect must in all cases look past the present management structure of a Golf Course, to ensure his input will not be wasted in the fullness of time. In all likelihood, the golf course will still be there long after any current managers, committees or owners are gone. A good Golf Course Architect will feel responsible for any piece of land he is involved with, regardless of the present day management or financial constraints that are currently attached to it.

What this means is if the club won't fund the Golf Course Architect to do a Master Plan, and the Architect still wishes to be involved, he should, under his own steam obtain enough data, and do enough research to know in his own mind that anything he has a part in building will not be wasted and can form a part of a future, optimised Master Plan of great stature.

Time after time this issue comes to light. Cash strapped Golf Clubs believe they are saving money by not paying to get a high quality Master Plan in place, which all staff and committee can use as a roadmap to excellence for years to come, ensuring positive progress regardless of changes to finances and personnel.

Master Planning is an investment that *all clubs* should make. The extent of the plan may range from a total re-alignment of every golf hole over many years to a historical record for the already great Golf Courses to remind everyone how they should be maintained. It is an unfortunate paradox that those clubs who most need a Master Plan are generally those that have the least ability to invest in it.

Golfers are a fanatical type. They will travel great distances and part with good money to play a great course.

If your golf course has inadequate money, it is most probably not "great" and therefore has a reduced capacity of attracting a large number of well paying patrons.

If a Master Plan to greatness is in place, and administered accurately and well, over time every one of the precious few dollars that can be spent on maintenance and Golf Course improvements will be spent on items that are all working towards a common goal. It will start off slow, but over time – and it may be many years – the momentum will grow exponentially and the last half of the course improvements will occur several times quicker than the first half.

Scheduling Of Improvements

It is the responsibility of the Golf Course Architect to advise the client and contractors not to "bite off more than they can chew" with regard to upgrading works. Those who are inexperienced frequently under estimate golf construction works and I regularly still meet people who are amazed that Golf Course Architecture and Golf Course Construction exist as professions. People often say things like "I thought a golf pro would just tell some people where to mow the grass."

Golf construction works that are thin on finance and expertise risk appearing worse than what they are replacing, regardless of how good the long term strategy is. Widespread negative opinion amongst the members will derail such a program, regardless of how successful it ultimately would have been.

Concentration of all efforts to progressively upgrade small areas to completion using high standard construction techniques is the best way to ensure a minimum of waste in maintaining & resurrecting previously partly finished work. As well as that, it illustrates in no uncertain terms to all doubters (and there are always many at the outset), the high standard of the new work and the obvious disparity between that and the existing course.

Diagram 7 shows an example of a Master Plan that has been successfully completed, and which has facilitated the execution of a resolution enabling management to proceed with an onsite upgrading process. The plan has been conceived with due consideration for both internal and external boundary issues such as real estate, as outlined below.

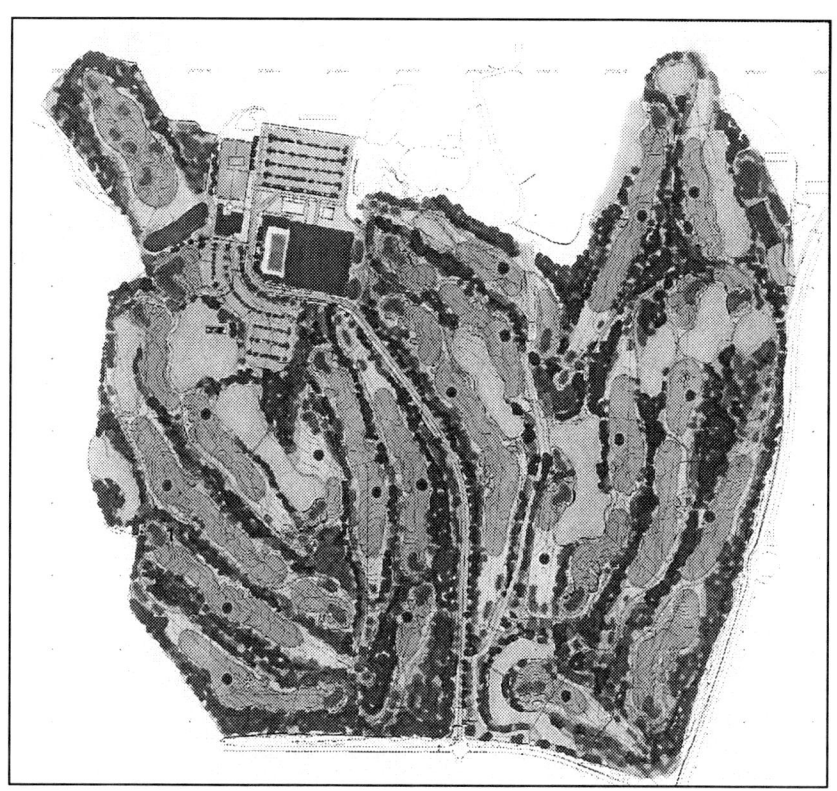

Diagram 7. Typical Golf Course Master Plan.

Real estate, however, has been both friend and enemy to Golf Course Design for some time. Encroachment of houses can severely effect a golf course, but conversely, demand for enhanced real estate has spurned the development of many more golf courses than might otherwise have been built.

3

Golf And Real Estate

As alluded to previously, it seems that on the surface, Golf Courses and Real Estate is a marriage that won't last. In many instances, the two disciplines are almost like archenemies, however this is I believe most prevalent in areas where common boundaries became that way by accident.

Nowadays it is very rare indeed that our Golf Course Design activities do not give at least some thought and allowances for real estate or residential properties; be they existing adjacent properties, or proposed. We have already looked at the typical issues likely to come up on existing courses with built-out boundaries, and how we minimise their negative effects, but on a new layout, the approach is very much different.

On older, existing Golf Courses, areas of shared boundaries are generally to be minimised where possible because in crowded conditions, the more residents there are living on the Golf Course boundary, the more potential exists for disagreements.

In planning for Golf Course/Residential developments, one is usually attempting to maximise the golf course frontage to real estate, as that is generally where the developer gains the most value from inclusion of a golf course in his development.

The main differences in circumstances which make this possible are as follows:-

    a) Well planned, integrated developments are built to attract people who *want* to live on a golf course, as opposed to those who previously only ended up living on a golf course by chance, and who do not rate their shared boundary as a benefit.

    b) Optimum golf course routing and generous buffers, designed in as a part of integrated developments, minimise the negative effects of shared boundaries.

c) The relationship between golf course and residential is set up in an optimum manner to create spectacular views of the course from the houses. More often than not, the houses will be set at higher levels than the adjacent fairways with views framed by well-maintained trees and shrubs.

d) Nowadays, many developers are putting together Legal Documents that must be signed by all buyers acknowledging there is a risk of some stray balls entering their property. This helps reduce the potential for future disagreements, and ensures everybody is aware that the very occasional stray ball is a fact of life.

The success of a golf/residential project, given that the appropriate development attributes and design skills are in place, such as location, construction expertise, and marketing, depends on the abilities of the Golf Course Architect and Real Estate Planner to maximise the site as a whole.

In the same way that we must consider the whole golf course layout before we proceed to design one new green, we must also consider our whole site, including real estate, roads, and all other elements, which must be included and be made to harmoniously co-habitate with the golf course.

The Golf Course Architect and Planner must work as one for the initial part of the planning phase, to define the optimum balance of all items, which firstly - *must* be included, and secondly - which *can* be included. A gradual working-up of the shape the project should take can thereafter be conducted, including site analysis plans, input from market research indicators and preliminary engineering input, prior to making any design decisions. Working hard in the early stages to identify all constraints and indicators as accurately as possible will enable a very clear and useful site analysis plan to be compiled. With an accurate and detailed site analysis plan as an aid, many of the design decisions with regard to land allocation ie. The location and arrangement of different items that are to be included - becomes obvious.

It may appear slow and overly meticulous in the beginning, but everyone, especially clients need to understand that this extremely careful and thorough approach in the initial stages is a major and very cheap investment when compared to the cost of the whole project. When dealing with construction costs, one seemingly inconsequential idea could lead the development process down a path that can save millions in development costs, to say nothing of the time savings related to getting the planning correct in the first instance.

Conversely, one slip of the pen or a rushed job could result in missed design opportunities, which could cost the client a great deal, in both time and outright development expense, to say nothing of potentially lower sales premiums. The reason this fact is lost on most people is that they only ever get to see the final result as it turns out, and have no idea what it could have been.

I personally have difficulty in coming terms with the ramifications of this concept. Intelligent clients should never quibble about fees for their key designers, unless they doubt their ability (in which case they shouldn't hire them).

Key designers such as Golf Course Architects and Planners are really there to anchor the chain of events that follow along the line to either success or failure. I have seen Golf Residential projects in obscure locations have great success due mainly through the self-promotion and positive word of mouth comments that occur fairly readily when a good product comes along. I have also seen many great projects in prime locations spoiled by ridiculous design decisions.

Intelligent Developers select their key consultants carefully, pay them a reasonable fee - and on time. They respect their opinions and design decisions, whilst ensuring they communicate a solid reasoning behind each decision. This allows consultants to maximise all site opportunities and therefore create successful projects.

Clients who treat their consultants poorly risk removing the spark required (at least on a subconscious level) for them to create greatness.

Key Golf and Real Estate Design Elements

Designing the layout of adjacent land uses in the Golf/Real Estate situation should be an extension of the basic design parameters employed in laying out the golf course.

Use of the existing site attributes where possible will, like the golf course, usually make these elements more efficient to construct and usually make it more pleasant to live in or visit. In any case, such an approach will make the connection to the golf course at its boundaries more homogenous, and therefore more pleasant and of higher quality.

We have already established that there is a certain value in golf course frontage, and this can be further accentuated if some of the virtues of a good golf course, such as natural terrain, and possibly landscape and shaping, flow through into other parts of the development. This is a very real way of raising the premiums that can be obtained on all land in the development, not just those pieces with direct frontage to the golf course.

It must be remembered also that not everybody wants to live in a house with direct Golf Course frontage. However almost all residents like to drive past and see glimpses of well-maintained and very green and natural golf courses as they travel to and from the front gate of their housing estate to their home. Likewise, they will like to make use of parklands inside their estate, which have been designed and developed to appear naturally beautifully, like a Golf Course.

It is a known fact that in comparison to other developments, all dwellings in a closed Golf/ Real Estate development attract at least some premium. The level of this premium is directly related to the planning and design of the overall layout in relation to the level of skill with which the Golf Course integrates with adjacent land uses.

Using the Lay of the Land, In Allowing For Real Estate

Although it is not necessary for Golf Course Architects to know all aspects of town planning, it is, I believe, essential that a good Golf Course Architect appreciates the basic requirements in laying out roads and Real Estate.

Likewise it is important that the planner has some appreciation of the requirements of the golf course, but this is perhaps not quite as important as the other way around.

When laying out a Golf Course, there is usually a multitude of ways that a layout can be compiled on any one piece of land, and when these choices are there for the Golf Course Architect, he needs to be able to make them in a fully informed manner. This will ensure these decisions assist in gaining the best result for the planning and design of the adjacent land uses, beyond simply gaining good views of the golf course from the interface boundaries. After all, the adjacent land uses and their subsequent rate of sale is most probably what is funding the Golf Course.

By this, I do not at all mean this should reduce Golf Courses in quality, size or other attributes in favour of Real Estate. In almost all cases there is no need for this trade off situation, or win-lose mentality. Sure, the developer will almost always want to minimise the land area to be consumed by a Golf Course, but once a general understanding has been struck in that regard, there is no reason why a win-win situation cannot be achieved. It is simply a matter of the key consultants putting their respective egos to one side, taking on a sympathetic view to the needs of other design disciplines and the attributes of the site. If this can be achieved to a sufficient degree, a feeling of excitement will begin to take hold of the design group, and real synergous design solutions will begin to come forth.

This is what every project should have. Clients who know how to cultivate this feeling of trust and mutual respect between themselves and their key consultants are doing themselves and the land a great service. And it doesn't cost a thing!

Issues that should be remembered by the Golf Course Architect during this planning phase are as follows: Services (drainage, sewerage, etc), how roads need to be routed to properly intersect and service homes, commercial zones, etc, as well as the optimum size and arrangement for different land uses.

Real Estate

In creating pleasant and appealing sites on which to build dwellings, one needs to consider, among other things, the following: aspect, views, location and accessibility.

a) *Aspect*
Most Architects will prefer a north-south directional axis as the main aspect for a residential site. It is of course very hard to ensure every site on a housing development conforms to this, however it should be kept in mind that scope should be left for the designers of each house to take advantage of some reasonable variation of the ideal aspect.

b) *Views*
Views of the golf course element of any such development are of course paramount to the success of a golf/real estate project. The best way to maximise this is generally to position the real estate higher than the level of the adjacent fairway, thereby creating a kind of 'grandstand view' of the golf from each backyard. This concept normally works well from a drainage viewpoint in any case, however there is more to it than this.

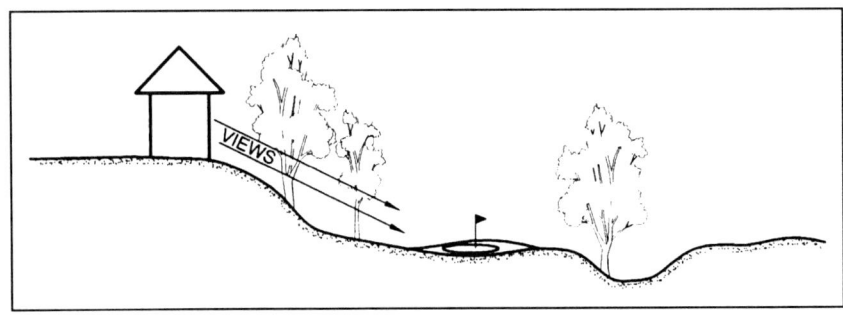

Diagram 8. Typical arrangement of Real Estate / Golf Course view Section.

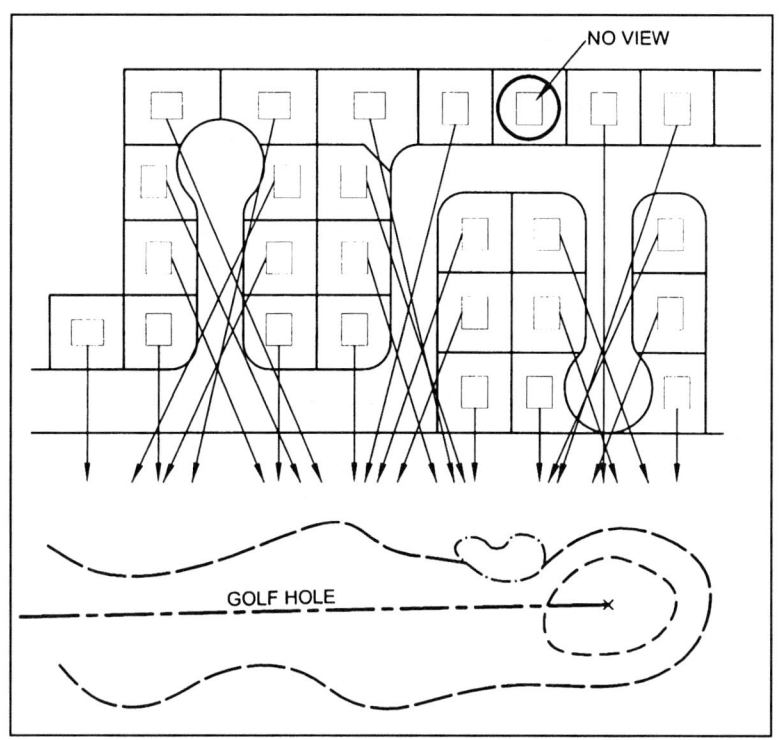

Diagram 9. Maximisation of golf course view options through road layout design.

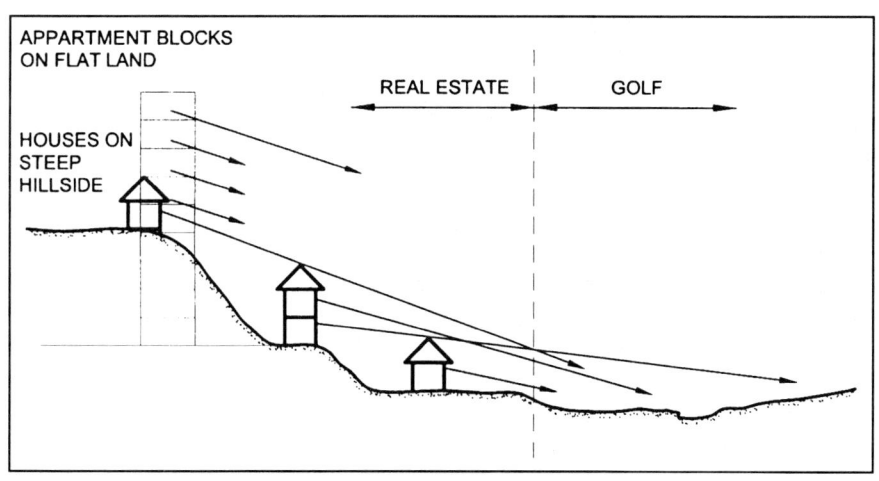

Diagram 10. Distant golf course view options utilising height differentials.

The distant views from those residences that do not have direct golf frontage are also a factor. As previously mentioned, not everybody wants to live right on a golf course boundary, and allowance should be made where possible to cater for that. Diagrams 9 and 10 give examples of how that can be allowed for in a two and three-dimensional manner, respectively.

Diagram 9 also shows the opportunities of creating much improved partial views of the course, whilst forgoing a minimum of direct Golf Course frontage, all of which would be calculated to give the best overall return. In this sketch, possibly 7 direct frontage lots have been forsaken, but the result is 3 lots with direct frontage and another 22 with partial views. Only one house out of 26 does not get a view, but the premium on this house is likely to be quite high in any case, because of the calibre of its neighbours.

Note also that while views from houses 3 to 4 lots away from the golf course will be fairly limited, the practice of putting a little stretch of road along the boundary of the golf in selected areas gives everyone a good view as they come and go from their house.

Diagram 10 shows a schematic illustration of how undulating sites can be utilised to create longer views of golf over the rooftops of the houses with direct frontage. Especially in a city environment, a view of a distant city skyline over the top of a 'green lung' such as a golf course can be a very sought after residential location. (Refer Central Park in New York, where an apartment with a view commands a not so small fortune).

In so far as the best short view options are concerned, a view of a golf hole across a lake is probably the most sought after. (Refer below diagram 11) Care should however be taken with aspect in warm climates to minimise the reflection of sun off water, which can make such residential sites uncomfortably hot and glary.

This pond-on-boundary effect creates an extra safety buffer (subconsciously for the golfer as much as physically), which works well for all concerned, and should these prime lots have a distant city or mountain view, they would be absolutely premium.

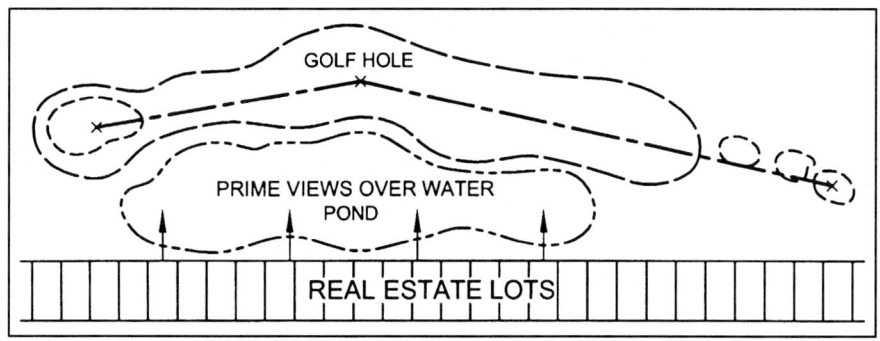

Diagram 11.Premuim Golf / residential sites, with a view of golf across water.

c) *Location And Accessibility*

Location of each residence inside a development and the balance of accessibility versus privacy are very important. Residents who buy into an up-market Golf/Residential development are likely to be the type who will want a degree of privacy, and the ability to completely remove themselves from the hustle and bustle of their work life, when they are at home. That is not to say that they require absolute segregation from everybody else. On the contrary the feeling of security produced by having neighbours fairly close by, is something many people favour.

Being continually annoyed by neighbours that are too close, or have the ability to look into the private space of adjacent landowners is something that must generally be avoided if at all possible.

The annoyance of living next to a road where the traffic is loud and fast is also a concept that is difficult to market.

People like to be close to conveniences such as schools, shopping centres and the like, but do not want to be caught up in the negative aspects of crowding and traffic that these public spaces create.

As in the design of a golf course layout, opportunities to use features of the natural terrain in a positive way to create the best of both worlds must be exploited whenever possible.

For example, a real estate precinct with a gentle gully might be able to be designed such that most of the public areas can be positioned low down on the gully floor, with roads radiating out to the surrounding hills, where the housing is situated. This radiation effect will evenly disperse all traffic and provide a height differential between the land use types. This will help to minimise the amount of noise of the public areas that spills into the residential areas. The result is a close proximity for all residents to public land use areas; whilst minimising the negative affects that these close public areas could potentially bring to their adjacent residential streets.

In siting a Golf Course and liaising with Town Planners, the Golf Course Architect should be sensitive to such issues and on the look out for potentially awkward land spaces that are hard to access or create negative impact on adjacent precincts. It may well be the case that from time to time the Golf Course Architect should consider ignoring small sections of the natural site contours and proceed to 'manufacture' a receptive section of a Golf Hole, in order to ensure the overall development operates at its most efficient for the fullness of time.

Indeed, on very flat sites or overly rugged sites there is often no alternative, and a good Golf Course Designer should have no problem achieving an excellent result, albeit for a slightly higher cost.

Siting Of Roads And Paths

Going hand in hand with the issues that effect location and accessibility are the roads and pedestrian reserves that service all areas. Like the centre lines of the golf holes, the roads are the skeleton of a residential development and their locations are paramount in insuring the overall success of most developments.

There is usually a reasonable amount of flexibility in the laying down of roads, - more so than in the laying down of golf hole centre lines, because the number, length and direction of the roads do not have to be as specifically variable as the golf holes. But having said that, it is not a matter of randomly aligning roads and there are several fundamental mistakes to be avoided.

A)   Intersections

i) *Intersections where roads come together at angles more acute than 90 degrees.* These are to be avoided unless good vision of the other roads can somehow be guaranteed. It is difficult for a human being, whilst driving a car to look further around than 90 degrees to the left or right before proceeding across an intersection. Furthermore it is frustrating and dangerous to do so.

T intersections where the intersecting road joins the continuing road on the inside of a curve, form a similar negative experience.

ii) *Roundabouts.*   Roundabouts in locations where traffic levels will cause cars on any or all legs to wait more than a few seconds should be avoided and replaced with traffic lights. These type of roundabouts can quickly become huge bottlenecks. Contrary to widespread opinion, roundabouts do not automatically improve traffic flow in all conditions, and should be selectively used. Generally they are great for areas of local traffic and light through-traffic.

iii) *Roundabouts With 3 Entry Points.* These will only function in quite light traffic conditions, in which case a standard T intersection with a give-way sign is usually just as good an option. In slightly heavier traffic conditions, traffic tends to bank up on one leg of the roundabout, which is frustrating for drivers.

iv) *Levels* – Siting of intersections on the crests of hills, where all intersecting roads cannot be seen from other intersecting roads should be avoided. Ideally, the intersection should be level with, or slightly below the level of incoming roads, to ensure early sightings of other vehicles by those approaching the intersection.

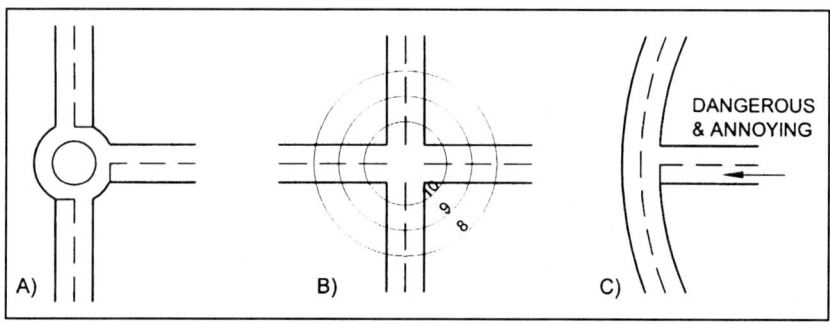

Diagram 12, examples of intersection types to be generally avoided in design. A) Roundabout with three points of entry. B) Intersection on the crest of a hill. C) Intersection on the inside of a curved road

B)   Roads

Siting of roads should be, first and foremost done in consideration of how to get traffic from one place to the next with a minimum amount of backtracking and a minimum amount of potentially dangerous situations.

Steep grades should be avoided if at all possible, and if required should only be for short stretches in areas where traffic will be going slow and where there is ample warning of the change in conditions.

Like Golf Course Design, the natural contours should generally have a major influence on the road structure of most developments. If roads can be routed to virtually conform to the natural contours, there is a good chance that the whole development will retain a fairly natural feel.

In recent years, in many places there has been a trend away from using fairly straight roads linked at the ends with connecting roads, which in most cases, on sites with gentle topography, is sound technical planning as it disperses traffic whilst maximising vision for vehicles as they approach intersections.

One often sees development plans where roads have been routed in symmetrical, winding arrangements, which can serve no greater purpose than providing an artistic appearing master plan. It must be remembered that the value of such preconceived, winding symmetrical road systems can rarely be appreciated at ground level. Issues such as site topography and the instinctive desire of humans to take the shortest practical route from one place to another, *should be* the governing factors of road layout design.

There is nothing more annoying than driving within view of your house, then having to drive much further, through a long-winded maze of slow curves and roads that double back on themselves in order to get home. This style of planning is not only annoying for the end user, but it wastes people's time, fuel, increases traffic congestion and increases the opportunities for traffic accidents.

Ease of practical use must surely be held as the most important design principle to be employed in laying out the more major roads of a development. Thereafter, interest can be added to this framework in the form of symmetry, curves, or any other stylised elements, as long as they have a practical and aesthetic benefit to the end user, by actually adding value to the concept. For example, on any undulating property, it is very unlikely that the spinal roads will be straight, in fact they are likely to have some curves in order to provide optimum access to all areas of the site, whilst minimising the work needed to make them function adequately.

It is unlikely however, that many pieces of development land will dictate the incorporation of a perfectly symmetrical road layout as its optimum solution. It may be decided, for example that since a reasonable amount of work is required in any case, it might be worthwhile to flatten a hill or fill a gully in order to widen & straighten an entry road, thereby adding a symmetrical or artistic element that will be obvious to the end user. Whether the layout of the rest of such a development is stylised will usually be of little consequence to the end user, as long as it is pleasant and functional.

The following diagram shows the layout of a 27-hole golf course with selected pockets of real estate in an inner city setting.

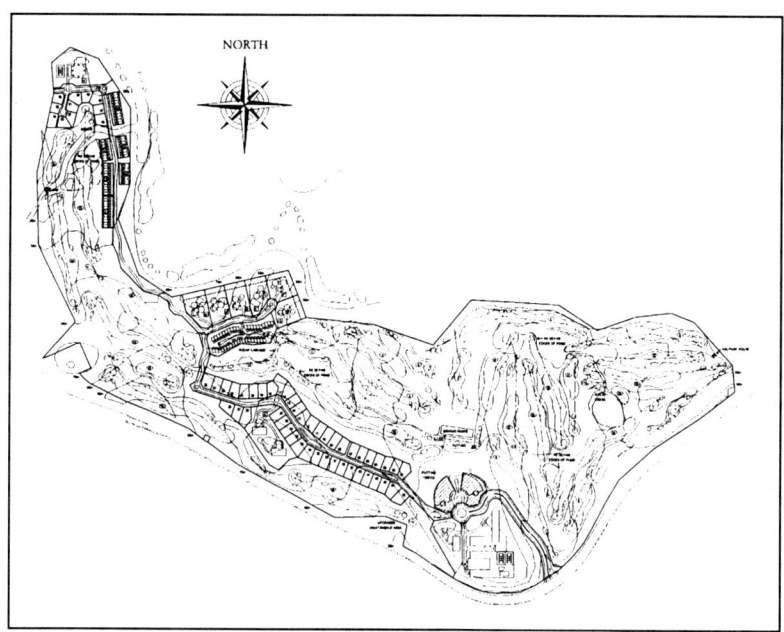

Diagram 13. Sample Golf/Real Estate layout on hilly land. Real estate layout courtesy of Grandwinter Resources.

This is an existing 27-hole golf course on very hilly terrain. A proposal was put together to redevelop the course into an 18-hole championship layout with a slightly shorter 9-hole, night-lit executive course.

Being an existing course, the members were keen to minimise Real Estate intrusion, and they felt the inclusion of fingers of Real Estate, even if well hidden, would be a backward step when compared to the purely core style of Golf Course layout that they currently enjoy. Items such as the clubhouse and entry road were essentially fixed from the start.

The location of the pockets of Real Estate and the main spine road are key to this plan.

The rugged nature of the site gave few options with regard to both siting of roads & real estate and locating returning 9-hole loops of golf holes in a manner that would not break too many of our "rules" of golf course routing.

The result is a win-win situation for both Golf and Real Estate.

The main road enters the site proper at the clubhouse area, where the proposed commercial centre on the left is situated on an existing flat, previously earth

51

worked site. The road continues on into the residential area, along the top of a long and rather high ridge. Approximately 40 Prime residential lots are situated on either site of this road, each with ideal North-South aspect and commanding Golf Course views, without appearing obtrusive to the golf course because of the large height differential.

The road turns right at this end of this ridge and curls its way downhill and left. To the right and fairly low down on some difficult and undulating terrain is the condominium site, which would be rather intensively developed. This land, slated for condos was too awkward for either golf or residential allotments without employing major earthworks. As such, it is perfect for high-rise apartments, as they have a relatively small base footprint, which can be easily situated on such rugged landforms. Space for 6 condominium towers is provided, which take in views of the 17th hole (with water) and to the North, over what also happens to be a golf course.

At the end of the spine road, is a medium density residential development, which will afford views of the golf course in a southerly direction from many of the houses, including distant views over rooftops for many residences at the northernmost part of this area.

For the most part, only minor, and fairly unobtrusive earthworks is required to build the roads and prepare building envelopes, and all real estate is sited to gain maximum sales premiums.

Like the residential aspect, the golf course takes advantage of the hilly terrain, rather than fighting it.

Many holes utilise sections of existing play zones, whilst we have been able to use the steep existing slopes as natural buffers along the boundaries with the real estate.

All golf holes are acceptable in relation to our routing models expounded under chapter 1, with only holes 4 and 6, which dogleg either side around a large hill, causing a little extra work to make them play optimally.

The practice range is sited close to the clubhouse, shooting north, and all starting and finishing holes of each 9-hole loop are within easily accessible walking distance from the clubhouse.

Overall, the course has a pleasant mix of golf holes, and while still steep in some small sections, the grades along lines of play are very much improved and acceptable from a playability viewpoint.

The following diagram is an 18-hole golf course/residential development on a very flat, low-lying site.

This site has a small stream running through it from East to West, where it discharges into coastal mangroves, and ultimately the ocean.

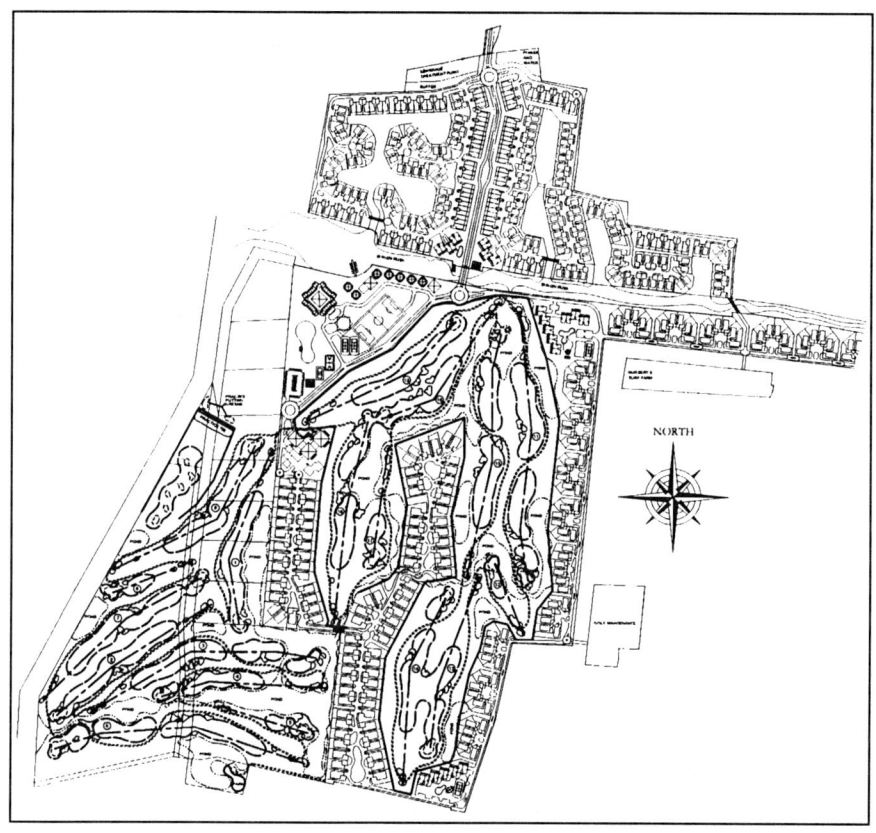

Diagram 14. Sample Golf/Real Estate layout on flat land. Real estate layout courtesy of Grandwinter Resources

Again, the access point to the site is fixed, from the North Western-most point of the site. Other issues which affect the planning of the development are as follows:-

-
- The western parcel of land is leasehold, and can only accommodate golf, as the lease will eventually be subject to renewal. As such it would be advisable to put a neat 9 holes of golf on this land, in order that this leasehold 9 holes could be omitted in the future, should the lease not be renewed. The clubhouse therefore must be located on the freehold land, but close to the boundary of the leasehold.

53

- The passage of the stream should under normal conditions not be impeded, and allowance should be made for the occasional flood, which comes down this stream. An extensive series of mitigation ponds is to be included in the golf course plan for this reason.
- Drainage from any area on the real estate to the nearest water body should not be farther than approximately 100 metres, to allow for minimum drainage fall without major earthworks. (Storm water from real estate will drain into the golf course as per standard practice)
- Feasibility studies indicated that approximately 500 residences would be required to ensure viability of the project, as well as a Hotel Complex.

The project is located in a tropical tourist area, close to a free trade zone. As such it will function as a holiday resort, and its residents will be a mixture of hotel guests, time-share holidaymakers, retired couples, and high-end corporate executives who work in the free trade zone. In keeping with the resort theme, all dwellings must have some kind of pleasant outlook, and integration between residences and open spaces such as the golf course must be seamless, as per any high-end tropical resort.

The resultant plan provides a highly optimised solution to all the required elements.

The entry road which, by necessity is rather long and winding will become a quite an impressive landscape feature rather than simply an extra cost. This will create feelings of wonderment and heighten the expectations of visitors as they enter the development.

Eventually the road will widen out to an impressively wide boulevard, with glimpses of well-structured resort homes on either side. At the end of the boulevard, a large 3-way intersection will give one the choice of going left – for residences, or right for the golf course and resort hotel. While one is making up one's mind, forward views from this elevated intersection will provide a panoramic outlook of the back 9 holes.

Turning left will lead motorists around the northern edge of the development, accessing Cluster homes with outlooks over either the river or the golf course. At the end of this road, are two rows of the most exclusive residences, on larger land packages. These outlook either east over holes 14 and 15, north over hole 16, or west over holes 17, 1 and over water and several greens and tees on the front 9 holes.

The residential element of the development is proposed to be strata titled, meaning that all road verges and spaces between Cluster residences will be shaped and landscaped to be an extension of the Golf Course. This guarantees a seamless integration of spaces, and with the golf maintenance team upkeeping all open spaces, a long-term strategy is in place to ensure the high class finish remains in place long after completion.

The hotel site is bordered on one side by a man-made lagoon on the edge of which will be several eateries and souvenir outlets. On the other side of the hotel site, the golf course will be clearly visible from most of the grounds and the Hotel tower will take in all of these relatively short views as well as the distant mountains to the north and the ocean to the south.

Overall, we have achieved optimum balance for all Real Estate, with every allotment having some kind of enhanced view, whether it is parkland, water, golf or a combination of these. The only slightly negative aspect of the plan is that the planners were not able to maximise double frontages for roads, meaning the total length of road is a little more than it otherwise might have been. The peculiar shape of the site made it virtually impossible to do better in that regard, however with the strata title arrangement, this is not such a major negative. Due to the fact that since all internal roads will be maintained by the body corporate, under the strata title model, they do not need to specified as wide or be built with as much expensive infrastructure as they otherwise might be. There is also an unavoidable east-west aspect to some of the prime residential allotments, which will have to be allowed for in the design of the houses that eventually fill these spaces.

With regard to the Golf Course planning, aside from the general planning issues already described above, there was very few specific onsite conditions effecting the routing of the golf course, as the site is quite flat.

Allowing for the through-flow of the river and flood mitigation, the site analysis process very much dictated (as it often does) the final location of the golf holes. We briefly considered siting some golf holes along either side of the river in the eastern finger of the site, but this was quickly dispelled due to limitations on useable space in this area, and difficulties in providing returning 9-hole loops to our ideal clubhouse location.

The resultant golf course layout utilises essentially a core layout on the first 9 holes, which also houses a practice range and enough space for marquees and the like, such as would be required for a tournament situation.

The second 9 holes utilises a basic dual fairway arrangement, common in situations where one is endeavouring to provide a reasonable amount of golf frontage without consuming too much land.

The layout allows for all technical requirements in a way that will enable them to appear naturally occurring (ponds waterways, minimum earthworks requirements) whilst all golf holes are routed in such a way they do not break any of our basic guidelines for golf course routing.

4

Strategy

We are the "Robin Hoods" of Golf. Wherever possible we steal (challenge) from the rich (low handicapper) and give (encourage) to the poor (high handicapper)

After general consideration of the layout of a Golf Course and its interface with surrounding land uses, the next phase of design would usually come in the form of consideration of the playing strategies of each golf hole. The above introductory sentence sums up in the simplest terms, the way strategy is generally incorporated into our golf course designs, and it is with this in mind that virtually every design decision regarding strategy is made.

Strategy when applied to golf is a term that is I believe, severely misunderstood and misused by a great many golfers, golf course superintendents, golf professionals and even golf course architects.

Although the Robin Hood analogy is by far the most accurate that I can think of to describe it, it is in reality not quite so simple. After all, who are the real rich and who are the real poor, and who are we to judge them? This question was probably also at the root of Mr Hood's problems. As such, in our context, the incorporation of strategy is probably best described as: *The process of giving options, through design to all standards of golfers as often as possible during their round of golf.*

The question of golf course strategy for us is two-part. Firstly, what is an *acceptable* strategy? And secondly, how do we implement it?

Firstly, and as an introduction, let's think of strategy at its simplest. In playing a golf hole, a golfer theoretically analyses what is before him and matches the strengths and weaknesses of his game to that challenge. This enables him to execute his shot making in such a way as to give the best possible chance of negotiating the golf hole in the fewest possible strokes.

A golfer therefore strategises his play, both in general terms (ie. "My game is too erratic so I'm going for the safe plays today") and on a shot by shot basis, which invariably involves a more specific, and in-depth analysis. This process will occur to some degree on all golf courses so long as they have a fairway, which is at least a bit easier to play off than the rough, and a hole on a green, which provides a target.

So what then, is an acceptable strategy? To me, an acceptable strategy is one that gives options to all levels of players, and preferably more than one realistic option to all levels of players.

These options will come in different formats, for different standards of golfers. As was stated in the quote at the beginning of this chapter, in design we aim to challenge the better players and encourage the poorer players. This ideally happens in degrees, by the golfer *selecting for themselves* what degree of challenge and what degree of encouragement they should aim for in planning for each and every shot.

I will go into some detail about this shortly, but first I would like to paint a picture as to how this strategic formula might appear, to the average golfer. For this I will use Royal Melbourne Golf Club as an example, and my first experience in playing there.

At that time I was your average young golfer, with a 15 handicap, hitting it 200-220 metres or thereabouts off the tee. I had a typical fade and on my bad days, a wild slice. I was the product of a country golf course laid out through a remnant eucalypt forest, with limited summer irrigation, limited winter drainage, push-up greens, and only 14 bunkers, all of which were green-side bunkers and most at that time, with more gravel in them than sand.

Royal Melbourne, consistently rated as one of the top 10 Golf Courses in the world, seemed like a world away, and I felt out of my depth just driving down the highway to get there.

Teeing off, I felt glad that the first fairway was so wide and forgiving, and the approach shot to the first green, although long was achievable even for me, with a run-on long iron. The 2nd, 3rd indeed every hole seemed similarly wide and forgiving. For me, concentrating hard and giving such high respect for this fabled layout was enabling me to play a few shots under my handicap. By the back nine I was privately making my plans for turning pro and deciding to go for a bit more, I suddenly dropped several shots on a few seemingly innocuous golf holes. I went back to aiming at the centre of the fairway with my 3 wood and employing run-on approaches for the final stretch and managed to break my handicap by 3 shots. I was overjoyed at that but felt I could have done a lot better and was eager to try again.

My experiences that day represent to me the epitome of good strategic golf course design. With conservative and intelligent play, I was able to break my handicap but the minute I mismatched the level of my ability with the shot at hand, I paid the price. The fact that the options were given there for me to choose for myself was in itself an empowering feeling, but the variation of the challenges gave the experience even more memorability.

This variation, made up through the routing of the golf holes plus the set-up of the strategies is very much an important part of the experience. Each hole should be a specific and different experience, whilst fitting comfortably into the overall picture. Even now, many years later, I can remember each hole and many of the shots I played at Royal Melbourne the first time I visited. With so many golf courses, any course that can evoke that kind of memorability has some kind of a head start when golfers begin to talk about which courses are the greatest. – If you can't remember them, how great can they be?

This issue of memorability and giving each golf hole its own character is dependent primarily on a) routing of the golf holes, b) set up of the strategies, and thereafter, c) the earth shaping, finishing and landscape or other such cosmetic work employed to present these strategies to the golfer.

An Acceptable Strategy

The play options that were presented to me at Royal Melbourne were perfect examples of acceptable strategies, in that they *narrow* the perceived gap between the poorer players and the top professionals.

The hazards are for the most part positioned in order to guard the optimum line of play, that is the line of play most likely to yield a low score, providing one does not fall prey to one or more of these hazards along the way. Coupled with this are wide fairways positioned in most instances adjacent to these hazards, skirting around them and providing large 'safe areas.'

This allows for landing zones for lesser players that are as ample and forgiving as one will ever see in golf, enabling almost everyone to keep the ball in play in most instances. By playing safe to these areas one will usually be able to get the ball on the green if not in regulation then one or two shots more. From there, 2 or 3 puts will probably see most golf holes played according to handicap, or may be even occasionally under handicap. This scenario is very much acceptable and encouraging to average and poorer golfers. At no time are they forced to take major risks just to keep the ball in play and they can choose the level of risk they wish to take, on any shot.

Built into this seemingly friendly strategic set up is a set of more subtle design elements that challenge the better players, but which for the most part, make little difference to the average to poorer player.

- Locating hazards such that their effect is often compounded unless the golfer who plays from the hazard gives due respect and concedes at least half a shot, in playing their recovery conservatively.

- Simply locating hazards out of reach of most amateur players can be employed to some degree, however this can have a negative impact. In today's game, modern technology has given professional golfers so much distance and accuracy that locating a hazard at driving distance for the pros will in many cases negatively challenge many lesser golfers on their second shots.

- Building in subtle shapes and slopes into the green designs, putting a premium on ball position of the approach shot when it finishes on the green, is an example of an element that achieves this.

The poorer to average amateur golfer is almost as likely to 3 putt from either 10 or 30 feet, regardless of slope and subtle green shapes; due to poor technique, lapses in concentration or an inability to read the borrow of the greens. However, a low handicapper or pro will feel the pressure under such circumstances if he knows he needs to hit the ball close or leave an uphill put if he is to have a realistic chance at a birdie or tap-in putt for par.

In such a situation the pro golfer will need to take risks by hitting the ball close to hazards to enable the best line in for his approach shot, which might also entail flirting with a hazard. The lesser golfer will not even be aware of such issues and therefore, for him it is pointless to take such risks. As long as he is on or near to the green in regulation he will be relatively happy, as he will also have a chance for par, and sometimes birdie.

Under this scenario it is therefore possible for a pro golfer to see a particular hole as difficult, whilst an amateur will consider it as quite easy. This situation makes the amateur golfer believe that maybe there's not so much difference between their game and that of the pros. If an average golfer can sit in his living room and watch a pro golfer bogey a hole that he made an easy par on the week before, then the Golf Course Architect has succeeded in narrowing the perceived gap between the amateur and the professional. This allows millions of average golfers to be able to identify with their pro-golfer heroes as they follow their every move.

I contend this is one of the most important factors that enabled golf to become the major worldwide participatory and spectator sport that it is. Almost all golfers, from children to aged pensioners feel they can identify with the happenings on the pro tours. There are few, if any other sports where that is the case. I believe that we have the talents of a few old time strategic master designers to thank for that. Why is the US Masters such an amazing event? Because of the strategic design of the Golf Course Architect, Dr Mc Kenzie, which has made for dramatic play, and the ability of the masses to identify with it.

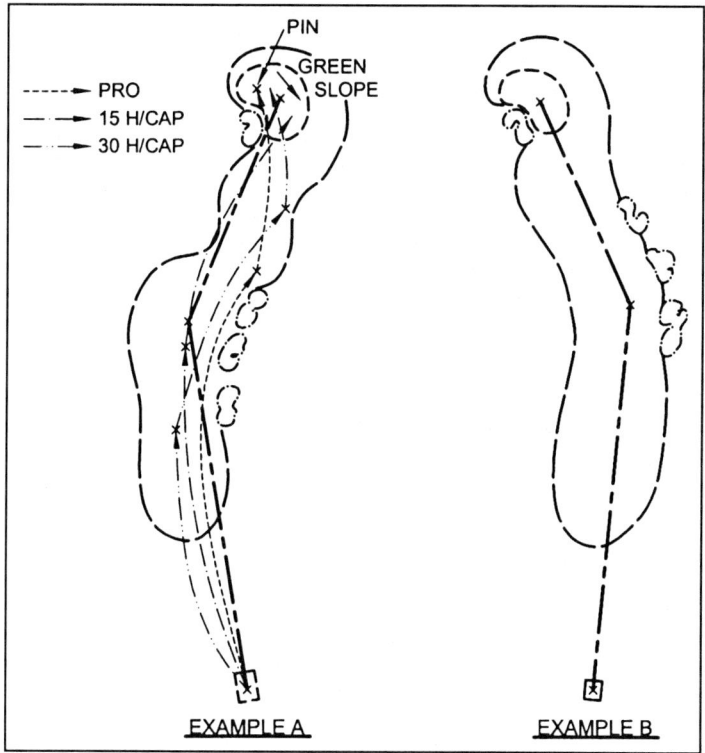

Diagram 15.Sample strategic par 4 golf holes.

Part A) of diagram 15 shows a mythical par four golf hole with the ideal lines of play for 3 basic talent groups, being the pro golfer, the 15 handicapper and the 30 handicapper, on what I would consider to be a fairly typically acceptable strategic golf hole.

61

I am including only this and the proceeding sketch of another par four (part B) of this diagram) on this section on strategy. Note that par 3's and par 5's are more or less either an abridged, or extended version of golf holes that play on strategies with similar *effect* as these. Please note the emphasis on the effect of these strategies, rather than the particular strategies themselves, which could be represented in any number of different arrangements. These types of strategies affect different types of players in different ways, which are generally as explained below:

The pro golfer - wants to hit it close to the pin with his second shot, and he will be looking to give himself the best chance at doing that as he prepares to play his tee shot. To achieve this, he needs to be hitting his approach shot to the green from a line that is to the right of centre of the fairway, to somewhat negate the slope of the green (which falls back to front and left to right). This line will also prevent him from having to hit over the greenside bunker which will gobble up his approach should it be a little short.

His ideal shot off the tee is therefore a fade, which skirts the fairway bunkers and hopefully finishes on the right of the fairway. From there, a slightly drawn mid to short iron will hold up into the slope of the green and leave him with a short uphill birdie putt.

The pro must select his level of risk off the tee. If his ball goes too close to the bunkers, and actually goes in one of them, he will have a difficult shot to get close to the pin. Attacking the pin from a fairway bunker is difficult, especially if the length of the shot is less than a full club, and could turn a possible par into a double bogey. If this happens, he would be best advised to play out sideways, or if his lie is good, play up to the right side of the green, leaving a regulation uphill chip or long putt and a chance at par.

To avoid the bunkers and go down the left edge of the fairway will leave a fairly long and difficult shot to any location on the green, as from this angle the bunker is more in the centre of the line of play, and the slope of the green will kick balls to the back right of the green as they land. Consequently, left edge of the fairway is no place from which to attack the green.

The pro is therefore under a reasonable amount of pressure regardless of where he endeavours to hit it. The smart play will probably see him aim down the centre-right of the fairway, and play to the centre or right edge of the green. From here he will be relatively assured of par and has an outside chance at birdie with a mid to long uphill put.

Bear in mind also, the potential situations under which this shot might be played by the pro golfer. Almost any pro golfer playing reasonably well will have an even chance at birdie on such a golf hole, should he be playing socially or practicing. Add the pressure of a major competition and this type of golf hole becomes a different proposition.

The average 15 handicapper - Playing most shots with a fade, the average 15 handicapper will endeavour to find the fairway off the tee, which should be easy enough to do, unless the dreaded slice comes into play. From here he will get a reasonable view of the whole right side of the green, and have an even chance of hitting it. Even if he decides to over estimate his skill and aim at the pin, his slice will most likely see him come up short right. Thus he will likely finish on or near the front of the green. His major sources of trouble will be the right side fairway bunkers, and like the pro he will be best advised to play up towards the right of the green, should his tee shot go in one of those bunkers.

The 15 handicapper should be able to bogey the hole on most attempts. Occasionally he will par it and maybe once a year he will snake a long birdie putt home.

The 30 handicapper - Like the 15 handicapper, the 30 handicapper should have little trouble finding the fairway off the tee, and being generally a shorter hitter, will probably finish short of the fairway bunkering. He will have little chance to get on the green in 2 shots, so the second shot is all about positioning the ball on the right side for the best chip approach angle.

From the finishing position of his ideally played second shot he will therefore be likely to have some kind of a short approach shot, ranging from a full wedge to a short chip. The beginner might have some difficulty with this and could skull it or shank it over the back or right. There's no major trouble back there save for a downhill putt, so this shouldn't have much of a negative effect on this type of player.

The senior golfer by comparison, with his more extensive short game experience is likely to thrive on this type of shot and shooting uphill will likely give himself an even chance at par by hitting it as close as possible. That's the reward for practice and experience, which is available to everybody. The 30 handicapper is therefore able to make many regulation bogies on this hole, as well as that he will make many pars, probably a few more double bogies, and maybe the occasional chip-in birdie.

Locations of hazards

Our sample golf hole, at probably about 370-400 metres in length is therefore playable, challenging and rewarding for all types and standards of players.

In looking at the plan of such a golf hole, if one was to draw an imaginary line from the tee to the most difficult pin position one will find that the hazards occur almost all along or close to this shortest route from the tee to the hole.

In positioning hazards that encourage as much variation in shot making as possible, this scenario often occurs. The ideal shot types for a pro on this hole is a fade off the tee, then a drawn second shot, at all times endeavouring to stay close to the optimal line of play. On this mythical golf hole the optimal line of play along the hole is quite straight, however, this is not always the case, and on golf holes with very distinct, multiple strategies, there may be more than one optimal line of play. Different tee locations and pin positions can also have quite a bearing on this. Indeed, on many links courses, with such complicated shapes and variable weather conditions, optimal lines of play vary greatly from day to day, and after hundreds of years of play on some of the older links courses, golfers are still coming up with new and different optimal lines of play.

We find that in design, it is best to keep the optimal lines of play, and therefore the playing strategies relatively simple at the outset, adding more and more subtle intricacies to them as the detailed design and construction processes progress. This enables all strategic elements to fit perfectly with the *actual* site conditions, not merely those that are assumed to be, according to survey, photographs and other site data.

Note in the example diagram that the location of the greenside bunker effects the approach shot to varying degrees based on the position of the tee shot. A tee shot positioned on the far left of the fairway has the bunker obscuring the view of almost the entire putting surface. This amount of interference becomes less the further right the tee shot is positioned, whilst always giving an option, regardless of where one hits one's tee shot.

A variation of this golf hole, shown in diagram b) above, as a dogleg left golf hole, dictates in simple terms a drawn tee shot followed by a drawn second shot. In reality, the topography will affect this and for that matter, all these strategic set-ups. With regard to this diagram, issues such as the following will come into being:

a) For golfers who can shape the ball through the air either left or right off the tee, a drawn tee shot hit up the right side of the fairway will achieve the best result, in terms of length and minimising the chances of the ball finding a bunker. However, it will also be possible to hit a fade, but one must be careful to select the correct line so as to make sure the ball does not trickle into one of the fairway bunkers.

b) The shape and optimum angle of attack into the green appears to favour a drawn second shot. In reality it is possible to design the hole such that it will either accept or possibly even favour faded approach shots from the right angle, to most if not all pin positions.

The point is that in most cases the detailed contour design can be used to moderate or even radically change playing options whilst still remaining in keeping with our philosophy of putting everything only where it fits.

One may also be wondering, in looking at diagram a) what a golfer might do who is a left-handed slicer, or a right-handed hooker. The answer is, play the hole conservatively and wait for other opportunities on other golf holes, because on a good course there will be just as many situations that favour those strengths as there are situations that detract from them.

A further point on strategic design - The little "story" about the strategies present in diagram a) should be able to be told to at least this degree on any well designed strategic golf hole (bear in mind that virtually no consideration was given in this commentary to the 3rd dimension). A good design must have a good and feasible story to it, and a good Golf Course Architect will be able to expound on the reasoning behind the treatment of every aspect of the design of every golf hole he is responsible for

The Modern Day Design Dilemma

Referring once again to diagram a), the average route shown as taken by the 30 handicapper in playing the golf hole, gives probably the best ball positions and angles that a short hitter would hope to achieve on this hole. As a Golf Course Architect endeavouring to encourage such short hitters, we try not to overly challenge these players by positioning difficult-to-play-from hazards in the locations where good shots by these players will be penalised.

However in today's design environment it is often difficult to give the short hitter a break in this manner. This is because with modern technology, the position of the professional golfer's average tee shot is very close to the position of the average 30 handicapper's second shot.

Club, ball and training improvements have, on average given the pros much more distance and accuracy. However these improvements have generally given the average 30 handicappers more consistency at relatively *similar lengths* to what they have always hit it. This effect creates a design dilemma in that is makes it more difficult to create designs that cater for all standards of golfers. Our standard design reasoning dictates that we need to challenge the professionals by inserting hazards at locations where their average tee shots finish, but unfortunately this also challenges the golfers with least ability to cope with that extra challenge, being beginners and high handicappers playing their second shots.

The result of this is that instead of "robbing the rich and giving to the poor," as designers we are under increasing amounts of pressure to rob from everybody and give to nobody. In the example shown, we can to some degree temper this through the inclusion of rough grasses or shaping of humps and hollows or other elements which in relative terms, don't hurt the amateur as much as the pros, however, our options as designers are becoming increasingly more limited.

I am of the opinion that with this, and the unbelievably precise play of the professionals, we are at risk of removing the ability of the masses to identify with the pros and therefore we may begin to see the demise of the game as we know it, on this basis, unless something changes. We will go into this in more detail in later chapters.

Unacceptable strategies

I will not waste time and paper expounding the negatives of poor design except to say that anything which highlights the disparity between the best and the worst standards of golfers is something which should generally be avoided.

For example, a tee shot with a 180 metre forced carry over water not only highlights the disparity, it shouts it from the rooftops. A pro golfer will barely even take a second glance at such an obstacle, as his tee shot sails over such a feature. The high handicapper will, with much embarrassment, probably go straight to the drop zone and play his 3rd shot whilst privately harbouring thoughts of going fishing next weekend.

A less extreme form of this effect are hazards that do not guard a preferred line of play. An example of this would be, with reference to Diagram a), to position bunkers on the left side of the fairway, short of the turning point. The only golfers who would ever end up there are those who already have enough problems *without* being in a specified hazard. These people need help, not further hindrance.

Sometimes I look at the location of bunkers on some if our newest courses and think that whomever positioned them did so by throwing a bunch of markers out of a plane at 30,000 feet.

Good designers position hazards where they will be regularly used by strategically thinking golfers searching for an advantage. Hence the well worn and frequently misused term " Risk-Reward strategies".

Fairness

If acceptable design strategies are employed, the whole concept of "Fairness" fails to be a valid issue in golf course design.

One of the reasons why golf is so popular is I believe, because it is a very accurate analogy of life itself. Looking around at the truly successful people of the world (and by success I do not mean money alone, I mean true happiness and fulfilment) are there any such people who got to that point by complaining about things that are "not fair"?

Truly successful people, as far as I can tell, are not those who worry about whether they have been treated fairly or not, but are those who do best at negotiating the inevitable tough situations, whether fair or not, and moving on. Life is not fair, but those who do not dwell on that, and persist in the face of adversity, get what they deserve sooner or later. That is, they make their own luck.

The game of Golf is very similar. Any successful, long-term golf professional will tell you that success in their field is dependent mainly on persistence; self-belief and the willingness look internally to seek out and correct one's own weaknesses. Natural talent is very much a secondary issue, and 'fairness' of the things that happen along the way doesn't really rate a mention.

Playing golf also fits this analogy. Golfers who get the best out of their ability on any given day are not the ones with the most ball striking talent or ability. They are the ones that take advantage of their good luck, and minimise the effects of their bad luck.

Acceptable golf strategies give golfers options when they find themselves in challenging situations. They *allow and encourage* golfers to take the appropriate measures to minimise their bad luck; in fact in many ways, they allow golfers to choose whether they would like to risk having some bad luck. Any hazard in golf, regardless of its location is therefore theoretically acceptable, as long as golfers are given a signal as to its existence and the option to allow for the minimisation of its effect.

There is no point designing golf courses that are so penal that all potential patrons would prefer to go fishing. Golf courses with forced carries of 180 metres is akin to killing off all the players in a game of life - Pointless, and you could say - not fair - but that's beside the point.

Analysing Terrain In Working Up Playing Strategies

In looking at the processes involved in siting of the golf holes in chapter two, we have, at least in a very preliminary manner made general, mental allowances for the earthworks and other requirements needed to set up each play zone to an acceptable level.

The next step, after a finalised 'stick diagram' in which all golf hole centrelines are in place, boundaries are settled and all space allocations for adjoining land uses are deemed optimal, is to enlarge our view of the golf course design to a bigger scale, and look in detail at the playing strategies of each golf hole.

We will assume, again for the purposes of this exercise that we are dealing with a gently undulating parkland style of terrain that has possibly some tree cover and at least some natural features such as rocks, and small scale gullies, humps and hollows that may be able to be utilised or accentuated as natural features.

This exercise, which is generally undertaken and annotated on paper in plan form, is an expansion of the vague ideas and strategies that were previously thought out as a part of the planning phase. This exercise however, is not undertaken without actually having the tee, interim and greens points pegged onsite and the centrelines cleared to about a 10 metre width. When this is done, The Architect can undertake a meaningful hole-by-hole site inspection to get a more definite picture of "where things want to go".

It is amazing how a survey plan, although very accurate, does not fully portray the properties of a piece of land big enough for a golf hole. In particular, the survey rarely gives any indication of the overall location of the golf hole, meaning how it relates to its surroundings. Technical fact shown on paper in the form of survey contours can appear totally different onsite due to optical illusions, depth perception issues and the effect of the greater landscape on one's perceptions of the section of it on which a golf hole will be constructed.

This centre line inspection procedure is possibly the most important single day (and that's all it should take for an experienced designer) spent onsite for the duration of the project. This day, more than any other is when the designer's true talent and experience comes to the fore.

Personally, when I undertake this experience, which I regard as one of the most pleasant in the profession, I am careful to set it up such that it is undertaken in the most relaxed atmosphere possible. I usually do not tell the client exactly what I am there for, but just to simply give me a golf cart, (for an existing course) or a 4 wheel drive (for a new course) or a good pair of boots (for a very rugged site) and leave me to it.

I try to choose a nice day in terms of weather, when all the best virtues of the site, such as plants and animals will be on full show. For existing golf courses I try to schedule it on a day when there are few golfers, or better still, a designated maintenance day when the course is closed.

I arrive in town the night before, try to get a good night's sleep and wake up early, hopefully rested, and get to the site at a time when an early morning round of golf might begin.

I go first to the clubhouse location where I evaluate it in general terms, make any notes about general site preparation, earthworks, or improvements (in the case of an existing facility) that might spring to mind, and then proceed to the first tee location.

This is the point where we complete the planning process of a golf course and instigate what might be called the design process. This is the time when all the experience, skill and creativity of the Golf Course Architect needs to come to the surface, as it is the time that the general set-up of all playing strategies as well as the imagery or appearance of each golf hole is conceived. It is therefore important, as a designer, to put oneself in the right frame of mind to encourage lateral thought and creative ideas.

Clearing the mind, ridding oneself of all preconceptions, taking in the surroundings, the scenery, the sounds, the smells, I begin to ask myself two questions.

1)   What features should be build into or which existing features could be used to create a playing strategy that would appear naturally occurring?

2)   What is it about this hole that will give it its own distinctive personality and memorability?

What happens after that is hard to describe. As Deepak Chopra, the famous spiritual writer refers, it could be explained as action through inaction, or non-doing. The subconscious imaginative mind goes to work, sifting through potential ideas and solutions that might suit the image at hand. I cannot say it is a "slotting in" of a solution that has been used before, because by clearing one's head and flooding oneself with the senses of that location on that day, that minute, that mood, one is creating a totally unique set of circumstances from which an equally unique selection of ideas is able to leap forth.

On an undulating site, the two key questions referred to above might hold equal weight. But on a site that is flat and devoid of any noticeable features, the primary question is memorability, and thereafter, the formulation of a detailed strategy of how to go about constructing the chosen features in order that they will appear naturally occurring and will complement an acceptable playing strategy or strategies.

In any case, after asking oneself these key questions, one, possibly two and on rare occasions, three conceptual ideas come forth of a scenario or scenarios, which could be implemented to provide naturally appearing images of the golf hole at hand. It is usually quite easy for me, as the Golf Course Architect to instantly choose the most optimal solution, and the other options usually do not see the light of day. This chosen image will have its own set of particular properties that will enable it to be memorable in the context of the other golf holes which make up the course.

At that point I would quickly and usually excitedly sketch in plan form, on my survey plan, the way the golf hole might set up, noting approximate profile of the proposed fairway, tees as well as general shape and orientation of the green. We are thereby either confirming or redefining the golf hole strategies that were initially and vaguely conceived as we laid down the centrelines. Notes describing key design goals and directives for subsequent detailed design are added to ensure that I will be accurately reminded of the chosen scheme when we are back in the office converting these ideas to working drawings. Photographs of each proposed golf hole taken from tee and landing zone(s) completes the record taking exercise.

This process is, as mentioned, a further, more detailed investigation of the assumptions that were made during the centre-line planning phase, but it is undertaken in a manner that allows for easy amendment of those initial assumptions based on a more in-depth evaluation of the actual side conditions. It is set up to enable the bulk of all design changes to be made prior to the site being substantially disturbed, such that most, if not all of the precious natural site attributes can be retained and worked into the final design. We usually request a 10 metre wide clearing line down each centre line, which in secondary growth tropical jungle sites is the minimal requirement just to obtain any kind of feel for the lie of the land. Conversely, on existing golf courses there is usually no need for clearing

It is quite common at this time to make slight amendments to the centre line locations, and we might occasionally move green, tee, and landing node pegs 5-10 metres in any direction to better accommodate and accentuate the existing and proposed virtues of any particular golf hole.

We also consider access, namely the location of cart paths, maintenance tracks, and walking golfer access ways and sketch their proposed locations on the plan. Requirements for drainage are considered if critical to strategy, although for an experienced designer, drainage goes hand in hand with any design solution and as such is considered almost automatically and simultaneously.

In undertaking this exercise we are allowing the natural features of a site, however small, to make their way into the subconscious mind of the designer, where they are used to trigger a thought process, thereby formulating, almost instantly, a unique golf hole image and strategy. In most cases the result involves using, or expanding upon what is already there onsite.

A hint of a ridge can be enlarged, for example, to fit bunkers into. A natural hollow can be slightly redefined to better drain storm water and house a drainage sump, whilst creating for instance, a "dead ground" scenario along the line of play which alters one's perception of depth

This strategy of utilising what is there is the best way to commence the design process because apart from triggering the formulation of unique design solutions, it also achieves the following:

i) It generally maintains the flow of floodwater in the same way even after the new golf holes have been formed, which is usually environmentally sound.

ii) It enables new shapes and features to be imperceptibly blended back to the original landforms at the edges of all new work. As well as looking good, this also helps to minimise the areas that need to be disturbed in order to create very naturally appearing golf holes.

Experience, a keen eye, and some of that intangible design acumen, applied to spot and then make use of whatever is already there -however minimal- for the starting point of a design solution is what ensures each golf hole is absolutely unique and memorable.

There's little more that can be said about this process in general terms because, as with most aspects of the profession, each decision most be taken with a whole bank of knowledge sitting in one's subconscious. This, however is a key stage of the process and one might like to bookmark this section and come back to re-read it after finishing the whole book.

There are many other points which I have yet to come to which form a part of the considerations of the strategic layout of each golf hole, such as shaping, drainage, bunkering, green design, tee design, and a host of other generalised issues, some covered in this book, some only obtainable through experience.

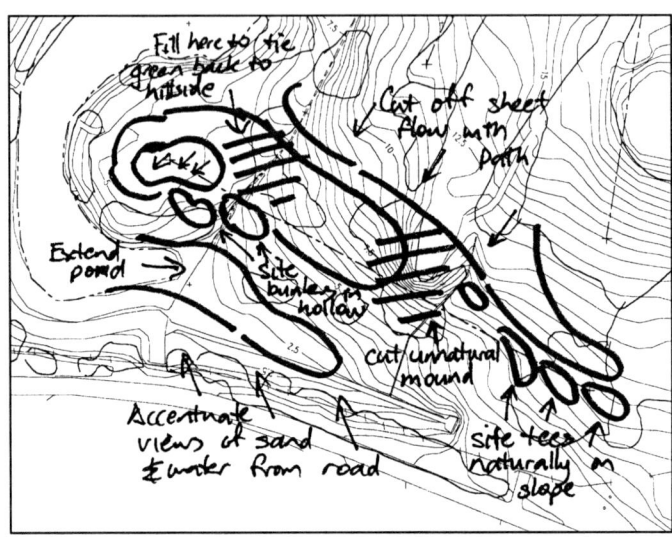

Diagram 16. Sample of onsite design sketch. The design contour plan and final golf hole image can be seen in Chapter 6 on page 115.

The Final Master Plan

The end result of this onsite process is the information used by us to compile the final Master Plan. We have touched on this under the section on planning of the layout and I will add to that here, now that all the processes in its formation have been expounded upon.

This plan is the final diagrammatical, coloured representation of the golf course in its optimum state, with all relevant issued considered.

For a new golf course, it will appear like the promotional layout plans one often sees for golf projects. The survey contours are shown lightly, the greens tees, bunkers, fairways, rough, landscape, ponds, clubhouse and maintenance facility are all shown in full colour. The golf course boundaries are accurately shown, as are the golf hole centrelines, and the scorecard. We usually include at least part of the surrounding land used to illustrate the interrelationship of these areas with the golf course.

Many people produce plans such as these for purely promotional purposes, without carrying out the relevant site checks. On very flat country this can work, although one can never maximise the value of the surrounding landscape without conducting a meaningful site inspection. On hilly country, hastily produced plans of this type can be meaningless. One ought to be wary, especially if no underlying survey contours are shown. If survey contours are shown, it is relatively easy for the trained eye to check the validity of the plan based simply on the issues raised in the preceding chapters.

For the final Master Plan of an existing course, a lot more base information is generally shown, in addition to the survey contours. The final proposed features will be coloured as per for a new course, but there is a need to show existing fairways, greens, bunkers, tees, paths, trees, etc, such that golfers who are familiar with the course as it is, can more easily visualise the location and extent of any proposed changes.

On a new course, the final Master Plan clearly represents the work in planning that has been done to date. It is often hung on a client's wall, or in their land sales office and used as a promotional tool.

On an existing layout, the final Master plan is all this and much more. Not only does it annotate the layout and strategic design work done thus far, it provides, together with the Master Planning Report, a roadmap for the future.

The Master Plan, is an accurate, true to scale representation of the way the golf course ought to be. It is a snapshot of the future, and it is the one document that can be used as the basis for logistical planning for every step taken towards achieving that end goal.

Adoption of a well-prepared Master Plan by a membership golf club enables that "road map" to be 'set in stone.' This ensures that, regardless of changing staff and committees, all ideas and proposals to make changes to the course can be checked against that document to ensure these changes will not be wasted in eventually realising the Master Plan.

The Master Plan enables sections of the work to be budgeted in detail as well as physically planned such that the level of disruption to playing golfers can be accurately estimated in advance and minimised.

It enables ground staff to "get a head start" on various peripheral issues prior to mass disturbance of a particular area that might require major works.

All in all, a Master Plan is a unifying document, which pulls together all the ideas and issues, and puts them on one piece of paper in a format that is readable and understandable by all stakeholders. Although it should be periodically and professionally reviewed, (say every 10-15 years) it is the best way to ensure continuity in the life of a golf course.

As previously stated, I am of the opinion that every golf course should have a Master Plan of some type. A golf course is not like a building. A building can essentially be well built by carefully following a detailed set of plans, and when it is finished, it normally begins to degrade until such time as it is either demolished or renovated.

A golf course, on the other hand is a living thing. It cannot be easily constructed by simply following the plans and when it is completed, it will, if lovingly cared far, evolve further into an even more beautiful and natural ecosystem, much like a freshly planted seedling grows into a beautiful tree, if treated well. But even if a golf course has been perfectly designed and constructed, the people entrusted with its evolution need to know clearly what they are striving for, otherwise the only way to go is backwards. As the old saying goes, "if you don't know where you're going, any road will get you there."

For the classic and great old golf courses of the world, this might consist of comparisons between old and new aerial photographs, with some small allowances for the progress of modern ball and club technology, together with a long-term landscape replacement strategy.

For the middle aged but technically outdated golf course, this might consist of the replacement of every green and every tee, drainage and shaping of every landing zone and the establishment of some new play zones. Whatever the case, the situation should be quickly made clear, such that wasting of time and money on tangential issues can stop, in favour of a focused effort with everyone pulling in the some direction.

And so ends my commentary on all specific issues related to planning. Although fairly abbreviated, we have, I think, laid the foundation for good design. The centre line diagram is the skeleton of the golf course, and the Master Plan its x-ray.

Once the Layout and strategies are in place, we can proceed with the detailed design of the golf holes.

5

Detailed Design

Shape

Anyone who has read about, been involved in or taken an interest in golf course design and construction would be somewhat familiar with the word 'shape', as applied to golf courses.

Shape is applied or created by specialist machine operators who endeavour to construct the smooth, free flowing land forms that one associates with a high quality golf course.

Golf course shaping has evolved into what one would historically term a profession, although as far as I know, there is no recognised qualification that a shaper can obtain. Inexperienced onlookers generally underestimate shaping. The reason for this is that a good and experienced machine operator in the normal definition will not understand the *theory of shape*, because it is totally contrary to almost any other form of earthmoving and machine operation.

Other forms of earthworks such as road building, dam construction, and preparation of building sites are all about turning natural features into specifically engineered features, which is distinctly *out* of sympathy with nature.

Golf course shaping involves ensuring that every square inch of the works area is finished in a manner totally *in* sympathy with nature. Under this scenario, a highly experienced machine operator in the traditional sense of the word can be as much of a hindrance as a help, as his experiences are vast, but only in a style of work that is totally contrary to that required on a golf course.

The question becomes not "can you drive a machine?" but more importantly, "can you visualise the plan?" *The key to successful shaping is knowing what it is one is endeavouring to create.*

In order to do this in a manner which not only provides for the production of the features according to the Golf Course Architect's plans, but which takes the opportunity to refine and improve on the shapes represented in them, one must understand the theory of shape.

The Theory Of Shape

Many times thus far we have alluded to the fact that using nature as the basis of as many design decisions as possible creates more unique variation than any human mind could ever concoct. In looking at the theory behind the shapes that we employ to define, accentuate and sometimes totally construct these features, we again look to nature.

The earliest golf courses came to be on land that was severely wind affected. The effect of wind on almost anything unstable, such as sand, water, snow, or clouds gives us our first clue regarding natural shapes.

In very simple, generalised terms this effect of wind on such unstable particles is illustrated in the following diagram on the next page.

Wind, carrying particles such as sand or snow horizontally across a flat surface suddenly strikes an obstacle, such as some grass, a stick, a rock or an irregular landform. When the wind strikes this obstacle, turbulence is the result, and the wind flow nearest to the obstacle is affected. At this point, the effective velocity of the wind slows down and it loses its grip on some of the particles, which fall to ground, the bulk of them on the windward side, close to the obstacle.

After a while, the pile of particles grows to a point where it has a greater effect as an obstacle to the wind than the original obstacle. Thereafter, the pile of sand or snow becomes a self-propagating, growing mound (or ridge, depending on how the shape of the original obstacle and its surroundings effects wind flow). Referring to parts b) and c) of the diagram, the crest of the mound is moving gradually windward at this point in time, as the shape becomes self-propagating.

At a critical stage, depending on the adhesive qualities of the respective types of mediums, different particles begin to act in different ways. Refer parts d) and e) of the diagram. Snow for example, being generally more adhesive than sand will tend to compact more and more on the windward side of the shape, as the section of the profile nearest its crest tilts progressively higher or at least becomes longer. (Depending on the properties of the particles and the specific terrain and wind patterns).

76

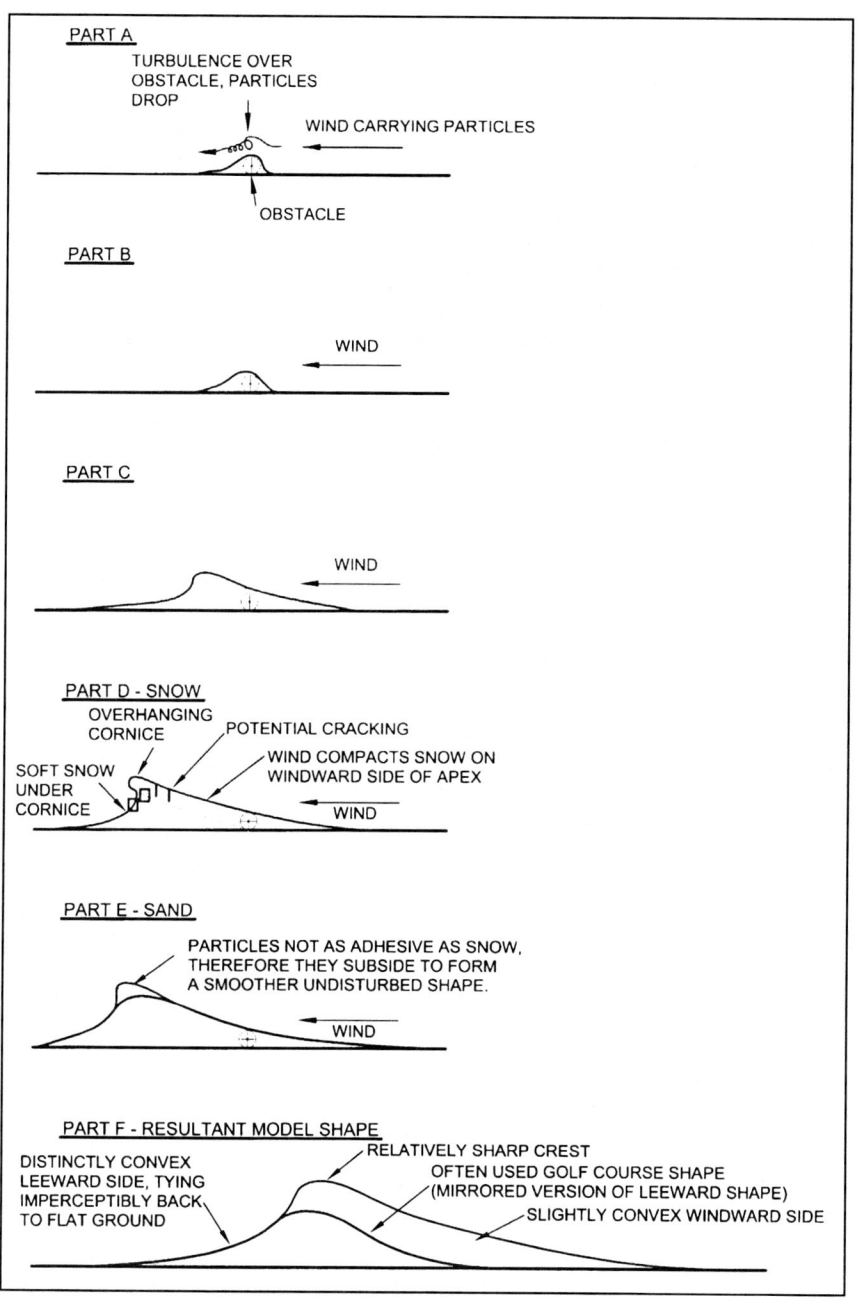

Diagram 17. A simplified example showing one mode of shape formation in nature.

Underneath this progressively forming, wind-packed slab is a bed of very soft snow, which has fallen without wind effect on the windward side of the ever-shifting crest.

This wind-packed slab grows much heavier than its underlying foundation. (Because more snow particles are being packed into a smaller comparative space by the wind). The crest becomes more and more pronounced with no snow under its edge (a cornice). Its growing weight, the unstable foundation and a difference in texture between the top slab and the underlying snow may cause cracking of the slab, which falls/slides into the soft snow beneath. The result is a chunky, but generally rounded windward side, or in the extreme (if the crest is on a steep hill) an avalanche in which most of the feature slides away downhill along with potentially more snow from both above and below it.

Sand (refer part e) of the diagram) generally reacts in a much more fluid manner due to its particles being generally less able to adhere to each other. The particles therefore subside in a much more gradual manner, if at all, because unlike snow, a hardened and heavier layer rarely forms on the leeward side, save for what a shower of rain might cause, but its result is unlikely to be as dramatic as for snow.

The resultant model shape (part f) is, I think you will agree a very familiar one. It is inherent with aspects of images of the great sandy deserts of the world, sand dunes at the beach, waves or swells about to break on the shoreline, clouds swirling on a windy day, snowdrifts forming on the roadside, tails of countless animals, erosion in a river bed, a well toned - even a badly toned - human form, the list is endless.

Its is worth noting that the general shape as described is open to an extremely wide range of variations depending on the particle types and localised conditions. In fact, it would be fair to say that no two of these shapes anywhere in existence would be exactly the same, because every instance of natural shape formation has its own unique set of conditions.

The main point I am endeavouring to make, however, is the formation of a relatively sharp apex followed by a long concave slope joining imperceptibly back to a flat plane.

Before moving on, I would like to draw attention to the shape of eroding mountains, to reinforce the value of this shape in reverse terms. By reverse terms, I mean that in our snow drift/sand dune example, a shape was being built higher, or being created. In the case of an ancient mountain range, a large shape is being made into a smaller (or lower) one, or to put it another way; a shape is being gradually dismantled.

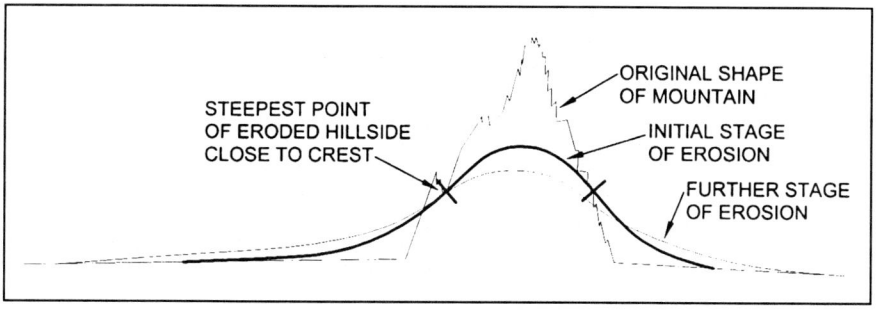

Diagram 18. Schematic of eroding mountains.

The above diagram shows a section through a schematic mountain range. It began life millions of years prior as a pushed up pile of rock and debris caused by the clashing of the continental plates. Shape in our context had little to do with its formation.

Over the proceeding millions of years, long after the continental plates stopped pushing our theoretical mountain higher, it will continue to erode. The smooth curved shapes drawn over our theoretical mountain range profile indicate - albeit in a vastly over simplified manner - the way the mountain might erode over time.

The top of the mountain peak, having the least amount of stability and mass whilst being subjected to the most extreme wind and weather conditions, would erode at a very much quicker rate than the sides of the mountain. Particles of this peak, both large and small, would slide or wash down over the steepest side sections of the mountain. The heaviest ones would settle at the very foot of the mountain, whilst the lighter, smaller particles would be washed further away by the fast flowing waters running off the mountain sides.

Their final point of deposition is dependent on their size and weight coupled with the volume, speed and therefore strength of the running water. As the water runs further away from the mountain, over previously deposited material, the gradient of its flow becomes gradually less and less. Its velocity therefore also gradually decreases and as it does so, it gradually drops, or deposits particles. The larger ones are generally deposited closer to the mountain and the smaller, lighter particles further away.

The theoretical result is a shape similar to that of the leeward side of our theoretical shape described in diagram 17). It has a rounded top with the

79

steepest section of the slope just under, and close to the apex, and then a long, logarithmic type of curve, petering out to an eventual flat plane.

In reality, of course, one can rarely see a perfect example of this in its entirety. The variation of particle size and weight that makes up a mountain, as well as the unevenness of its formation means that different sections of a mountain erode at different rates. This causes the formation of gullies and ridges. The ridges, being generally of harder substances, tend to conform more accurately to the original profile of the mountainside, while the gullies, if taken in a long section would conform more accurately to our typical shape.

Because these gullies concentrate the flow of run off, eroded material is often carried well down stream, not in a wide sheet flow, but in a narrow gully or river situation, to where it might be deposited at a river delta or a flood plain.

An infinite array of examples of these shapes is present in all hilly or mountainous country. A very old land like Australia has numerous examples of round-topped hills and mountains. Newer mountain ranges such at those present in New Zealand or Europe give good examples of these rounded shapes in their foothills, where fairly freshly (in geological terms) eroded high mountain slopes have sculpted the lower elevations in such beautiful and intricate ways that they would surely be considered as contrived, were they to be created by man.

As an ever-learning student of golf course design I never fail to be uplifted and interested by experiencing the terrain nature has created. Continual observance of these unique natural formations and in particular, how they link together, is particularly useful for a Golf Course Architect, whose creative mind is capable of but a small fraction of the variation that is present in nature. With a window seat on plane trips flying over a mountain range or a desert, for example, one can view large sections of extremely variable terrain, all in one image.

This general shape as explained above is what I regard as the basis of a large portion of the design shapes that we might implement on a golf course, however it should be remembered that golf course design is more than simply building a bunch of mounds of this shape all over a piece of land. In fact on many of our designs, you will be hard pressed to find an example of an actual, freestanding mound of the shape described here. The description above merely explains from where the shape was borrowed, but it is the components of this shape that is the key to shape in the context of Golf Course design.

By the components of the shape, I mean the combination of a sharp curve (as is found on the apex of our sand dune) followed by a long gradually flattening curve, found on the leeward side of our sand dune. By combining shapes in this free flowing and very natural format, one stands at least an even chance of having the final product appear naturally occurring.

The key then, from this point, is to compile & communicate the design elements in such a way that one can ensure the intent of the shapes will be in keeping with the image and strategy as previously defined. Concurrently with that, the design must allow for all of the technical issues such as drainage, irrigation, paths, golfer access, landscape, etc.

The process of addressing this is what one might term the commencement of the preparation of the detailed design.

Detailed Design Plans

Detailed design consists of many different things to many different designers. Some do little more than have a chat with the construction supervisor and machine operators before they start. Others do onsite freehand sketches, concurrently with regular amendments to earthworks, in order to gradually work up the design onsite.

As an international design organisation, we operate in a very much-varied cross section of locations, each with its own set of cultural, environmental, contractual and communicative issues. We therefore choose to employ a system that is as specific and particular as we can make it, without losing the flexibility, which still enables us to obtain the optimum result through amending the designs onsite if desired.

Regardless of the level of design skill and advanced methods of representing designs, there will always be a need for some personal onsite adjustment in order to ensure that the golf holes 'come to life' in a way computers and machines alone just cannot achieve. Although our designs are very specific in nature, onsite adjustments are often undertaken, but more in the form of amending or changing the smaller elements inside the framework of our detailed design, rather than making wholesale changes to our overall design concepts for each golf hole. This is the benefit of carrying out a very structured detailed design and plan production exercise. Under this scenario, the overwhelming majority of potential design issues are solved prior to commencement of construction.

In many parts of the world where golf development is happening, the only definitive and accurate common language that can be used in golf course construction is surveying. By this, I mean if an artistic piece of golf design work can be reduced, for the most part to a scaling and set-out exercise, then most features can be put in place in their rough form at least, by almost any civil contractor, if need be.

This is by no means an ideal situation, because regardless of how expert they are at normal civil works, any civil contractor will have a continuous stream of problems and issues until they hit upon the best process required to get the job done on any given site. This usually takes the construction of 1 or 2 golf holes to full completion for the better contractors, but unfortunately, some never get it.

We are continually looking for ways to further refine and better present our designs to make this "teething process" ever better and easier. But in the worst case, where a contractor is totally unresponsive, a definitive set of plans that facilitate a formal contract with an accurate Bill of Quantities, combined with high calibre shapers, and supervisory staff, will always enable us to obtain a very good result, in any location with any civil contractor.

The secret then is to create a set of plans that can be totally dissected and put back together if need be, by the contractor as they endeavour to find the best way for them to complete the tasks at hand.

Like the final product we are endeavouring to create, we regard these plans as a work of art in themselves, as they are -in effect- a working model, positioned at the cross over between art and engineering.

The best way to transform our design thoughts into mathematical equations is by representing them in contours. Contours can be put into a computer, and used to create terrain models that can be digitally compared to a survey terrain model in order to accurately calculate earthworks volumes. Contour models can be used to make computer-generated images, in order to accurately check lines of site.

Contrary to popular belief, computers presently cannot create contours to a sufficiently accurate or useful level of detail or finish to portray anything close to the essence of our designs. Quite frankly, I don't see that happening until a computer is invented that can read creative thoughts. At this time a computer's usefulness is limited to calculating quantities, representing images and as a drafting tool to reproduce designs. All of these tasks require the use of design data that must still be first conceived and then translated to some kind of useable media wholly by human thought and action.

Design Contours

In order to be able to translate an imagined form into a detailed set of design contours, one must first be aware of how our basic shapes appear in contour format.

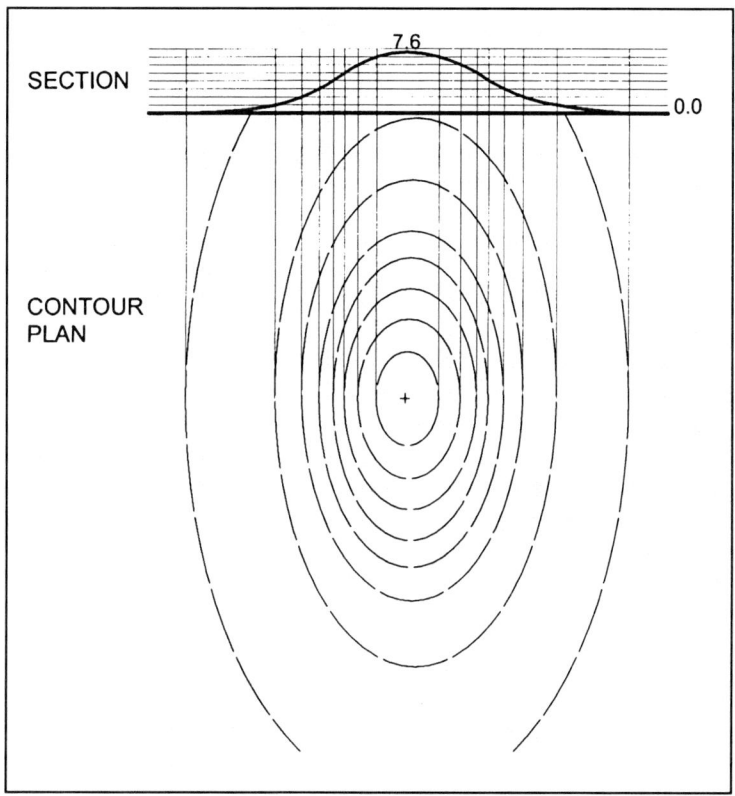

Diagram 19. Section view and contour plan of typical mound shape.

The top of diagram 19 shows a section through an elongated (in plan form) mound of typical proportion and shape. The mound is 7.6 units high; the unit type is inconsequential.

A grid has been drawn through that mound showing where the contours, representing each full unit, would intersect the surface of the mound. These intersection points have been projected down, where a plan view of this mound has been drawn, by matching up the intersection points on either side of the section view.

The important points that should be noted regarding this plan of a typical mound are as follows:-

1) Moving from the left edge of the mound towards the centre, the distance between contour 0.0 and contour 1.0 is quite wide. This represents a fairly shallow incline at the base of the mound as it begins to deviate up from the horizontal.

2) As one moves closer to the centre of the mound, the contours become gradually closer together, until at a point maybe 2/3 to ¾ of the way to the peak, they are at their closest. This indicates the steepest part of the concave slope on the side of the mound.

3) After reaching the steepest point, the contours widen out slightly before reaching the highest point of the mound.

These three steps together indicate the imperceptible tie in of a mound to its surroundings, the concave side of the mound and the convex top, which is the general pattern of shape for ridges and mounds.

It is this gathering of the contours in the key locations, in harmony with nature that is the key issue in creating naturally appearing shapes. This does not only apply to mounds, but to all shapes one creates in detailed golf course design.

Beauty Of The Contours

I mentioned earlier that we regard our detailed design plans as a work of art in themselves. By that I mean we strive to create contours that are pleasing to the eye when looked at in isolation as well as, most importantly, how they relate to the other design contours around them.

To a trained eye, a mere glance of a plan for a couple of seconds will, without analysing the meaning of the contours, enable the viewer to immediately pinpoint any badly formed contours on an otherwise acceptable plan, the result of which could well create disharmonious clashes of three dimensional shapes onsite when it comes to construction.

In simple terms, this could be described as departing from the basic laws of nature and creating shapes that would have little chance of generating themselves naturally, and therefore not appearing as naturally occurring.

In realty, it is sometimes necessary for Golf Course Architects to contrive small sections of the shape of the land to a certain extent, especially in remodel situations where one is endeavouring to make the most of existing features and where cost is a big factor. However, if the golf holes have been sited skilfully, the contrived shapes as designed will have no need to *appear* unnatural, to achieve the desired goals with regard to strategy and playability.

By skilfully widening and narrowing the spaces between contours, one is able to gradually create shapes that naturally tie into one another, whilst allowing for the desired lines of sight. Well-executed contour design facilitates very naturally appearing locations for bunkers, greens and other hazards to create optimum challenge and playability conditions, whilst allowing for paths, drainage and other hard items to be incorporated imperceptibly.

A Glaring example of one such situation, which should always be avoided and would be picked up in the plans, is the siting of a hollow (low point) at the end of a ridgeline.

This design procedure, illustrated in part A) of diagram 20 on the following page, is almost a sure-fire way of ensuring a contour design will appear contrived, when constructed.

This situation rarely occurs in nature, because a minimum amount of water will be shed directly off the end of a sharp ridge, to a point where the hollow is in this case situated, making it unlikely that such a hollow would form in that location.

Most water will shed off either side of the ridge, and collect at one of 2 locations adjacent to the point of the ridge, on either side. In this way, hollows are most likely to form at these locations, meaning that contours 5 & 6 are likely to encircle these points.

If the resultant hollows are to be located on the floor of a valley, as opposed to a ledge part way down a slope, a ridge is likely to be located opposite the first ridge, making up the slope on the opposite side of the valley (Refer part B) of diagram 20).

If the hollows were to form the basis of a ledge part way down the slope, the contours below the ledge would likely continue to fall away from the nose of the ridge, in a rippled shape that echoes the ridge and the hollows on either side of it. A flat area or even a slight mound might be present on the ledge opposite the ridge before it drops further away (Refer part C) of diagram 20).

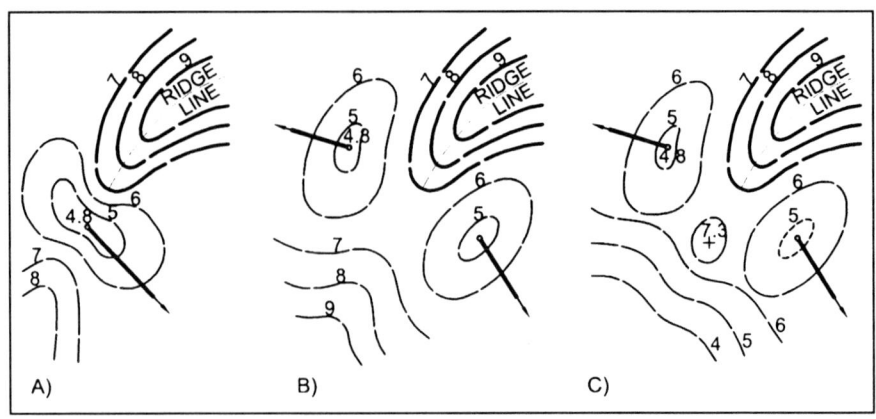

Diagram 20, Part A) shows an unnatural contour solution of a hollow opposite a ridge. Parts B) and C) show two natural solutions with hollows adjacent to the ridge.

When one understands the general concepts of what is acceptable and what isn't, in this context, one can see that good golf course design is perhaps not as "free and easy" as many people believe. The shape of each contour has a huge effect on the way the next contour can be positioned, as well as the proportions of the spaces between contours. It is therefore imperative to make the first contour in a design a good one. This is not always easy to do, and I remember that as a budding designer I would quite often sit in front of a blank piece of design paper for some hours whilst trying to make a start.

As many examples of these unnatural landforms exist as do examples of natural landforms, and it is pointless to expound on them here. Anyone who takes an interest in this subject can easily train themselves to pick up on them, by applying logical thought processes of shape formation, drainage and erosion to any landform.

One must imagine being reduced to the size and properties of particles of water, or soil, and mentally track the process that such particles would take, under the localised conditions of the site in question. For example, take any area of landform, not specifically shaped, but with some minor irregularities to its surface profile, and assume it is easily erode-able, and that reasonably even applications of wind and rain are applied.

Over time, the localised irregularities are accentuated or obliterated, transforming them into shapes of totally different proportions, which continuously tie themselves together as one harmonious set of shapes that, without intervention will proceed to change indefinitely.

It would be a wonderful luxury if we, as designers were able to use these 'talents' of the weather, in a widespread manner on the design and construction of our golf courses. One can imagine earth-working the area for a golf course, leaving it at the mercy of the elements for a period of time, before returning, re-evaluating the design and proceeding to fine shape, drain and grass the course.

In reality one rarely has the time to wait, and the process would in today's world be rightly considered environmentally unacceptable.

In designing naturally appearing golf courses, we are trying to make our designs appear as if we simply flattened some small areas for tees, and mowed the grass on landforms that were essentially already created by nature. On what we term great sites, that is indeed what can happen, however, on 99% of sites with which we work, the natural scale of the landforms is not ideal for the playing of golf, and thus it has to be created.

For example, a truly natural golf course built on a flood plain will be totally flat. By today's standards this is considered unacceptable from both a golfer interest point of view and a maintenance point of view. For example, if it is too flat it will be prone to drainage problems, as well as several other issues.

But viewed out of the window of a jet aeroplane at 30,000 feet, that flood plain might appear as a small flat area at the base of an extensive mountain range, or in giant's terms, an ideal tee site for a natural uphill golf hole.

So in the context of the creation of a new modern day golf course on a flood plain, technically, all shapes created will be contrived. It is the challenge of the golf course architect to use all the modern day techniques available to him to create design systems that not only appear naturally occurring, but which in time will reach a balanced state that enables them to function at least as harmoniously as the site did prior to any human intervention. Or in other words, the Golf Course Architect must, through employing techniques such as natural shape, strive to create a "new or improved nature" on each and every site.

This is obviously much easier to do on a degraded site such as a quarry, and becomes more difficult the more pristine the site is, however even on a large percentage of sites with delicately balanced natural ecosystems, well designed golf courses can be an asset.

History has shown that while golf courses consume a lot of land when compared to other forms of development, their soft nature enables them to become readily preserve-able nature reserves, which, in contrast to many nature reserves, can actually be accessed and utilised by a large number of people in a very controlled manner.

Nowadays most people agree that areas of natural indigenous land in any location should be retained wherever possible and kept as near as possible to their 'original' conditions. The question then becomes, since nature is forever changing, - what is the 'original' condition.

Take for example the situation with the Australian Aborigines, which, archaeological evidence tends to suggest, migrated to Australia via a now defunct land bridge in the north east of the continent, between 40,000 and 100,000 years ago. Who knows what the continent was like before they got there, but one change that they made was to undertake periodic burning of large tracts of land, in order to renew the vegetation and the life it supported. This practice occurred for so long it has become to be viewed as 'natural', but for those who regard human intervention as unnatural, it surely must be categorised as long-term abuse of the environment.

The real question therefore that can be asked of golf courses and the shapes that they are comprised of, is not 'What is natural?' but 'What is naturally *sustainable*?' In light of the experiences of the oldest civilisation on earth -the Australian Aboriginals- there is no reason to suggest that a well designed golf course in a natural environment is, all things considered, just as naturally sustainable as any naturally evolving nature park.

Getting back to this idea of "unnatural shapes," it is a concept that is probably unheard of by many; however most golfers are aware of the existence of unnatural shapes, at least in a subconscious manner. Golf holes that you just don't like, even though they may have good vision and a reasonable set of play options, quite probably have some "unnatural" shapes that are easily visible, and which are picked up by most golfers in very general, hard to explain terms. It's a bit like art, and the old saying of "I don't know much about art, but I know what I like".

There are times, of course when all designers have a need to break these rules to some degree, and create on unnatural shape in order to physically make a golf hole function. A good designer will be able to disguise such a shape in order to either put it in a context that will make it a positive attribute, or sufficiently hide it by manipulating lines of sight, landscape and other moderating factors.

Designs that demand this are possibly some of the most challenging design undertakings of a micro nature that an Architect will face. These situations most often arise on remodel projects where it is necessary to tie new work back to existing work of a less than ideal nature, which is either too costly to change in its entirety or has other restraining factors. This is one reason why remodel projects are, in my opinion, among the most challenging areas of golf course design that an Architect will face.

Links Golf

The game of golf has grown and evolved to such a degree that its almost as if there are now two types of golf, links golf and parkland golf.

Anyone who has honed their playing skills on a modern day parkland course with lush, manicured turf and benign weather conditions is in for a substantial shock when first setting foot on the links courses of Britain and Ireland.

The differences are quite vast and becoming more so through improved turf maintenance practices, which have their most noticeable effects on the inland courses. Modern day design ideals, in terms of playability and safety generally see the traditional links courses adhering to very few of our commonly held design conventions. In most cases they have little need to comply due to the compensations made by their specific environments and site characteristics. This is illustrated annually by the British Open, which is always played on the most traditional of links courses and always viewed as a valuable and worthy test of golf.

But what of the traditional links golf and does it have a relevance to modern day design of golf courses, both coastal and inland? The answer, I believe is a resounding yes, the properties and values of links golf are more relevant than ever. This is so for many reasons, not least for its use as a kind of measuring stick or barometer of change. Indeed, Links golf could well be utilised more frequently for this purpose as we map the future of the game. Proponents of advances in all aspects of golf, including golf course design, maintenance, playing equipment and rules changes would do well to frequently check them against the values of traditional links golf, which are the values that originally set that game on its route to becoming as popular as it is today.

In analysing this further one might start by looking at some of the obvious differences that are regularly encountered between traditional links golf and modern day parkland golf.

Wind – a typically pleasant and breezy day at St Andrews, the "home" of golf would equate to a howling gale at most inland parkland courses. This has several major effects on the way the game is played. Generally wind challenges a golfers estimation of distance and direction, more specifically in the following ways:

Crosswinds and Taking Aim - Wind is invisible; it reacts with the local environment and landforms and blows inconsistently in gusts and in different strengths at different altitudes. This makes it impossible for a human to accurately estimate its effect on a rolling or flying golf ball in the context of playing a golf shot. In short, it adds an extra element of chance and luck to the game.

Judging Distances - A typically stiff coastal wind that is not blowing exactly across the line of play on any golf shot; that is a wind that is either helping or hurting the flight of the ball to some degree, can obviously make a huge difference to the distance that one is able to hit the golf ball. On downwind shots average players, let alone pro golfers have been known to reach par 5's with a short iron second shot, and into the wind, mid length par 3's can become unreachable in one shot, for virtually everyone.

Turf condition – Coastal links golf is by definition played on sandy, free draining soil, which generally cannot support plants that are much more substantial than grass.

The type of turf that grows there, when kept short, tends to be very firm underfoot, which promotes bounce and roll of the golf ball, more so than on heavier inland soils.

This type of soil also promotes golf notable for the absence of trees, the concept of which tends to be opposite to that of inland courses where trees are most often an integral part of the design and play considerations.

Rough – The rough on most links courses, consisting of seaside grasses in their natural state can only be described as very penal. In fact, one can bounce a ball a mere 2 or 3 metres off the fairway and never even find the ball, or if one does, it can be so difficult to play that one often wishes it hadn't been found!

Shaping – The land shape of most links courses are much more varied and radical than one is likely to find on inland parkland courses, given what can be termed as naturally appearing in each scenario.

A links setting can conformably accommodate -in context- shapes of varying scales and degrees of irregularity that facilitate many more play options and design variations, which in the vast majority of cases can only be positive for the playing of the game of golf.

This ability to naturally encompass a wide array of shapes, especially considering the "naturalising" factor of strong winds during construction and ongoing maintenance enables links courses to absorb man made and often contrived design changes that over time appear for the most part, quite seamless and naturally occurring.

The shapes and features of the Old Course at St. Andrews have been documented in great detail over the latter parts of last century up until the present, such that any changes made to it would now be instantly recognisable. Prior to that, however, over a long period of time many design changes were made to the course. Many of those were not recorded at all, and others are noted only through printed descriptions and narrations, which are always open to much interpretation.

Despite these changes, nowadays it is virtually impossible to isolate where the man-made features end and where the non-man-made natural features begin. This is interesting considering that many design changes would have been made during times when the notion of creating naturally appearing shapes would not have been any kind of major design consideration.

Drainage – As sandy links land is for the most part free draining, there is generally no need for inlet sumps and sub-surface pipes to gather storm water from the play zones. In accordance with "shaping" above, this means that a multitude of different shapes can be retained in place, regardless of whether they trap surface run-off or not. This is a vastly different situation to a course built on heavy soil, where every water-holding depression must be property drained, for the sake of maintenance and playability.

Casting aside the effects politics and history (which tend to make landmarks of happenings on golf courses more so than the golf courses themselves), pulling all of these factors together, and combining them much like one would a mathematical formula, what kind of a game would we ideally be playing, if it were based solely on these typically links type conditions?

My guess is there would be a few notable departures from how the game is presented nowadays on televised professional-events, in the following ways:

Chance – Would play a much greater part than it does in today's game. Hard surfaces, gusty wind conditions and variable shapes mean that seemingly perfectly executed shots can bounce into the very penal rough. This would be seen as unfair if it happened on most inland course but it is expected in links golf, and the best players are not necessarily those who play the best shots, but just as importantly are also those with the greatest mental fortitude to overcome bad luck.

Distance – Length of golf holes would not be such an issue as it is today. A stiff breeze in any direction severely alters the effective length of most golf holes and makes estimating of effective distance less exact. Not being able to reach a par 4 in two well struck shots or conversely, being able to get on the green of a part in 4 in one shot is not such a major issue like is in parkland golf. Indeed, the concept of par for golf holes would tend not to be so important.

Nowadays we tend to observe unwritten rules about design lengths of golf holes and par figures. The value of par 4's of less than 280-320 metres are questionable, with a par 5 of less than 450-470 metres likewise. Links conditions can provide more flexibility in this regard, and give modern day pro golfers a chance to hit long irons off the fairway, which in today's game is rare on parkland courses.

Scoring – Like the concept of par, counting every shot that is played over the course of a round of links golf often does not give an accurate reflection of how successfully the course was negotiated. Two players could hit virtually identical shots landing within 2 feet of each other with one player's ball kicking to the centre of the fairway whilst the other kicks to an unplayable position in the rough.

Under stroke play, the first might go on to score a birdie, par or bogey and be left waiting while his playing partner looks for, and then attempts to play his ball, running up a score that renders the remainder of his day of golf virtually null and void, as he thereafter has no chance of posting a competitive score. Not to mention the time delays and frustration associated with looking for and then attempting to play balls in deep rough.

The solution to all of this, of course was Match play. A disaster on one hole means loss of only one hole rather than the waste of a day's golf. Golfers also play matches against another player, which makes golfers more conscious of the other golfers around them, adding another dimension to the self-absorbed nature of play that stroke play encourages. It also encourages more variation in shot making, as a golfer who sees himself with little chance of winning a hole is likely to try an extremely daring shot in a last attempt at an improbable win. Most golfers would likely never attempt such feats in stroke play far fear of ruining their whole round.

As well as that, one is not obliged to play all 18 holes if he is having a bad day. Players leave the course when a match is won or lost, which in the extreme is after 10 holes, but usually at least 13 to 16 holes are played.

Hundreds of years ago, this was in essence the game of golf, and it was play under these conditions that made the game popular. I am not for a minute advocating we forget about the modern game and revert back to these roots, because right or wrong the game has evolved and it is pointless to look to the past as if it was somehow better.

We do, however have a responsibility in helping to shape the future of the game and much can be taken from the past to assist us in that endeavour. In playing golf on the old links courses, in typically windy conditions, throwing away your scorecard and playing against a close friend at Match play, one can gain a general feel for the traditional roots of the game, in particular the interest, the excitement and the human factor.

There is a sense of freedom that one experiences when one knows that a single shot hit into deep rough cannot spoil the whole day, when one embraces chance as a factor in the playing of the game and when par is not an issue. The most important aspect of the game is what happens to the golfer and his partner as they play the golf holes, regardless of what is written on the card.

It is, I believe, left to the modern day Golf Course Architects to keep this feeling at the forefront of their minds and endeavour to inject the positive elements of the roots of the game into its modern equivalent by design, whenever possible.

Design strategy in links golf

A study of links golf reveals an unbelievable array of golf hole playing strategies that are relevant to modern day design of both links courses and parkland courses.

Like an appreciation of how the traditional game was played, one cannot simply duplicate the strategies and reproduce them on another golf course. Rather, it is the essence of these strategies that must be absorbed. It is a feeling of how they make the golfer react on experiencing them that is the key issue to be taken by a designer in experiencing these strategies.

The ability of links golf in accommodating a large array of naturally appearing shapes on any one golf hole also gives rise to the concept of multiple strategies. Over time there has been much discussion generated on how best to play many great links golf holes and the options can be quite distinctly different.

My personal design approach is to work up strategies from a simple platform, enhancing them as the design is created, according to the specific attributes of the particular area of the site with which I'm working.

In this manner the experiences on any one links golf hole may influence design decisions that I might make on many other golf holes. That is not to say I would design several golf holes that are similar to one I played on in Scotland. Rather, an individual element of a golf hole, tucked away in the memory banks might come to light and be used as inspiration. This inspiration or starting point for the design of a golf hole can work to instigate the design process, but the end result will always, without fail finish up being vastly different to that section of the golf hole from which the catalyst sprung forth, for a multitude of reasons.

In summary, it is not particularly the landform itself that one is "using". We have spoken enough about them and in any case, the dimensions and shape are simply the by-product or more accurately, the means by which we process one element of the overall experience. It is the experience itself that we are pursuing, and there are an endless number of very unique ways that the different experiences can be portrayed in design.

Links golf, in my experience, simply gives the most widespread and varied examples of these experiences in a relatively small and easy to see area, in a format that is easily accessible and appreciated by golfers and Golf Course Architects.

It is perhaps for this reason that golf courses are not revered until somebody famous, and preferably a whole string of famous people achieve unusual feats on them. It is the experience of the golf course, (ie. what happens on it) that one gains through playing it or watching others do so, that is the most indelible and intangible of things. In the extreme environment of links golf it is easy to create unusual memories. A good Golf Course Architect is simply one who is able to take the essence of these experiences and use them to advantage in design of new golf courses.

*   *   *

Thus far we have looked at the basic design approach in very generic fashion, as applied to the planning for design of a mythical parkland style golf course.

I have made many generalisations, and will no doubt be seen by many as oversimplifying certain aspects of the design process or concentrating too much on one area at the expense of another. Admittedly, it is very difficult and probably impossible to accurately stress on each aspect of the design process when in reality, that process is always individually tailored and is quite often turned on its head in order to best suit the individual constraints of each particular project and situation.

I have endeavoured, thus far to provide simplistic, and possibly over simplistic generalisations about the design process, in order to provide some semblance of a "storyline" if you will, such that the information is presented in a format that is easy to remember and compare to the reader's own real life golfing experiences.

This is without doubt not an ideally accurate presentation for each and every design situation one might come across. I believe it is however, more useful and memorable than a collection of hundreds of points that would be impossible to put into context unless you are the one who thought them up or at least processed them, in the course of solving a real design situation.

The remaining information I would like to expound upon will be best presented as a series of design examples, and short commentaries on pertinent issues. These issues are those I see as being essential in building up the basic bank of background knowledge of good design. However there is no "usual" or specific stage along the design process where they come into play, and as such it is difficult to work them into my aforementioned "story line".

For example, technical knowledge of subsurface conditions in a particular area might affect the optimum amount of cut and fill, thereby affecting design issues such as the routing of the golf holes & the detailed contour design.

The issues are therefore best presented as examples to be contemplated and then stored in the back of one's mind, to be called upon as and when the situation dictates, usually to assist in solving a more mainstream design issue.

6

Application Of the Design Principles

Detailed contour design is one of the single most important aspects of design and is one area that I believe cannot be generalised about with any great rate of success. The final design contours are in effect, the final result of all the issues of this book -and more- when applied to a specific design problem. They are, in essence what this whole book is about, and I believe it might be best to take in a short analysis of some of these solutions in order to confirm and cross check the issues raised and the degree to which they might affect the design outcomes.

All of these examples are taken from one project and it should be remembered that these solutions are tempered, to a large degree by the specific constraints and generalized design decisions that were made to produce what we as designers considered to be the best result for the circumstances.

The major design related issues for this project are as follows:-

1) *The Site* – Was an existing golf course, which is to be upgraded to better cater for the changing needs of its membership. The land is quite spacious by modern day standards, and in one large, almost square parcel, giving adequate opportunity for creative layout design solutions.

2) *The Landforms* – The natural landforms had been altered to some degree by the construction of the course that was occupying the site, and these changes had been made in a style that might largely be considered unnatural for the most part, according to the standards put forth in this document. Nonetheless, these changes had not been widespread, and the general, large-scale landforms were still present. These consisted of rather bold features of a scale whereby only one or two large features could be accommodated by any one hole. For example, a hole might play down one side, then up the other side of a valley thereby utilising only one natural feature.

3) *Site And Local Conditions* – There is a level range of 20 meters over the site, which is located in a tropical region with an average rainfall of over 3m (10feet) per year. This rain often comes in the form of heavy storms and 3-4 inches in 1 hour is not uncommon.

In addition, the soil condition can only be described as bad, it consists of peaty clay in low areas and black and white pottery style clay in the higher areas with very sparse areas of topsoil – pH of the soil ranges from 3.0 to 5.0.

4) *Golfer traffic* - It is projected that golfer traffic will be high, some 4,000-6,000 rounds per month. Consideration of potential wear around high use areas such as green and tee surrounds is therefore paramount.

5) *Status* – The club is known as the premier club of its state, and as such the standard of the golf course is to reflect that. It should be able to be maintainable at consistently high levels and able to stage Major tournaments whilst catering for day-to-day member use.

6) *Client* - The client is not corporate and operates under a club committee system. Any major decisions must go through the committee, or in the extreme, a General Meeting. This can be a little cumbersome but it does ensure that all decisions made are done so in the best interests of the club and in this case, in the interests of creating the best possible golf course for the allotted amount of funds. This is the biggest key issue dictating success or failure. The client, be they corporate or club, must have the best interests of the land and the golf course at heart. Money really is a secondary issue. With this in place and a competent designer, success should be achievable every time.

7) *Budget* – Was just barely adequate to remodel the whole course and was by no means extravagant.

8) *The Course Style* – Because of the strong traditions of this premier club, the spacious nature of the site, and the very bold nature of the natural contours, a very natural, bold, broad, "big" style was implemented. The design took every opportunity to make the golf holes look wider, and the shapes look broad, in keeping with our natural design ethos. In practice onsite, our design implementation consisted of smoothing out previously unnatural shapes as well as creating subtle areas of interest in the shaping, mainly in relief, in selected areas such as the foreground of long, naturally appearing ridges. Consequently, there are less than 10 freestanding mounds on the whole course that actually appear obviously as such. Most shapes are in the form of ridges, swales and hollows that meld

imperceptibly with the natural terrain. Most features such as bunkers are in readily visible locations and the final profiling of greens, bunkers, aprons, tees and fairways is a major factor in creating the overall natural image of the golf course, making it appear to have had little human infrastructural change made to it.

9) *Existing Site Attributes* – As always, these were to be maximised where possible, but not to the detriment of the final product.

10) *Playing Strategies* – The course is designed to be a stern test of golf for everyone who plays it, without being downright demoralising for amateurs. The deeper strategic thinkers will probably generally play closer to their potential, however the course will for the most part, actually appear tougher than it plays,.

11) *Peripheral Considerations* – Unlike many golf courses that are built primarily to facilitate other things such as real estate, there was very little peripheral consideration required here. Items such as the entry round and clubhouse were reconsidered and upgraded but only in order to facilitate and complement the aims of the golf course redevelopment.

I regard this site as extremely challenging because of these attributes. Heavy rainfall means it is virtually impossible to cut bunker faces any higher than maybe one foot, otherwise all the sand will wash from them during storms. This means design & placement of bunkers for optimum vision and interest is an extremely delicate affair.

The drainage must be impeccable to cope with such high rainfall and extremely poor soils. Acidic soils mean the treatment required to successfully grow turf must be well considered; and areas of long, steep slopes and heavy rainfall further exacerbate turf propagation. In addition we had a contractor who was totally inexperienced in golf course construction, in a country where English is not the first language, although it is widely used.

In short, almost everything about this project except the goals of the client and designer seemed to be working against the prospect of a positive design outcome. I have deliberately included it as the subject of my examples because it illustrates that despite all of this, a top quality product can be the result. In this case, the result is some of the best work I have had the pleasure of being associated with.

In today's hi-tech world there are no excuses for not providing quality golf courses. It is simply a matter of the designer making sure that the client shares his ideals, thereby creating the basis from which all solutions can evolve. If this is the case, a good designer will always be able to produce a quality result, as all other critical elements will fall into place in accordance with this common agreement.

Application Of The Design Principles In The Detailed Landform Design Of Tees

As previously mentioned the idea of a perfectly flat section of turf, - such as a modern day teeing area - melded perfectly into a naturally undulating landscape seems like a severe contradiction. This is unless this flat area is to be on the crest of an extremely gradual rise, or as a part of a natural floodplain.

Human nature dictates that neither of these solutions are usually held as being particularly beautiful or appealing, and in fact, tees situated in such a manner on a new golf course would most probably be seen as a disappointment.

Technically speaking, in any concentrated play zone such as a tee, the major practical design consideration is to ensure that a minimum amount of floodwater flows onto the tee surface. This constraint ensures that most golf tees are set at a higher level than most of the surrounding ground, or at the very least have hollows or swales located nearby to achieve the drainage requirements.

This practice fits well with the benefits that raised tees generally give in terms of improved vision of the challenges that lay ahead.

In addition to these issues, there is a certain theatrical factor that raised tees generally add to a game of golf.

In fitting with our theory that each golf hole should be a separate challenge and experience of its own (in keeping with the overall fabric of the course), the teeing ground is the place where a golfer should obtain his first taste of that experience. As well as that, it should be the best, most optimum location from which to absorb the qualities of the golf hole. This includes a full appreciation of the golf hole, from the subconscious comfort levels, to the landscape, to the individual features, to the strategy of the golf hole, to an idea of how one might attempt to play it.

We are not saying that the tee should give golfers a complete view of all the intricacies of the golf hole, for this would eliminate much of the deceptiveness that is inherent in high quality design. Rather, the tee should be the optimum location to take in a balanced experience of all of the intricacies that make up the golf hole. And this includes the unseen areas of the hole that have been intentionally hidden by the designer in formulating the whole experience.

The feelings one instantly experiences when standing on the tee of any golf hole makes up the bulk of the image or memorability factor of each golf hole. On par fours and par fives a little more of this memorability is generated by images and feelings from locations further along the golf hole, but on par threes, the tee image is almost everything.

In conjunction with this, and working with it is what happens on the tee and more importantly, the build up to the act of actually playing the tee shot.

After finishing play on the previous green, the golfer is lead to the next tee, through a transition zone that is somewhat different to the play zone. This may range from a simple pathway, to a landscaped wonderland of flowers, wildlife and gently flowing water. In any case this transition acts to put the experience of the previous golf hole into the past, whilst preparing the mind for the next hole. On a high quality golf course, this preparation includes a certain build up of expectation, where the golfer will be eager to feast his eyes on the next interesting and thought provoking golf hole experience.

The golfer arrives at the tee and invariably will first walk onto the tee surface to take in the experience. This can be likened to a performer stepping onto a stage. He first does a "dress rehearsal" by surveying the challenges and imagining the type of shot he wishes to play, before selecting a club and preparing for the "performance".

He then executes the shot and the focus changes to the ball as it enters the picture, thus signalling the commencement of the physical experience of the golf hole.

In tournament situations, the tee truly does act as a stage. Spectators surround the tee at the back and sides, standing on mounds or slopes, or whatever will give them the best vantage point.

A "stage-like" tee is therefore quite beneficial for this type of situation. If the tee is set at a different level, or slightly removed or separated from the bulk of the spectators generally more people can get a better view, and the sense of theatre is enhanced.

Take for example, a crowd of several thousand people on a pond or creek edge slope, watching tournament golfers on a tee situated at a level below them, on the opposite side of the waterway.

The image is picture perfect, with green grass, water, etc. Because of the natural separation created by the water and the elevation differential, many more people are able to view the golfers play than would be possible should they be crowded around the rear of a tee box situated on flat ground.

The pre-shot routine and mental dress rehearsal is very much standardised for most golfers. In fact, almost all golf instruction regimes advocate a very specific routine that comforts the psyche & facilitates maximum attention and focus for the golfer, thereby giving him the best chance of executing a good shot.

This is particularly prevalent on the tee shot. The playing surface is perfectly flat, with no odd stances or overhanging tree limbs or the like, to interrupt the pre shot routine. It is therefore the one location on each hole where the golfer theoretically has the most control over the golf shot. Well designed tee sites are therefore good for the game and those that play it, as a good teeing ground gives everyone the best chance of playing the golf hole in a satisfying and enjoyable manner.

In such a standardised environment, the obvious challenge to the designer is how to create a naturally occurring look and feel on a set of tees which obviously need to be specifically located and unnaturally flat in nature.

The location of each tee is obviously considered in general terms during the planning stage, such that when it comes to detailed design, the optimum solution can be readily achieved. Ideally, each tee location should be on an area that naturally sheds storm water from around it, provides an ideal view of the golf hole and is of appropriate size to accommodate a set of tees.

With such a specific set of requirements, it is plain to see that even on the best sites, one rarely finds such natural tee sites that simply require a little bit of levelling before preparing the soil for planting of turf-grass. Given the normal modern day requirements for tee preparation, it usually does not constitute much extra work to completely manufacture (if required) the landforms on which the tees will be sited, so long as these landforms can be made to appear naturally occurring.

Some examples of the varying manner in which this can be done
are as follows: -

Diagram 21. Sample tee complex treatment on flat ground.

This tee complex is an instance where the landforms have been changed to give the impression that the tees were simply levelled off sections of a naturally good and fairly high vantage point. In reality, the whole area was originally quite flat. We slightly elevated the rear tee, cutting away the right side, to help provide that isolated "stage" effect, thereby accentuating the drama of the rear tee whilst facilitating drainage.

The front two tees were filled by approximately 0.5 to 1.0 metres each, then gradually feathered back to the existing, natural surrounding levels. A balance has thereby been struck, in creating teeing areas that are sufficiently raised to create adequate definition in the 3rd dimension, without having them appear unnatural.

Note also the path which threads its way unobtrusively in front of the back two tees, at a very gentle gradient facilitating easy access to the tees.

The photograph below shows a set of tees, which has also been "manufactured". The original profile of this piece of land was falling at about 1:5 through the area where the tees are now situated.

In the example below, fill has been introduced to create the tee "platform". The pertinent points to be noted here are: -

Diagram 22. Sample tee treatment on side-sloping ground.

a) ***The Location of The Path*** – It sits at the interface between natural existing terrain and the filled tee area. The alignment of the path conforms to the natural terrain, whist acting as a cut-off barrier, collecting storm water from the natural slope, thereby preventing it from flowing onto the tees. It sits as naturally as possible, masking the interface between the natural and the man made features.

b) ***The Shape and Level Of Each Tee*** – The shapes are determined to best fit the land form. They are not made up of pre –conceived shapes, but are free-form type shapes that fit together harmoniously, to best facilitate i) the tie in to the existing left side slope, and ii) A naturally appearing profile on their right side.

Note the tees step gradually lower, the closer they are to the hole, naturally tying into the left side, and giving an optimum view of the green from any tee. This is a function of good initial planning in that the hole was originally well sited with this in mind, which enables us to take advantage of this natural step down effect during the detailed design and construction processes.

c) ***The Tie In To The Natural Terrain On The Right Side*** – Although it cannot be seen in this photograph, the right side of the tee complex consists of a gentle slope down to the existing ground levels, at a similar gradient to our natural 1:5 slope on the left, enables this tee complex to appear quite natural. The repetition of the left side slope on the right, with a gentle tie-in gives one the impression that the tee complex might have been a naturally occurring landform. Maybe it was a small mound forming a part of the greater existing slope, on top of

103

which the tees were simply and easily constructed. This facilitates the "stage" effect of the tees in a naturally appearing setting.

Diagram 23. Sample treatment of a tee on a pond edge.

This photograph illustrates a tee that has been constructed as a part of a pond edge. This particular pond has been constructed on one of the lowest areas of this site, with its edges formed to create a naturally appearing slope of about 1 metre in height immediately adjacent to the pond edge. This gives a good opportunity to position a tee on top of this slope on what is naturally a fairly flat section of terrain.

The close vicinity and the level change between the tee surface and the pond create the theatrical aspect of the tee. This interface has naturally styled interest added to it with the use of gently curved pond edges echoing the shape of the tee plus the addition of aquatic plants.

It is impossible to imagine how much of this setting was created by man, and how much was originally in place.

Application Of The Design Principles In The Detailed Landform Design Of Fairways

More specifically, this refers to the design of landing areas, being the areas of the fairway on which most long tee shots land. This might take in the area starting some 150metres from the rear tee, and extending to the area taken in by the detailed design of the green and surrounds, some 30 to 50 metres short of the putting surface.

The goals to be attained in detailed design of these areas might be as follows:-

i)   *Strategy* – Design of the landform shapes, hazards, and all other elements to firstly create strategies that give options for all standards of players and secondly, position all shapes such that the optimum representation of these strategies are afforded to the golfer as he stands on the tee.

ii)   *Focus* – contour design in these landing zones must be of a manner that will focus the golfer's eye and attention on the key elements of the golf hole. This subconsciously gives the golfer a better idea of the strategy. I find that one of the best ways to achieve this, in terms of earth shaping, is to provide specific contrasts in shape style and scale where one wishes to create focus. As an extreme example, if the left side of a scene consists of broad shapes and the right side consists of a minefield of small scale humps, then the eye will be naturally drawn to the point of interface, which thereby becomes the point of focus.

A number of other tools can be used to create focus, such as water, landscape and grass mowing profiles, but in terms of shape this contrast is an important factor, and within the discipline of design of shapes there are several ways to create contrasts.

iii)   *Comfort* – As touched upon in earlier sections, reinforcement of the comfort factor should be considered as a part of detailed design. Indeed, where one is forced to employ an "unnatural" golf hole routing, detailed design of shape is possibly the major tool one can use to create the comfort factor.

Following are examples illustrating how these and other qualities have been attained.

The proceeding photograph and corresponding design sketch illustrate a mid-to-long par 4 of about 380 metres. The focus off the tee are the two right side fairway bunkers and the more intricate shapes that surround them, which appropriately draw one's attention to what is generally the optimum line of play for the tee shot.

From the centre-right of the fairway golfers can see most of the green surface. From the right side one also obtains a line to the heart of the green, between the large bunker short left of the green and the small greenside bunker at the back right. The green also is generally angled in this direction, giving the best chance to play a run-on shot, with the least amount of penalty for an approach shot that might drop short.

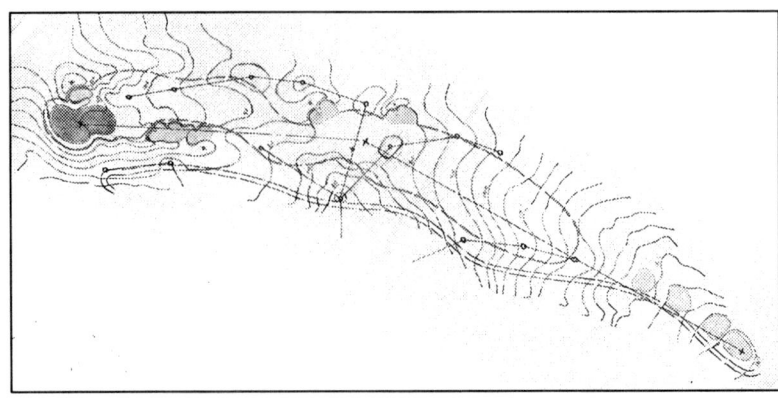

Diagram 24. Sample no. 1, fairway design plan (top) and final constructed image (bottom).

Balls dropping short will be a common occurrence due to:

    i) The uphill nature of the approach shot.
    ii) Dead ground between the left side bunker and the front of the green.
    iii) The substantial length of this bunker along the line of play.

    All of these factors will make the target seem closer than it is.

Note also the shape and contour of the green provides a very difficult pin position at the back right of the green. This pin is guarded by the shoulder of the right side, greenside bunker, which makes it impossible to get close to this position if approaching from the right side of the fairway.

We have therefore created a soft penalty on the left side of the fairway in the form of a deep hollow, which is mown as rough, and where golfers will get no view of the green and will invariably have an uneven lie. This type of penalty affects low handicappers and pro golfers much more than the average golfer,

106

as these conditions affect the ability of good players to judge distance and spin the ball. Whereas for the average player, he will still be able to advance the ball somewhere close to the green, as per normal.

Another feature that encourages the average player is the location of the lowest point of the fairway; in the downhill-uphill play arrangement of this hole. The 230-metre mark measured from the back tee marks the lowest point of the fairway, and all fairway area short of this, slopes down towards it. This means that any shorter hitters landing anywhere on the fairway, and especially shorter than about 200 metres (at the steepest part of the slope) will likely get a healthy forward kick-on which could reduce the distance of the approach shot by a couple of clubs. Conversely, longer hitters flying the ball more than 230 metres off the tee will likely get very little run, as their balls will be hitting an up-slope. This helps to "bring the field together" somewhat and give all types of golfers more of a reasonable chance.

This hole illustrated in diagram 25 is an extremely difficult proposition by anyone's standards, playing slightly uphill along its length of 420 metres.

For the tee shot, the golfer's attention is drawn to the pair of bunkers clustered and set into the right edge of the fairway, which also marks the point where the hole doglegs to the right. The lie of the land falls from left to right, signalling the dogleg. Extra filling on the left side and another bunker on the left beyond the dogleg, have further accentuated this.

At the 255-metre mark the fairway terminates, and is replaced by a steep side slope of rough. 25 to 30 metres further on, the fairway resumes, slightly more narrow and at a lower level with a pond skirting its right edge.

The fairway snakes its way around the lake edge to the right where a section of fairway some 50 metres wide at the 340 metre mark gradually narrows as it climbs to the front of the green.

Some of the pertinent design features are as follows:

At the 230 metre mark, a slight ridge cuts the fairway diagonally, meaning that any tee shots that land to the right of the ridge will get a kick on and to the right, to what might be termed position "A" off the tee. This will, however require landing the ball in quite a small area (shown circled). Landing anywhere on the fairway beyond this area will most probably see the ball finish either in the rough, (with a hanging lie) in the bunker long left, or in the extreme, off the end of the fairway and into the water.

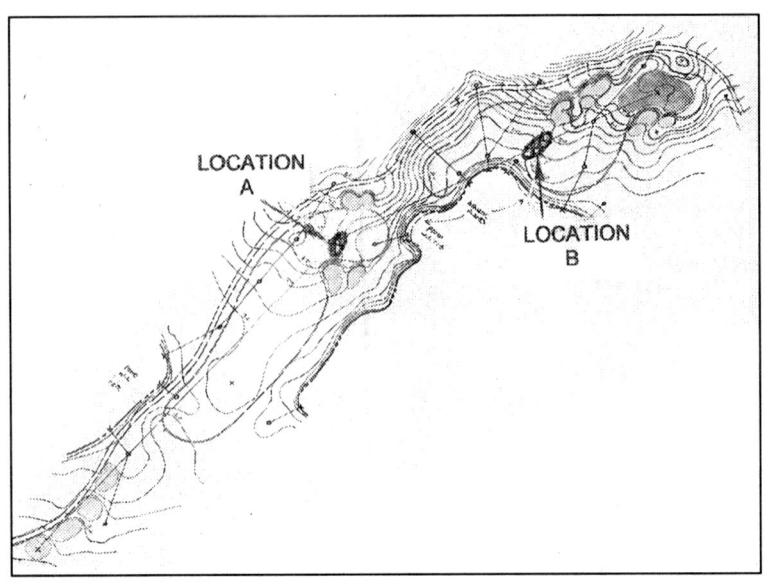

Diagram 25. Sample no. 2, fairway design plan (top) and final constructed image (bottom).

For the shorter hitter, any tee shot between 170 metres and 210 metres in length will be directed at a section of fairway some 40-45m wide, as opposed to the section of fairway from the 220-255 metre marks, which narrows to 20-25m wide. The right side of the fairway, as close as possible to the fairway bunkers is the best place for an average golfer to finish with his tee shot. For a large percentage of golfers the green will be out of range on the second shot, and it will be a matter of positioning the ball as close as possible to the front of the green for a regulation uphill chip. The main priority will be to leave the

108

second shot to the right of the two bunkers positioned short left of the green, which generally requires one to fly one's ball over the edge of the pond for the second shot. This will provide a good view of the putting surface and a good line of play to almost all pin positions.

Flying the ball over the edge of the pond requires 2 shots totalling 330 metres in length, which is quite acceptable for anyone playing from the back tee. Those who have been able to hit close to the fairway bunker will have cut the dogleg by some 10 or so metres. From here they might, on occasion be able to fly a long club 180 metres to the front left of the green where they will get a kick-on from a receptive plateau just next to the bunker, rolling the ball to the heart of the green.

For the low handicappers and pro golfers, shooting for the second section of the fairway off the tee will be for the most part, considered too risky. Most will feel obliged to take on the fairway bunkers, but as previously explained this also will require a very accurate tee shot. From here, the best one could hope for is a challenging shot of some 170-180 metres to the heart of the green.

Most golfers would do best to play this hole as a short par 5, where playing to the "fat" parts of the fairway, one should be able to score a 5 on most attempts and will also have an even chance of scoring a 4. In any case, the hole is not easy for the average player, but he can take solace in the fact that the hole is just as difficult, if not more so (in relative terms) for the low handicapper or pro golfer.

The contour design is quite simple in that the right side of the fairway is generally the best place to position a ball, along the first two-thirds of the golf hole, with the centre-left best for the last one third of the hole, conforming basically to the shortest route. The design contours have been widened on the right side, creating receptive areas on which to land balls and hit from. This is in keeping with the natural shape in that the terrain would normally level somewhat at the pond edge, resulting in a fairly naturally appearing set of images.

Shapes around bunkers, and sudden changes in level have created areas of focus. Location B for example shows a significant level change in the fairway. Balls immediately left of this area will get no view of the putting surface and will have to fly 2 bunkers to get there, while balls on the right side will get a clear view with no obstacles in front. To get to the latter location however, one must fly the pond edge with the second shot. As such this is a good example of risk/reward design. Location A is also a critical area of shape, in ways similar to B.

The comfort factor was present for the most part on this hole before any shaping was undertaken. The most significant design elements that add to this are: a) Framing of the optimum target zones of the fairway and green by bunkers and water as well as b) Fitting the play zones snugly beside the left side slope, giving the impression that most balls hit left will trickle back towards the fairway.

Generally, the contour design is quite minimalist in nature, in that no major features have been created aside from substantial bulking out of the left side slope at the landing area and the creation of a naturally appearing green site. The natural contours have been slightly amended in order to facilitate drainage and affect the bounce of the ball as it lands in the key zones on what is a golf hole with multiple strategies.

The next example, illustrated by diagram 26, is a par 4, which appears early in the back nine of this course and is the shortest par 4 on the course, at 320 metres. The hole appears to have been in its setting for a long time, but in actual fact it is the only totally new hole on the course, consisting of a totally filled area except for the green site.

The hole has a slight left to right dogleg, and the main feature is the storm drain that separates the green and its immediate surrounds from the fairway.

The hole plays as a dogleg to the right, with the green angled left to right across the line of play.

The focus for the tee shot is the fairway flanked on the left by a bunker set into a mound and on the right by a long swale at a level slightly below that of the fairway. The fairway doglegs slightly right at the bunker and drops a little downhill, before terminating at the waterway. One is made aware on the tee that a good tee shot will be one which just misses the bunker to be turned slightly right by the left side mound into which that bunker is set. This forms the basis of the comfort factor for this hole. The best tee shot is one which starts left, and fades slightly, thereby accentuating the value of the above mentioned landform.

The green reflects this strategy by generally best accepting balls hit from the left side of the fairway. This strategy also has an in-built regulator to challenge the good golfers and encourage these poorer golfers, which is as follows:

Without the drain crossing the fairway many low handicappers would be considering an attempt to drive the green. Since the waterway makes this unacceptably risky, it is a matter of positioning one's tee shot to gain the best distance and line to the green.

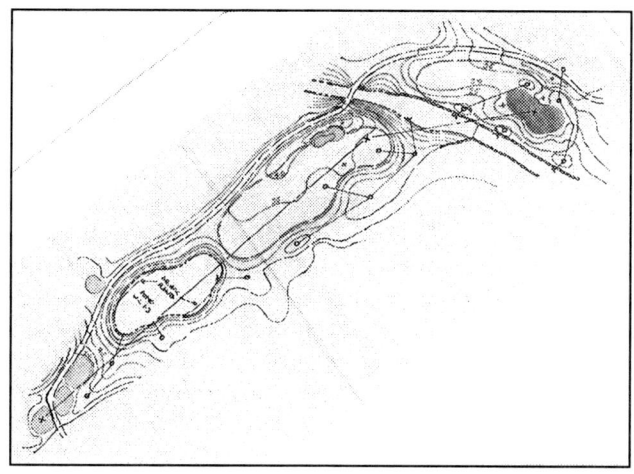

Diagram 26. Sample no.3, fairway design plan (top) and final constructed image (bottom).

The angle of the green and its detailed design dictates that the best line in is from as far left as possible. Also, for a good player, a full wedge shot of 80 – 100m will give the best control on the approach. A shot 80-100m from the green on the left is somewhere close to the fairway bunker. Good players therefore have to take the risk of going in the bunker in order to obtain the best approach position. A long drive that is still in the fairway must, by definition be hit further right to what is a poorer angle of attack with a less than full shot. Most golfers consider this to be a much tougher approach shot.

This strategy encourages the lesser golfers; in that those who hit it less than 220 metres off the tee will likely get a better chance at successfully hitting their second shot onto the green because of an improved approach angle and more optimum approach distance. Even shorter balls that finish on the right side of the fairway will generally be at an advantage to the 240m shot that finishes on the right side of the fairway.

The contouring of the green surface reinforces the strategies found on the fairway. The green is fairly narrow across its width from back left to front right, and slopes generally in that direction. There is a slight level change halfway along the green and the back pin position slopes subtly away from the line of play, making attacking shots to that location very difficult. Approach balls that fall short or go long when hit from the ideal left-side line will have a regulation chip-on approach. Balls that fall short or go long from the less favoured right side approach line will either go into the storm drain in front or be left with a very tricky downhill chip shot from behind the green.

Because of all of this, higher handicappers, who are oblivious to the design subtleties, are more likely to score well on what is quite a short par 4. Low handicappers, on the other hand, playing under pressure and who have to be concerned about ball position in order to score, will find this hole much tougher than many other longer holes.

Application Of The Design Principles In The Detailed Landform Design Of Greens

Following on from the above description of the short par 4, I have included a copy of the green plan for that hole, which is, in essence a more detailed version of the section of the hole comprising the green and its immediate surrounds.

On this hole the plan took in the whole area bordered by the storm drain and as mentioned previously, its design reflects and accentuates the shot values as set up in the strategy of the fairway.

This green contouring is quite subtle in nature. As the putting surface is quite small at 440 square metres, we do not want to "eat up" all the potential pin placement areas by incorporating steep slopes or level changes, as we might on a bigger green in a location more befitting of such undulations. In addition, our basic design flavour is to appear quite simple at first glance, with the incorporation of subtle design features that will only be apparent to those who take the time to study the best way to play each hole.

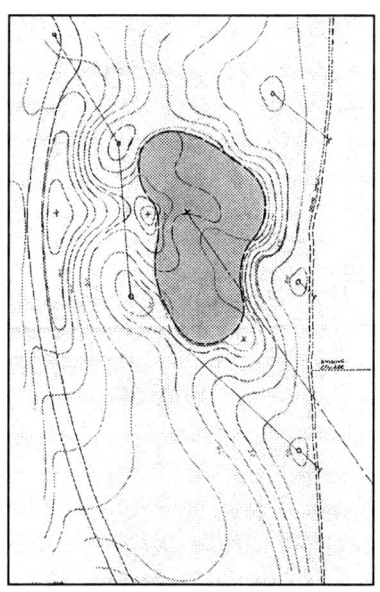

Diagram 27. Sample no.1, green design plan (top) and final constructed image (bottom), looking down the fairway from behind the green.

This green, with its features as described above, appears very innocuous in nature, however it requires a very accurate approach shot for a chance at birdie. Any balls missing the back left or front of the green leave either a difficult downhill chip, or risk going in the water hazard, respectively.

113

The subtle level change in the green surface half way along its length assists the holding of balls played conservatively into the heart of the green, whilst the slope away from the line of play at the back of the green challenges attacking approach shots to this section of the green.

Contour shapes are very much in harmony with the simple lines associated with the stone wall at the front of this green, which, together with the small cascade below the green surface, serves as the dominating visual component as one prepares to hit one's approach shot.

Our aim in the design of this hole and its green was to make it appear very simple in the mold of an old style English parkland course, whilst incorporating enough subtle strategies to provoke much thought in the playing of it. We achieved this, I believe, and also succeeding in making the hole appear as if it has been there for many years, when in reality it was almost totally engineered.

This next example (Diagram 28) illustrates the design of a long par 3 hole, playing downhill by about 5 metres, over its length of some 185 metres from the back tees.

The green is set on a promontory surrounded by water, although the water is far enough from the line of play that it would take a very bad shot to lose one's ball in this water hazard.

The main aims in designing this green was firstly to make sure the green surface and its surrounds appear as a natural extension of the right side hill. Strategically, our desire was to give the shorter hitters a sporting chance, whilst still providing a suitable amount of challenge for the better players and longer hitters

We decided to employ a rather long putting surface angled slightly from front right to back left as it is played. This gave us ample space for a pair of 2 readily visible bunkers on the left side of the green and enabled us to tie the front right of the green surrounds to the greater right side slope in a manner that will benefit all types of players.

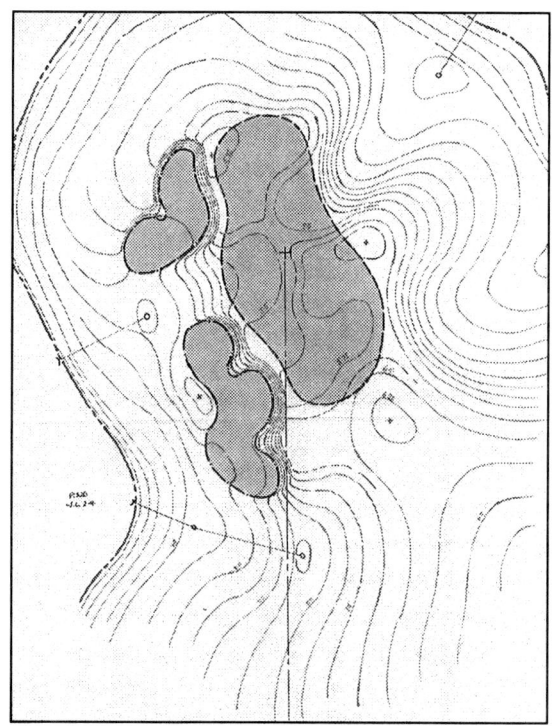

Diagram 28. Sample no.2, green design plan (top) and final constructed image (bottom).

This "tying in" of the ground to the right side hill gives a very natural appearance and creates an angled down-slope at the front right of the green surface. This enables shorter hitters to have a chance of getting on the green in one shot off the tee, by hitting the down slope, provided they can land their

115

ball on that slope some 140-160 metres off the tee, preferably with a slight draw shape.

In keeping with this, the green surface slopes generally across and away from the line of play, along its length of some 40metres. This will make it quite difficult to stop any ball that is hit to the putting surface off the tee with a draw shape. The best shot with which to hold the green surface will be a fade, however one must invariably fly this over the two left side bunkers and hit more across the angle of the green as opposed to along it. Consequently there is less margin for error, meaning this type of shot must be quite accurate in order to find the putting surface. The best type of shot for the good and long player will be a straight or slightly drawn shot that lands right at the front or just short of the putting surface. This type of shot should safely bounce on to the putting surface and roll to the heart of the green, thus reacting basically the same as the running shot played by the shorter hitter.

In this way the hole will be perceived by high handicappers as quite easy as far as longish par three holes go, whilst it will be quite treacherous for the low handicapper who is trying to attack the pin.

The shape of the green and surrounds accentuates the "trickle factor", which is used as a soft penalty for balls that are over-hit to the right side of the green. The grass is cut short in this area meaning balls will quite often run further away from the green surface, to face an awkward length chip to a downhill green slope that will invariably be blind.

On the left side of the green the contouring allows for the bunkers to sit nicely below the green surface in a very natural manner, giving the appearance that they have been there for many years. The length of the green surface has given us many opportunities to create several interesting putting possibilities, with 6 or 7 distinctive and very interesting pin positions, each of which has the capacity to alter the approach that a golfer may take off the tee.

The next example, shown in diagram 29 is the green complex of a long par 5 of 530 metres. The hole plays downhill along its length by some 10 metres.

A good tee shot by most standards of players will leave them in reach of two pot bunkers positioned in the middle of the 2nd landing area some 120 metres from the heart of the green which is separated from the 2nd landing zone by water.

Pro golfers and even good mid to low handicappers will regularly hit tee shots of 300 metres in length on this hole, as an accurate drive that just misses 2 fairway bunkers will receive a healthy kick-on down the slope towards the pot bunkers.

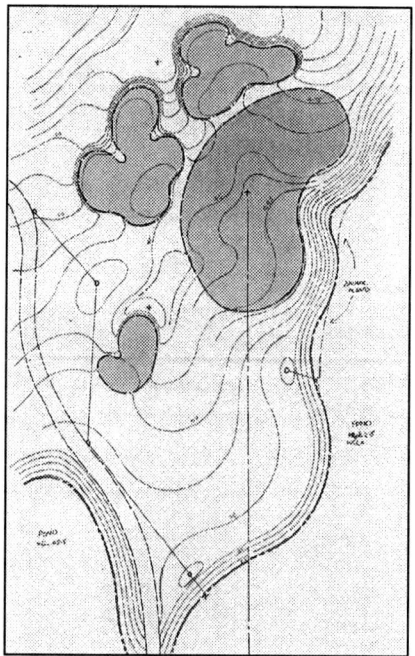

Diagram 29. Sample no.3, green design plan (top) and final constructed image (bottom).

Unless the tee shot is hit perfectly this kick on will tend to direct balls to the left edge of the fairway, which is not the preferred angle of attack to this green, especially when hitting a long club. Most golfers who have just hit a 300-metre drive will feel obliged to go for the green in 2 shots, however the smart play will be a short iron to a place somewhere to the right of the pot bunkers, leaving a regulation wedge shot up on to the green.

117

The green design plays with this temptation that was created by the long drive scenario. Although there are 3 bunkers surrounding the left side of the green, the whole area appears very spacious, with a rather wide and inviting section of fairway short of the green.

In reality, the actual useable target area is quite small, and a less than perfect approach shot landing short may well either finish in the short left bunker, or run across the face of the green to the right side slope and water. The subtle message for most players is "don't kid yourself and lay it up", because a long left bail out shot that finds any of the bunkers or the rough will leave an extremely tricky chip or bunker shot to a downhill green surface with water beyond.

The contouring of the green complex has been made to appear like the green and surrounds ties naturally with the left side slope. In actual fact, quite an amount of fill was introduced on the left side to give this impression, and the right side lake edge was totally redefined and re-shaped to portray this seemingly natural and relatively simple looking structure.

The green surface falls generally from left down to right, with a slight concave shape to the front, a receptive hollow in the centre and a stepped up rear portion housing a rather small pin position.

The green surface is quite receptive for the most part, to any balls approaching it from the right side of the fairway, as one will be hitting more directly into the gentle up-slope of the green. This angle of approach also somewhat negates the effects of the bunker short left of the green surface, and just as importantly, the shapes into which it fits. For example, to hit the right shoulder of that bunker from a left side approach shot may see one's ball skip across the front of the green towards the water. Conversely, hitting the same feature from the right side approach angle will likely kick one's ball into the heart of the green.

The green surface has 4 basically different pin placement areas, at the back, the front, the middle right and middle left, with numerous subtle variations that are designed to create a degree of indecision in mapping out one's strategy for playing the hole. For example, a back or back left pin position is probably best approached from the left side of the fairway, but a middle-left location is definitely best approached from the right side. Subtle pin placements somewhere in between, create indecision and encourage creative shot making.

The first ever bunkers apparently came to be on the first links courses through the erosive effects of wind acting on areas of sandy terrain that had been stripped of grass cover by animals taking shelter from the elements.

If this is indeed true, one can surmise that these animals, mostly sheep would be taking cover in positions lower down on the dunes, or at least in less windy positions somewhere under the crests of these sand dunes.

This fits fairly well with the way modern day bunkers are most often positioned, nestled fairly low down in sheltered or semi sheltered landforms. It is considered quite strange for bunkers on any course old or new, to be perched atop mounds.

The original bunkers must have been fairly uniformly rough in nature with no real defined edges and probably quite often no real way of knowing whether your ball was inside or outside, which is quite a contrast to the way bunkers are often defined nowadays. Similarly, in days gone by the locations of bunkers were probably not analysed in as much detail as they are today. Indeed, in links golf or on any golf courses that are prone to consistent strong winds the *effective* location of a bunker could vary by 100 metres or more, on any 2 respective days. Therefore in many cases it would have been pointless to worry too much about being very specific with their locations, aside from ensuring that they fit comfortably into their landforms and are easily maintainable.

Nowadays golf course designers are obliged to consider all golfer types in all weather conditions and as such the design of one of our most recognisable design features – bunkers, has become very much multi faceted. Apart from their traditional use, simply as a hazard which is somewhat more difficult to hit from than the fairway, bunkers are now also employed for a number of other reasons, such as the following:-

1)   *"Strategic" Bunkers*

This is where bunkering is used to set up risk-reward strategies, whereby one can evaluate the degree of the negative potential effect a hazard might have on the way the golfer proposes to and is able to play a golf hole. This is in opposition to possibly the crudest from of bunker use, being where bunkers are built in penal locations, thereby indiscriminately doling out a penalty to the golfers who happen upon them without giving the golfer any option to minimise their effect.

Some blind bunkers and bunkers that sit laterally cross fairways might fit into this latter category.

2) *"Catch" Bunkers*

Especially in fairly steep terrain, bunkers are often employed on the low side of the optimum target line to catch mishit balls in order to prevent them running further into trouble. A bunker shot, regardless of difficulty is always preferred to a lost ball or a ball that runs into a water body and is often better than a long recovery shot from a location well away from the optimum line of play.

3) *"Sighter" Bunkers*

Bunkers are often used to assist in defining the extent of a landing zone or to mark the turning point of a dogleg fairway. They also help the architect to either clarify or deceive the golfer's depth perception and help give an individual character to every scene, thereby adding memorability and helping to build the comfort factor.

4) *"Aesthetic" Bunkers*

Bunkers have evolved to a point where their look and chosen style adds great aesthetic value. Most great and well recognisable golf images have distinctive bunkers as a part of them, and the beauty of the bunker held in isolation or as part of a greater scene can do much to help portray a great golf hole and assist in making it photogenic.

Indeed, many great golf holes would function quite well in a strategic sense without their bunkers, but would appear decidedly bland and lacking of focus.

One can imagine that most bunkers are designed to serve more than one purpose, and indeed it is possible to have some bunkers which serve all of these purposes as specified.

This brings us to an important design issue. My own personal belief is that each bunker that is included in any design should be there for specific reasons and should see regular use. I therefore try to use bunkers quite sparingly in most cases, but when bunkers are used, make sure they have maximum impact, both strategically and visually.

Diagram 30. This pair of bunkers in the centre-left of the photograph serve 4 purposes. Strategic - by guarding the optimum line of play. Catch - by stopping running slice balls from going into the pond on the right. Sighter - by dominating the view of the fairway from the tee. Aesthetic - the inclusion of tongues and noses around them adds visual interest.

Bunkers In Relation To the Optimum Line of Play

As mentioned in earlier sections on strategy, it is quite common to find most bunkers positioned somewhere close to the optimum line of play along the length of a golf hole. This usually gives these bunkers the most strategic value and therefore the most frequency of use.

Bunkers that are set well away from the optimum line of play may occasionally be employed as catch bunkers but should, as a rule, never be included as a purely aesthetic feature. For the small percentage of cases where aesthetics play the major role in a bunker's existence, the bunkers in question should contribute greatly to the balance or comfort factor of a scene.

If one finds that a set of bunkers looks so great in a location a long way removed from the optimum line of play, one might be best advised to alter the optimum line of play to give these bunkers an additional strategic worth, rather than simply include the bunkers as an ornament.

This type of "ornamental" golf design is something I believe needs to be guarded against. This concept, as well as too many bunkers or indeed too much shape can in many cases dilute the focus, confuse the golfer and take away the comfort factor.

Clustering Of Bunkers

Having said this, it should be stressed, however, that clusters of bunkers; that is, including more than one bunker in any location is often the best way of meeting strategic as well as visual design requirements.

Imagine, for example that one decided to use bunkers to create a strategic challenge on the inside of a dogleg on a par 4 golf hole, and one wanted golfers of most standards, at least say handicap 15 or 20 and below, to have to deal with that challenge on the tee shot.

In order to achieve this with one bunker, one would require the bunker to stretch from say the 200-220 metre mark, through to maybe the 270 metre mark, or a bunker of around 50-70 metres in length. This is a big bunker by anyone's standards and one may find it more applicable to build 2 or 3 smaller bunkers in the desired location for the following reasons.

- It is more cost effective to use more than one bunker in order to cut down on the area of sand that needs to be created.
- By implementing 2 or 3 bunkers of each say 15 metres in length with say 15 metres of space in between, one can create the same strategic effect as one big bunker with possibly half the sand area, easing maintenance issues.
- The location of the bunkers(s) is unlikely to be totally flat, and as such, more than one bunker can be used to effectively extend the total hazard to cover uneven terrain. Especially in heavy rainfall areas, there is a limit to the amount of gradient in the base of bunkers that one can implement, in an effort to position bunkers on slopes. Breaking bunkers down into smaller sections, each with a more flat base, alleviates this.
- Clusters of bunkers generally give more opportunities for creative shaping to either hide or accentuate sections of the bunkers and the spaces between them.
- The natural look. In most cases, well-positioned clusters of bunkers, located possibly under the brow of a ridge, look the most natural, as if they have evolved there by themselves, just like they might have on an original links course.

Its is usually possible to make a cluster of bunkers appear as one bunker if desired, or alternatively make them appear more separate or staggered. In any case, even on sites where a very broad style of shaping is employed, clusters of bunkers give the designer opportunities to play with depth perception and create the "unknown" factor in ways that add interest and intrigue.

Note the first sample picture under the previous section on tee design where two bunkers clustered on the inside of this dogleg on this fairway appear close together. In actual fact they have some 20 metres between them. This type of design alters depth perception and creates a hint of indecision about the bunkers from the tee, due to the unseen areas that are thus created.

Bunker Levels

In temperate climates and areas with relatively light rainfall and good quality bunker sand, designers have the freedom to position bunkers in a wide variety of locations.

In general terms, possibly the biggest and most important factor in designing the levels of bunkers and their interface between the sand and the turf edge is ensuring that optimum amounts of the bunkers are visible at the locations from where they are designed to be viewed.

In dry, conducive climates and sites, where storm damage poses minimal risk, we find that one can design with the emphasis almost completely on strategy. This is because one can be safe in the knowledge that should vision of the sand in a bunker be a problem, it will be quite easy to make an adjustment during construction, with minimal ill effect to the final product.

In these dry climates it is possible to locate bunkers fairly high up on hillsides where they will be viewed from several metres of elevation below, and still get good glimpses of sand. This can be achieved simply by slightly increasing the gradient of the base, tilting it toward the line of play, or by cutting the sand/turf interface line higher on the turf face. Where heavy rainfall is not a factor, these types of amendments will have no adverse affect on the ability for the bunkers to remain easily maintainable in that configuration.

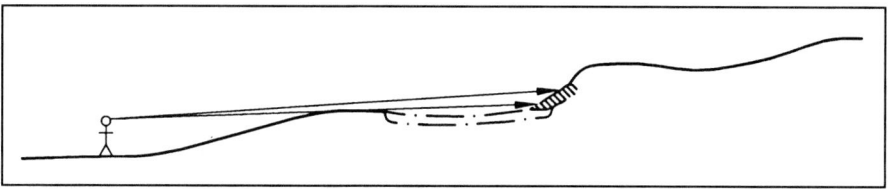

Diagram 31. The effect of higher sand faces on bunkers to improve viewing.

In climates with high rainfall and the propensity for heavy storms these type of luxuries are not available. One must aim for -ideally- flat bunker bases such that the sand will have little propensity to wash away from the turf edges during storms.

Sand bunker faces must be almost non existent, and we find that any slightly higher sand faces are best achieved by slightly thickening the depth of sand at the edges rather than putting a steep gradient on the bunker's base.

Sand faces in temperate climates can be very high, and several metres are not unusual. In a tropical climate 8 inches to 1 foot (30cm) is usually the maximum one could realistically hope to achieve and readily maintain.

To further minimise sand washing in high rainfall areas, one must also be careful to design bunker surrounds such that an absolute minimum of storm water from surrounding areas runs into the bunkers, especially at high velocity from steep surrounding faces.

A well constructed bunker can in fact handle quite a lot of storm water landing and even running into it, provided it does not travel at a high velocity which will displace the bunker sand particles. Water with suspended solids such as silt that flows into bunkers also must be guarded against as the addition of these particles progressively lower the bunker's ability to allow moisture to move vertically through its sand layer and into its sub-surface drainage structures.

With these kind of constraints to contend with, I regard the tropical high rainfall environments as the most challenging in which to design bunkers that not only appear natural and free-form, but which have good visibility and which will remain in free-draining condition without regular, costly and time consuming reconstructive maintenance.

Any designer who has succeeded in creating naturally appearing bunkers in this sort of extreme environment is, I believe well qualified to design high quality bunkering for virtually any location.

The reason being is that the designer must possess a heightened sense of appreciation for the levels of his design and a deep imaginative sense of how to implement naturally appearing design variations in an environment with very tight design constraints.

Simply by positioning the sand level of all bunkers on a golf course at levels equal to or lower than those levels of the locations from which they will be viewed will virtually guarantee all bunkers will be visible.

Whilst this idea can be kept at the forefront of the designers mindset, it is however not always a practical solution, and when it is, it must be implemented with a level of creativity that adds more to a scene than simply a blob of sand.

The photographs of the design examples used in this chapter illustrates some examples of how we have gone about endeavouring to create variation and interest with bunking, in a tropical environment. We have attempted, on this particular project used in the examples, to create a bunker style that is well adapted to the local environment whilst drawing some comparison to a more traditional look associated with some of the older parkland courses in more temperate climates.

A good designer will be able to manipulate bunker shapes and surrounding landforms in consideration of the lines of sight to make tiny sand faces appear much bigger, and hide sections of bunkers to give the illusion that more radical shapes are present than is actually the case.

This type of design requires a very much deeper than normal appreciation of balance and proportion in a golf hole scene which is very difficult to totally predetermine purely with contour design. Whilst all elements should be able to be well positioned by a competent golf course architect in the course of the contour design process, it is usually necessary to slightly amend the shapes onsite, in order to obtain the optimum balance, which will best highlight the desired features.

This is dependent more on inherent skills, which are refined by experience. These traits are difficult to define to any degree through text.

Application Of The Design Principles In The Detailed Landform Design For Paths

Most modern day golf courses, with anything more than a very light traffic load will require protection of their high wear areas, being areas that are most frequently accessed by golfers as they play each golf hole.

It has therefore become standard practice to include sections of formal paths in these high wear areas, most notably at the side and rear access to greens and tees, and the linkage between each green and the next tee.

One might think that the positioning and alignment of such structures would require little in the way of design. Indeed paths on golf courses usually serve their purpose best if they are not at all memorable, but simply facilitate the unhindered playing of golf.

This does not mean paths require less design consideration than other aspects of a golf course. On the contrary, as a hard item routed through a natural, undulating collection of landforms, paths and golfer access ways must invariably be one of the *primary* design considerations along with the golf hole strategies, golf hole imagery and drainage.

On a course in a temperate climate with moderate traffic, the extent of the formal pathways might only be minimal, in order to access tees and greens. But anywhere with a heavier traffic flow or in high rainfall areas, and with propensity towards motorised golf carts it is wise to allow for a full-length path running adjacent to the play zone of each golf hole.

The design challenge in these latter cases (which nowadays consist of the majority of cases) is to strike a balance between bringing the paths as close to the play zones as possible without having them affect the playing strategy or impact visually on the golf holes.

We also endeavour to align the paths such that they take golfers to where they want to go in the most direct manner, without having the alignment appearing too straight or unnatural.

The basic guidelines for roads and intersections explained in chapter 3 apply to golf course access paths in a smaller scale, however intersections and the like rarely feature on a golf course.

Using A Cart Path

On many modern golf courses use of golf carts is compulsory. This enables the average time taken for a round of golf to be reduced, whilst giving improved access for the elderly, young or infirm whilst no doubt contributing extra revenue through cart hire fees.

From a design viewpoint it gives a little more flexibility in routing the golf holes, as there is no need for each tee to be within easy walking distance from the previous green.

In driving a golf cart around a golf course, it is my experience that most golfers become very lazy, and if you allowed them they would drive to within 2 or 3 paces of their ball, including on tees and greens! While this is probably not in the true spirit of the game, where one would ideally obtain a good measure of physical exercise during a game of golf, I'm afraid golf carts are here to stay and we need to allow for their use as we design modern day golf holes.

I must admit that in lush tropical conditions and hot weather I am thankful for use of a golf cart, however I do admit to becoming a little frustrated if I cannot easily access my ball in my cart when it lands on the fairway.

In alignment of cart paths, one must consider the needs of the golfer not only as he accesses his ball, but also on route to his ball.

When one plays golf on foot in the traditional manner, looking at the target and evaluating the next shot consumes a reasonable part of the time taken in walking towards the ball after it comes to rest. As a golfer, this is a healthy habit to get into, as it firstly helps one to find one's ball, and thereafter helps to better prepare for the shot at hand. This presumably gives a better chance of hitting a more accurate shot, and in any case the whole process generally helps to speed up play.

One should ideally still be able to undertake this process when using a golf cart, despite the fact that one tends to move to one's ball quicker and has to also consider the location of the ball of the person who is riding next to them in the cart. It is therefore preferable to design golf holes such that golf carts can be driven fairly closely to the fairway landing zones, and preferably on them, at least in dry weather. This is also applicable for shots to be played from locations outside the fairway, for which a good golf course drainage design should enable access for golf carts for all but the wettest of conditions in the wettest of climates.

It is inadvisable to allow golf carts to be driven on the greens, tees or their surrounds, however good design will make it more practical for golfers to leave their carts on an adjacent path and walk a short distance to play their tee shots and putts.

Good cart path design is a function of this issue: - Frustration by golfers, causing them to consistently break the rules and leave the paths in these areas is a sign that the paths obviously do not practically deliver the golfers adequately and conveniently close enough to the play zones. Obviously there will always be a minority who will want to break the rules regardless, but it is the majority of patrons doing the same things that causes the worst kind of damage.

Luckily there are several design solutions that offer the best of both worlds. Referring to the second sample photograph regarding tee design, one can see this set of tees is situated very close to the adjacent path. In this case it would be pointless for anyone to leave the path in his cart and drive any closer to the tees, for he would then be on them. We have prevented carts from going off the path with the inclusion of a section of kerb, some 150mm (6") high, along the path directly adjacent to the tees. The path is double width in this area to provide parking space for carts with through-access for course marshals, maintenance machines and the like.

The path itself does not detract from the image of the golf hole, because the line of play from any tee towards the target is angled away from the path, making the path a part of the peripheral image whilst on the tee.

Looking towards the green, a section of the path is visible adjacent to the green on the left side periphery, which disappears as the path makes its way to the right side, behind the green in line with the target zone. Additional landscape planting will partially screen, if not totally hide the section of visible path.

Where the path goes behind the green, it also has a widened section with a kerb in similar fashion to the tee. This is situated some 3 or 4 metres behind the faces of the rear greenside bunkers, making access to the green from this area not further than 15 or so metres down a slope which in any case, would be impractical to drive a cart.

The path has been rendered invisible in this area by the placement of naturally shaped soil against the kerbing as well as slightly angling the level of the path back towards the hillside. As well as reducing the field of vision of the path surface to zero, this also serves a dual purpose in trapping surface drainage run off as it travels drown the hillside behind the green complex, thereby preventing storm water from running into the bunkers and onto the green. The storm water in this case is channelled along the path edge and into a sump inlet set into the path edge behind the left edge of the back left bunker. Dual use of these hard surfaces in this manner is an intelligent and cost effective way of -in this case- assisting overall drainage of the play zone.

Locating paths on the high side of golf holes which play alongside a slope, is generally an intelligent design approach. Not only can one cut off virtually all storm water running down the slope, thereby easing drainage and maintenance issues on the play zones, but golfers who drive along such a path will get the best possible views of the golf hole from the highest vantage points, thereby reducing their needs and tendencies to leave the path.

Paths And Contour Design

As mentioned above, the location (which side of the hole) and the general alignment of the path is one of the first design decisions that I personally make when it comes to contour design. It is important to set out in one's mind the basic design goals and then set these as constraints prior to commencing with the design process. Paths, which facilitate golfer access are obviously a major initial consideration, and must be addressed early in the design process.

It does not matter how great a golf hole is, if it can't be properly and easily accessed by those that use it, its enjoyment and playability factors will not be optimised.

Once the general locations of the paths are decided, we proceed with the detailed contour and drainage design. During this process, the final alignment of the path is drawn in, in sympathy with the design contours. The free-form nature of the contours makes it quite easy to incorporate paths with gentle curves to their alignments, which we regard as ideal for aesthetics and practical use.

Dead straight sections of path tend to clash with the natural shapes and one's eye is automatically drawn to them and consequently away from the golf strategies.

Overly twisty sections of path can be dangerous to drive on, and increase the incidence of people slightly cutting corners, which means adjacent areas of turf are prone to wear out and look untidy. In addition, it is difficult to take in the scenery and analyse your upcoming shot if you have to keep your eye closely on a twisty cart path. These factors are the main reasons why we regard winding cut paths with sharp corners as a negative influence on a round of golf.

A minimum and consistent width of the paved surface should also be employed which will enable golfers to easily drive on these paths without continually having the wheels of their golf cart drop off either side. We find that with the average speed and width of a modern day cart, and allowing for a gently curved path alignment, a width of not less than 2.2 metres (7 1/3') should be employed.

Disguising The Paths

Our aim, in attempting to produce very natural golf designs is to make items like paths as unobtrusive as possible, and there are several ways this can be achieved.

As a general rule, we try to position all paths where they will not be seen on the optimum line(s) of play from the key areas, such as from the tees and landing areas of the golf holes. Unfortunately it is not always possible to make all paths totally invisible from these locations. For those that are visible, we try to ensure their locations are well to the side of the optimum line of play and use other methods like landscape to soften their look.

Where a path has to cross in between one's viewing location and the optimum line of play we do our best to hide the path through adjustments to shaping. At a distance of 50 metres a 2.2 metre wide path viewed side on only requires the earth to be raised less than one foot (300mm) on the near side for the path to be invisible. In a well-considered design this type of shaping can be simply and easily made to be a part of the natural landscape.

Paths That Cross Fairways

In designing a full-length cart path for a new or existing golf course, it is quite common that there is a need for a path to cross one or even a few fairways. In aligning cart paths the first concern is always for the safety of the user. Golfers expect to be able to drive along a path without having to worry about stray balls or other dangerous conditions. And if such conditions are prevalent then like driving a car, a road sign should warn users.

In design we are always trying to locate paths along the edges of play zones on the opposite side to an adjacent golf hole, which plays – especially off the tee – in the opposite direction. This minimises the risk of unsighted golfers being hit front or side on by stray and fast flying balls from adjacent golf holes, as they drive innocently along what they assume to be a safe path.

In many instances a path must cross a hole somewhere near half way along it, in order to best achieve this.

In situations like this we try to position the crossing where it will have the best chance of benefiting the lesser golfers or at least the shorter hitters.

We therefore try to make the crossings at maybe the 120-150 metre mark, to benefit those who might miss hit their tee shot, giving their ball an encouraging bounce along should it hit the path. Alternatively we try to position the crossing out of range for the pro, possibly at the 320-350 metre mark, (but who knows for how long this will be out of reach?). We then have a chance to provide a benefit to the shorter hitter on his second shot. In all cases where paths cross the fairways we ensure they are made very much invisible from the landing zones. Because of this and their locations they rarely have an effect on normal strategic play.

On a par 5 the path might even cross twice, and far from being a negative aspect, if the crossings are positioned well it actually gives a benefit to golfers driving carts, as it facilitates views of the golf hole from both sides and the centre of the fairway, without ever leaving the path.

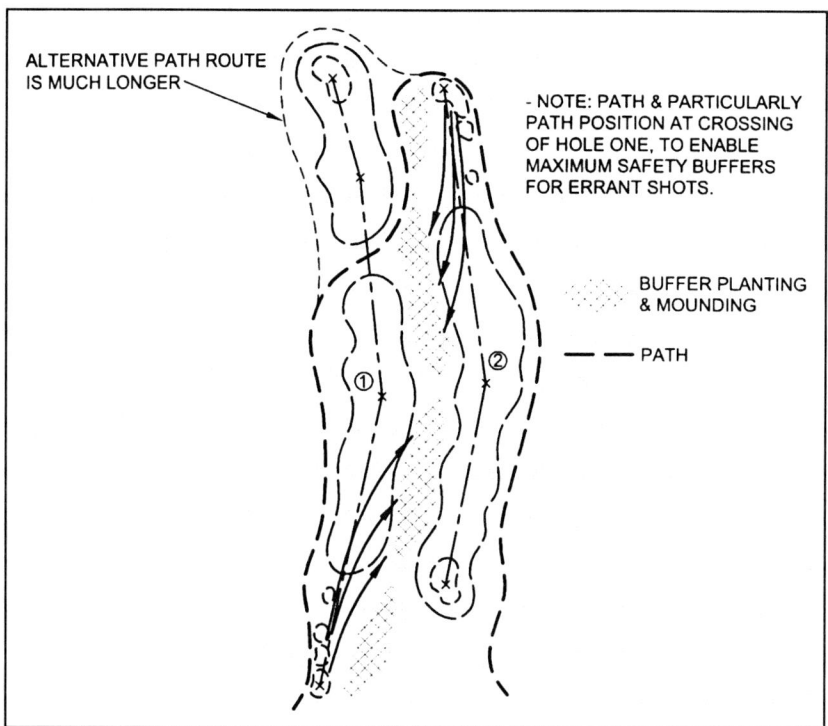

ALTERNATIVE PATH ROUTE
IS MUCH LONGER

- NOTE: PATH & PARTICULARLY
PATH POSITION AT CROSSING
OF HOLE ONE, TO ENABLE
MAXIMUM SAFETY BUFFERS
FOR ERRANT SHOTS.

BUFFER PLANTING
& MOUNDING

PATH

Diagram 32. Strategically positioned path locations and fairway crossing on a par 5.

Application Of The Design Principles In The Detailed Design Of Landscape Planting

Golf course landscape is often seen as a contentious issue. Traditionalists and proponents of links golf might argue that there should be no landscape, especially trees, added to a golf course site because the first real golf courses, the links courses were by definition virtually devoid of trees.

In those types of "linksy" coastal dune environments I would for the most part agree with this statement that trees have no place, because they do not naturally grow there.

Looking at what naturally belongs on a site is I believe, the key issue. To grow a pine forest on the links of St. Andrews would be whole-heartedly viewed as sacrilegious. But likewise, felling every tree in any forest to make way for a golf course would nowadays also draw mass discontent.

131

In keeping with all our general design philosophies we try to put together a landscape concept that both preserves and strengthens an existing natural ecosystem, or rehabilitates a degraded or nonexistent natural ecosystem.

Contrary to the beliefs of many of the anti golf-development movements, intelligent golf course design strives to stabilise and preserve large areas of natural and rehabilitated land.

When these areas are included as a working part of a high quality golf course facility they become sustainable for the long term, as they thereafter come under the umbrella of the club management. A well-designed and constructed golf course will be popular and if managed well, it will be profitable, meaning that the means to ensure long-term preservation of such areas of ecological significance will have been achieved.

Many examples of this phenomenon are present all around the world. The mere existence of links golf has made for the preservation of countless areas of natural sand dunes in areas that no doubt would otherwise have been built up with houses and factories.

Melbourne, Australia is a sprawling city with a fairly low overall density. Its famed "Sand Belt" golf courses, all established on a unique stretch of native sand country are possibly the only examples of any size where one can still experience areas of the original, natural landscape.

I am of the belief that this design mindset, which encompasses much more than a rigid, traditionalistic view of how the game of golf ought to be played, is the only way to ensure that golf courses are environmentally friendly. It also ensures that much variation is present in new golf course designs, driven by the unrivalled creativity of nature, which is always there in any place to be discovered and brought forth by the designer.

This natural theory therefore renders as obsolete the question of the use of trees and landscape on golf courses. If trees and flowers are naturally occurring in the environment, which includes the golf course, then I believe they should be included and allowed for in the design of the golf holes.

Landscape, like shaping and bunker styling is a site-specific issue that cannot simply be generalised about.

On links style land the landscape might consist of nothing more than a mix of grasses and possibly some low shrubs. A tropical setting might lend itself to the use of dense leafy trees and bright colourful shrubs, but all of these decisions depend on site and project specific factors, which vary even between projects situated side by side in the same climate.

Design Of Areas Of New Planting

As with most other aspects of the design process, landscape planting has several specific functions, which are as follows: -

1)   *Highlighting* – Drawing one's attention to the strategies and optimum lines of play. This might consist of the planting of a particularly colourful or contrasting cluster of plants directly behind the optimum target line to highlight, for example, the turning point of a dogleg golf hole, or a particularly challenging pin position on a green.

2)   *Transition Planting* – On sites where an area has been cleared to make way for a golf hole, some additional, smaller plants might be required to create a "step down" effect from the bigger existing trees to new turf areas. This planting can soften the edges of the clearing line and "naturalise" the look of the clearing line similar to how a natural treeless area often appears in nature.

3)   *Back Drop Planting* – In areas where reinstatement of planting is desired, large areas of generally quick growing trees are often needed to create a natural backdrop for the golf holes and to quickly establish the basis of a self sustaining, naturalised ecosystem in out of play areas.

4)   *Planting For Golfer Comfort* – In the physical sense this consists of, for example the inclusion of shade trees in hot climates, strategically located where golfers are likely to wait before moving on. Carefully chosen species that can be planted close to tees, greens and fairway landing zones without creating undue maintenance problems such as excessive shade, root intrusion, surface roots, dropping of leaves or attraction of insects, will achieve this.

In cold windy climates, this might consist of the inclusion of selected species to provide shelter from wind.

With regard to the mental side of the golfer experience, landscape can and should be used to help create and improve the comfort factor we have spoken about so many times previously. Landscape should thereby be structured to exist in harmony with the shaping of each golf hole, using the extra height and structure of the planting to further emphasise the design elements and challenges. Large imposing trees, for example situated on a ridge marking the outside of a dogleg will give extra emphasis to that ridge thereby accentuating its visual effect, and if designed well, giving a more heightened awareness of the optimum target lines.

This type of planting comes in many formats and is very much situation specific. The Golf Course Architect will formulate many such Landscape design solutions in general terms during the process of working up the contour design of each golf hole.

5)   *Concentrated Feature Planting* – This consists of decorative planting and is often done with a combination of trees, shrubs and groundcovers. Although this type of planting incorporating flowers and the like sounds very appealing, it is often not practical, for the following reasons:

   i)   It cannot be readily planted anywhere where a golf ball is likely to land, because it results in either lost balls, slow play in looking for balls, and damage to the plants caused by golfers looking for balls. Feature planting can therefore only be readily planted in out of play areas, mostly beyond greens and behind tees.

   ii) Maintenance is very often labour-intensive and costly. For most clubs a balance must be struck in spending money on maintaining areas that do not affect the playability of the course. In locations where returns are high or labour is cheap it can be worth it, but in most places it is not.

   iii) Visual impact. In order to create an impact of sufficient magnitude to make it worthwhile, quite large areas must usually be planted. A golf course exists on a much larger scale than most gardens and parks, and to make an impact with shrubs behind a green, one might have to mass plant an area 50metres wide. This then relates to the question of maintenance, above.

While it is always a pleasure to use masses of colourful feature planting to frame our golf course images, one must exercise much forethought and only proceed with this concept if one is sure that all the ingredients are in place to ensure sustainability.

We generally find this type of detailed feature planting is often not so applicable to be used in featuring golf holes and play zones, for the above reasons. In addition, it can also have the effect of taking one's focus off the actual golf holes and challenges at hand. This is fine if the golf course is substandard, but that is not what we are about. As such we find detailed feature planting is generally best used in the transitions between play zones and other areas, such as around the clubhouse and car park, between the clubhouse, 1st tee, and practice areas, and especially on route from each green to the next tee.

These are all areas where one is not actually playing golf, and where one has a few moments and the best mental state of mind to take in these features. A well-landscaped natural waterfall situated beside a path leading you to the next tee will have a positive effect on your overall golf experience. It will help you relax before reaching the next tee, whilst not distracting you as you play the golf hole.

The Landscape Design Approach

The generalised landscape concept for a golf course will be formulated together with the concepts for shaping, bunkering and the like, before any design work begins.

Thereafter, the detailed design of landscape can only proceed after all other design is complete, at which time its major goal will be to strengthen and enhance the attributes of the golf course design, in accordance with the originally conceived landscape and general design concepts.

The detailed landscape design must be undertaken in close liaison with the golf course designer, if they are not one and the same person, and the Golf Course Architect must have veto powers over everything proposed by the landscape designer. The Golf Course Architect is the only one who has a truly intimate knowledge of whether the landscape designs as proposed will have an optimum level of impact that is perfectly complimentary to the overall design. The Golf Course Architect, in working up his detailed golf hole strategies, shaping, drainage and golfer circulation solutions, will have in the process, formulated some landscape images, both generalised and specific that will best complement all other components.

A golf course designer is very much designing the land areas from the ground up, so he has probably the best knowledge of what a fully integrated design concept should consist of, allowing for playability, maintenance, strategy, and overall image. He will have ideas of the type or look of plants required to best take advantage of the design levels and shapes. As well as that, the knowledge of what feelings each design element should evoke when viewed from various key locations are issues about which the Golf Course Architect will have a reasonable idea, even if he is not able to fully document the landscape planting design.

It is for this reason it is often best for all concerned that if the Golf Course Architect has the capacity to undertake the landscape design, he should do it. In the very least it should be done under the direct instruction of the Golf Course Architect, either in-house or by the Golf Course Architect directly supervising an outside Landscape Architect.

This situation of having the landscape designer acting under the direction of another designer has the potential to create differences of opinion, which can have a negative effect on a project. For this reason the Landscape Architect and the Golf Course Architect should be very closely aligned in a professional sense, with a high mutual respect for each others opinions, if not belonging to the same organisation.

This follows through into the onsite implementation phases. As previously mentioned, it is often the case that design adjustments are made onsite during construction of a golf course. In accordance with that, the Golf Course Architect must have the power to amend locations of proposed planting onsite in accordance with his design amendments.

The best and most ideal situation in many cases may be to delay the detailed landscape design until all other elements have been designed and built onsite. This enables the designers concerned to accurately consider the actual site conditions and requirements after all the other amendments to the golf course design proper, have been made and implemented.

Unfortunately, this amount of time, and secondary interruption to a golf course is rarely available as golf courses are built and grown in.

Application Of The Design Principles In The Detailed Landform Design Of Water Features

Water features, consisting of lakes, ponds and the overland routes such as creeks, rivers and canals that connect them, serve very important roles on many golf course sites, both practically and aesthetically.

Nowadays, almost all golf courses are equipped with some form of automated irrigation system and as such, a water source from which to pump, is usually required.

On golf courses built over fresh water aquifers, that source can often be obtained directly from a bore or well. On most golf courses that are not built on a deep and porous sand base, an interlinked system of ponds and lakes together with an integrated sub-surface drainage system harvests and channels at least a portion of the storm water that falls on the golf course, for collection at an irrigation water storage pond.

In addition, the inclusion of various water bodies are often required to meet flood mitigation requirements, as golf courses are often utilised as naturalised flood regulation areas.

In all of these cases, the project engineers, and specialist irrigation sub-consultants calculate the volumes of water and basic water levels that are required to be observed and achieved in the detailed design.

It is up to the Golf Course Architect to input these factors as constraints in the detailed design equation, and come up with design solutions that are functional, economic, aesthetic, and environmentally friendly, whilst maximising the potential of these factors in terms of playing strategy and overall golfer experience.

If a pond is required for technical reasons, it is in most cases best incorporated as a working, strategic golf element, rather than having it separate to the golf course where it requires extra cost to build and uses extra space.

On very flat sites it is often required that earthworks be undertaken just to create surfaces with enough fall and differentiation of levels to adequately shed storm water, as well as creating interest, strategy and focus with shape.

Since it is usually more costly to import soil for this purpose, ponds and water bodies are often excavated onsite to win sufficient amounts of fill soil that is required in the normal course of construction. As well as providing soil, they also generally have the following positive effects:

a) They provide low catchment areas into which play zones can drain.
b) They provide irrigation water storage.
c) The inclusion of such water bodies is usually seen as a positive aesthetic and strategic asset.
d) They reduce the turf area of a golf course site, thus reducing overall maintenance costs.

Technically, the formation of the water bodies must be specified by a civil engineer, based on the local conditions. As designers aiming for a naturally appearing and easy to maintain water body and edge, The Golf Course Architect usually works in conjunction with the Project Engineers in order to achieve something similar to the following general characteristics.

1) *An immediate pond edge of no steeper than 1:3*

A 1:3 slope (3 metres horizontal for 1 metre vertical) on a pond edge usually gives the following benefits:-

a) It is not too steep to walk up and down without fear of slipping into the water.
b) It is accessible by the required maintenance machines.
c) It is shallow enough to be able to be readily constructed with all except the most unsuitable of soils, and requires a minimum of costly, engineered slope stabilisation techniques.
d) It can facilitate a naturally appearing pond edge.

2) *Underwater services*

All inlet and outlet pipes adjoining the water bodies are to be located at levels below the normal water level, such that they are concealed to the casual observer. Contrary to what the logical thoughts of a good many people tell them, pipes will drain if their outlets are underwater.

3) *Minimisation of hard edges*

Where possible it is best to soften pond edges with the inclusion of aquatic plants and the like, and discourage the use of engineered hard edges except for specific situations, such as locating a green on the very edge of the water.

Even in situations like that we are nowadays trying to minimise the widespread use of formalised rubble walls and timber. In days gone by you would see vast lengths of timber retaining walls going in some cases almost all the way around a pond.

Most designs tend to appear most naturally appealing when these types of edges are broken up with rocky slopes, areas of turf and smaller sections of formalised timber or rubble walls. Under such a scenario, the small areas of formal wall provide visual focus, whilst appearing that they were maybe added to aid a small area of erosion, on an otherwise natural pond edge.

This is opposed to the widespread use of formal walls, which nobody can argue, is fully engineered and artificial.

4)   *Lake edge protection*

In some instances engineered lake edge protection is required, such as on large ponds in windy locations where wave action is likely to erode banks, or in irrigation ponds where large water drawdown leaves an exposed section of soil that is ugly and could be prone to structural failure.

Rockwork is usually the preferred medium in achieving this protection and it can be either set in mortar, or carefully laid dry on a compacted base, depending on the local conditions.

Where this rock is for protection of the slope from water drawdown we usually set a very accurate top level for the rock some 100-200 mm above the top water line. Although the rock can still be seen when the pond is full, it still appears natural, especially when the turf from the slope above is allowed to grow down and slightly soften the hard edge.

Where wave action is a concern, a mix of rocks of differing sizes is usually positioned along the water's edge, extending a few metres inside and outside the water depending on local conditions. The idea is to make the lake edge look natural, as if the wave action has eroded the bank slightly, to expose a rocky sub-surface. Indigenous semi aquatic plants help further naturalise the image.

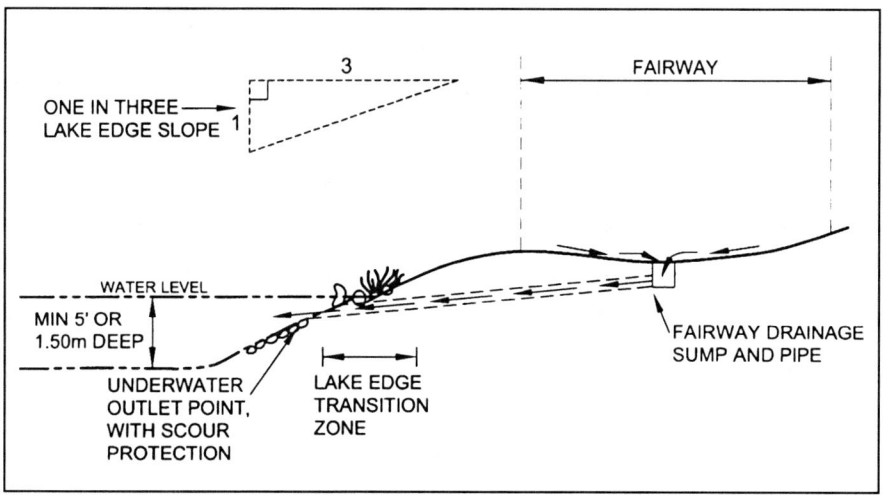

Diagram 33. Typical lake edge.

139

Quite often, a mix of these styles is employed and in any case, the concept is always changed to suit the local conditions.

5)   *Depth*

Overly shallow water, especially without much movement (such as in a flowing stream) will be pone to become choked with aquatic grasses and the like, due to the warm water conditions created by sun being able to penetrate through to the floor of the water body.

Where clear water is desired, a minimum depth of 1.5 to 1.8 metres (5'-6') usually alleviates this effect. This kind of depth sets up natural differentials in water temperature that prevents excessive plant growth and provides a healthier environment for fish and other elements of a self-sustaining ecosystem.

Designing for the Natural Positioning of Water Bodies

In locating a water body on a golf course such that it will appear natural, one must closely observe the surroundings of any potential water body in order to ascertain what might need to be done to make it appear natural.

On very flat sites, obviously there is little to think about, because one area is basically the same as the next, in terms of the amount of work that is required to be done.

On an undulating site one must be a little more careful, and on a site that is made up, for example, of a broad slope tilting to one general direction, selection of pond sites can require very creative solutions borne out of vast design experience.

Starting with the basic design requirements for irrigation water storage, as well as the desired aesthetic effects, the amount of water to be included on a golf course should be calculated early in the planning process such that it can be allowed for, firstly in the routing of the golf holes and secondly in the detailed design.

Looking again to nature, one will find that in all naturally occurring water bodies, they are virtually surrounded by land that slopes up from or is higher than the water level, except possibly for an overflow point, like you might find in a pond that forms part of a river in times of flood.

The main issue, then, in making a permanent water body appear natural, is in fitting it into the base of an area that gives it the appearance of a natural catchment, and ensuring that the surrounds of such a water body are all set at levels higher than the water level.

This, it could be reasoned is obvious, because to hold water the edges must surely be higher than the water. That is true, but to make it appear natural, the wall structure of a dam must be bulky enough to give it a natural appearance, as well as tying naturally to the landforms adjacent to the wall of the dam; which incidentally must also be quite bulky to make them appear natural.

In a natural gully situation it is relatively easy to position a pond, providing plenty of fill is put behind the "dam wall" to make it appear natural. Making the water level a little lower than you would if going for maximum capacity will also assist in achieving a natural look.

Possibly the toughest situation is putting a water body of any appreciable size, on the side of a slope, with no gully in which to position it. In this instance, it might be necessary to re-shape quite a large area, to manufacture a system that will look natural.

The examples as shown in diagram 34 are probably the minimum amount of work that is required to position water bodies naturally on two different types of terrain. Anybody with experience in engineering or agricultural dam construction will see there is an appreciable amount of extra earthworks required than would be the case if one simply wanted to create a dam, without consideration for how natural it might look.

But even in these examples, more work should be done to further naturalise the tie-in areas of the earthworks on the low sides of each of these structures, and if that cannot be done, visual softening measures, such as thick landscape should be used to partially obstruct the view of these areas and partially hide the tie-in areas.

Making Use Of Engineered Dams

Quite often, in remodelling existing golf courses, or occasionally in building a new one, it is deemed unfeasible to rework an existing dam, at obvious great cost for the sake of the look of maybe one or two golf holes, which are situated on its edges.

In these cases, one of two options is usually the best.

a)   Even on many engineered dams, the uphill side usually ties fairly naturally with the above slope, meaning any golf holes situated along this uphill slope can be shaped without too much bother such that the relationship with the waters edge appears fairly natural.

b) For golf holes situated on the downhill side of such a structure, that is, under the dam wall, any view of the water will immediately appear unnatural. How often, in nature does one get to look along the surface of the water when standing up? Not often, unless one is climbing a frozen waterfall. Therefore, from this side, it is best to separate and hide any view of the water one might potentially see from a golf hole. Dam walls should generally be shaped to appear with a smooth tie-in at their base like a hillside, and then mass-planted. This creates an image that for the casual observer appears like a hill with trees on it, and one is given no inkling there might be water at the top of such a hill.

For dams that are completely perched, that is where the water level is higher than all of its surrounds, dense landscape totally surrounding might be the best option, if the surrounds cannot at least be partially filled to create a natural tie-in to surrounding play zones.

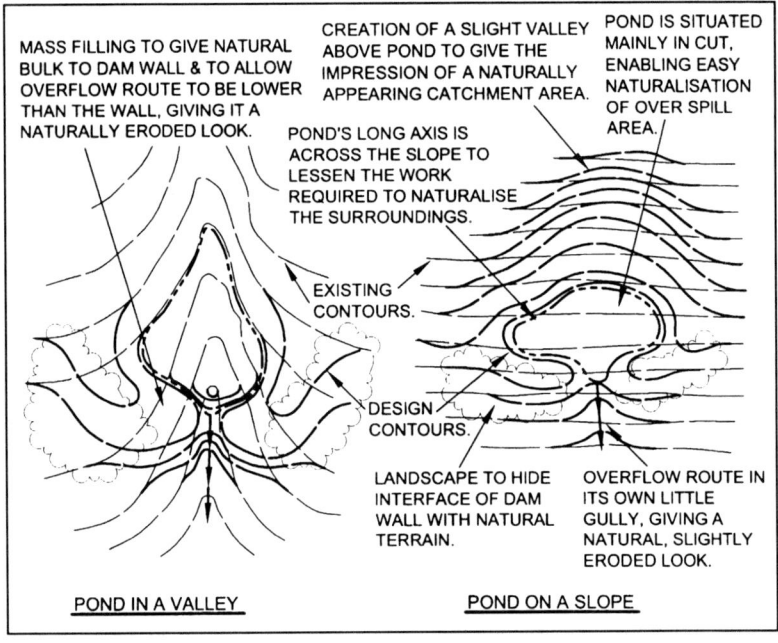

Diagram 34. Designing water bodies for natural appearance.

As is probably obvious by now, I am of the opinion that in general terms, if a golf course is to have water on it, then it should come into play. (Unless of course the water consists of an irrigation pond on a sandy links course that could never naturally hold water).

Once one has figured where the water bodies should generally be positioned according to the natural landforms and the layout of the golf holes, it comes time to design the water bodies in conjunction with detailed golf hole design, such that they perfectly compliment golf hole strategy.

Like most hazards on a golf course, I am of the opinion water should in most cases be very much visible when it comes into play. Water is a very penal hazard, where one doesn't often get a chance at a recovery shot and to rub salt into the wound, one usually loses one's ball.

For this reason, the incidences of hitting what one considers to be a good shot only to find it went in the water should be avoided at all costs for virtually all standards of golfers, in virtually all cases. This fact and our self-imposed requirements for making all features naturally appearing, effectively cuts down our options in terms of where and how water can be positioned on a golf hole.

Water cannot readily be positioned as a hazard on the outside of a dogleg golf hole, unless all areas from where one is hitting towards it are extremely elevated.

A water body on the outside of a dogleg golf hole on fairly flat country makes it impossible to see the interface between the turf and water. In fact, at 200 metres, with a 1.0 metre height differential between fairway and water and even with a 5 metre high tee, the water body must be at least 20 metres wide in order to see any of it.

In addition, water in a golf hole strategy is an all-or-nothing proposition. For this reason it is usually best used to guard the "tiger" line, encouraging people to hit longer over its edge on a fairway. Alternatively it might be used close to the edge of a green on the left or right, rather than penalising balls that were aimed conservatively away from the optimum lines of play, regardless of how bad the execution of such shots might have been. Golfers who hit those types of bad shots will already have enough trouble recovering without losing golf balls in water. Water is usually best used angled across the line of play, in order that golfers can choose for themselves just how brave they want to be, therefore how much water they want to attempt to carry.

This is not to say that ponds should never be located beyond a landing zone. On the contrary a pond is often, for example, cut in front of a green giving golfers the choice to lay-up short of the pond or risk going into the pond by playing close behind or beside it. The key issue is to ensure the playing strategy and the location of the waters edge is clear and obvious. The presence of water will thereby be an element that is challenging golfers to make a good shot, rather than giving the worst type of penalty to a shot that is already well away from the optimum line of play.

If we have no choice but to put a waterway on the outside of a dogleg we try to give plenty of width to make it effectively out of play, or provide thick rough and catch bunkers to help stop balls before they roll into the water.

It is however not simply enough to position a large water body on the inside of a dogleg, where it can be readily seen. One must make sure that most, if not all of the edges of the water body that fall inside the target zone are visible from the hitting areas. In terms of playability, we regard it as most unacceptable if a golfer hits a ball down what he considers to be a perfect line right next to a pond, only to have it run over a small ridge and into the water.

Diagram 35 is a generalised sketch illustrating the most and least preferred arrangements for providing vision of the edges of water bodies.

Shapes Of Water Bodies

The shapes of water bodies, namely ponds and lakes are for the most part dictated by the scale and shape of the land in which they will become a part of. The edges of ponds usually reflect the shapes that border them, and are therefore, to a large extent, dependent on the generalised philosophies with regard to shape and the desired imagery of the course. A very wavy pond edge will likely not appear fitting beside simple, broad fairway shapes. Likewise a simple lake edge might not match a particularly intricate set of fairway shapes.

In design, we generally try not to use perfectly straight pond edges, unless for a specific purpose and we try to add interest with the pond edges along optimum lines of play. We add interest, and play on the fear of the unknown by hiding small sections of the pond edges, but not so much as to create the negative effects portrayed in diagram 35.

In essence, ponds can be almost any shape, as long as their surrounds are suitably formed to reflect that shape and give the natural impression the shape of the pond is the evolutionary result of the formation of its surrounds. As Golf Course Architects, we use this free-form framework and shape ponds to best serve our strategic golf hole requirements in a setting that will appear interesting and naturally beautiful.

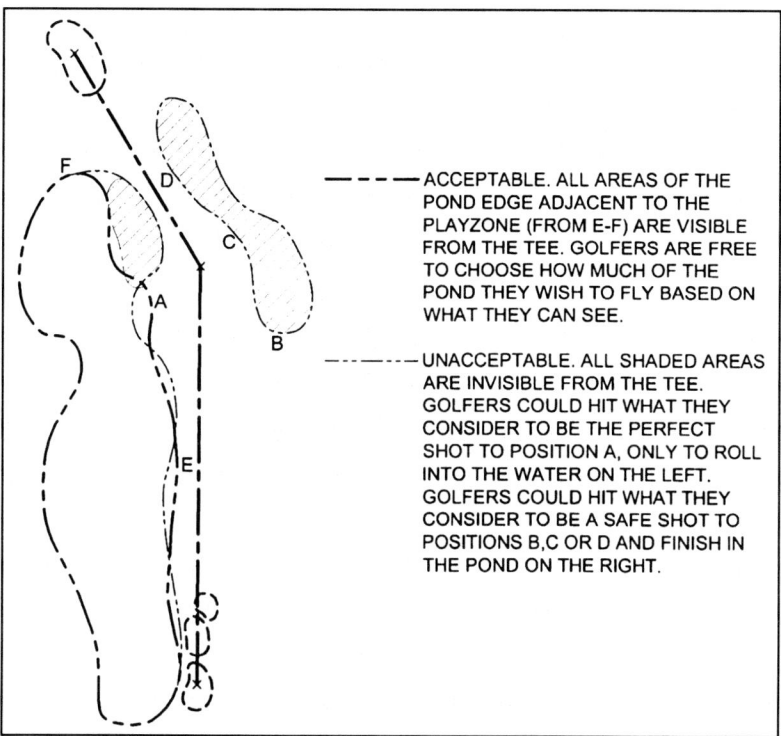

ACCEPTABLE. ALL AREAS OF THE POND EDGE ADJACENT TO THE PLAYZONE (FROM E-F) ARE VISIBLE FROM THE TEE. GOLFERS ARE FREE TO CHOOSE HOW MUCH OF THE POND THEY WISH TO FLY BASED ON WHAT THEY CAN SEE.

UNACCEPTABLE. ALL SHADED AREAS ARE INVISIBLE FROM THE TEE. GOLFERS COULD HIT WHAT THEY CONSIDER TO BE THE PERFECT SHOT TO POSITION A, ONLY TO ROLL INTO THE WATER ON THE LEFT. GOLFERS COULD HIT WHAT THEY CONSIDER TO BE A SAFE SHOT TO POSITIONS B,C OR D AND FINISH IN THE POND ON THE RIGHT.

Diagram 35.Pond edge lines.

Design Of Waterways

In considering the design of the waterways that connect the ponds, and facilitate overland movement of excess water, I often consider two basic types of natural moving water.

1) *The mountain stream* – The mountain stream runs through sometimes-steep terrain, staying close to the valley walls. Directed by the bases of the ridges that terminate in the valley floor, the mountain stream's direction of flow is forever pulled one way and then the other, as if subservient to the hard rocky shapes that limit its every move.

    It cannot escape downwards, for long ago it scoured its base to the hard bedrock below. Only rarely can it muster enough energy to change its

145

surrounds, but that usually only results in another huge load of debris falling into it, which again must be negotiated by its waters.

For the must part, the rocky mountain stream has given up trying to change its surrounds and has settled for a constant, moderate flow that has smoothed its rocky base and allowed fish to thrive happily in its waters. It has allowed fertile soils to be deposited on its banks, with grasses and shrubs allowed to grow close to its trickling flow.

2)   *The flat land river* – The flat land river is a lazy animal with time on its hands. Where it could simply flow directly from A to B, it chooses to take the scenic route, forever doubling back on itself, sometimes taking an alternative direction. It moves easily through its soft soil base, and likes to play with its surrounds, forever re-shaping the edges of its chosen route.

On occasions when it becomes too big for its own bed, it rarely becomes angry, but simply turns itself into a sea, slowly edging its way further away from its banks.

On most occasions it is happy in its own, rather vast and spacious home, forever re-shaping its look, like a woman trying on new outfits.

As we design waterways in the golf course sense, we are probably, in most instances tending to design more along the lines of the mountain stream, as we usually use rocks to protect the base and sides. In following, the surrounding shapes are usually used to define the path of the waterway, in a similar, if less pronounced way than this occurs in nature with the mountain stream.

It is worth remembering, however, the shapes and tendencies of the flat land river, as one lays out a stream, and in particular the way such a river evolves, and changes, in flood.

Imagine a river running through country made up of sand and silty clay. In times of heavy rain the river level rises to near the top of its banks and moves down its twisty length much quicker than normal. As the water rounds the sharp bends in the river, its velocity erodes the bank on the outside of each bend. When the water hits this area, it chews off some of the bank, and turbulence occurs in the water as it bounces back off the bank towards the other side of the river. Here, as the flow slows somewhat, the water drops some of its silt and sand, on the inside of each bend, before proceeding towards the next bend. In this way the bends of the river grow evermore wider, and after the water level of the river goes back down to normal, one can see sand and silt deposited on the inside of each bend, at a slightly lower level than the river bank.

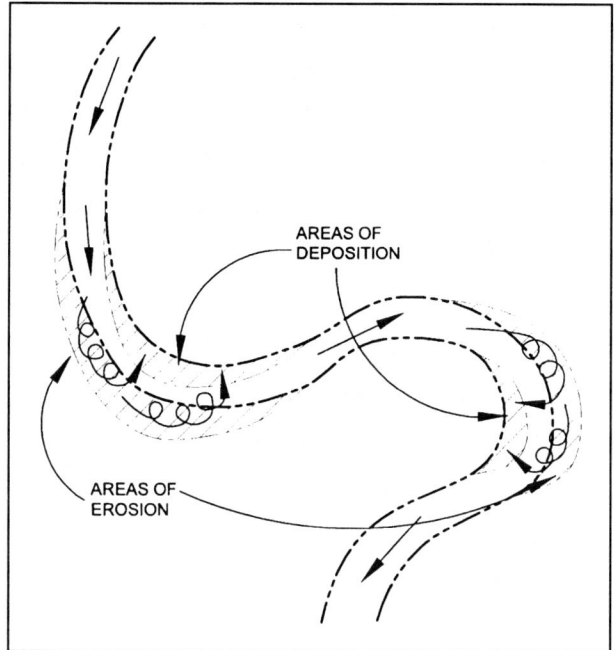

Diagram 36. Evolution of a flatland river

I find it useful to keep the knowledge of this phenomena in the back of my mind when routing creeks and the like, as it helps create very naturally appearing waterways, with bends and widenings in very interesting configurations.

Creating waterways That Rarely Flow

It is not often we are blessed with a water source that is constantly feeding our man-made rocky streams, unless we run a pump specifically for that purpose. Not every Golf Club has the wherewithal to be able to do that, and so we often need to consider how our waterways will look when no water is flowing.

A natural rocky stream normally will consist of small rock pools of water and stretches of very gradually sloped creek bed that will be totally dry if no water is flowing.

To ensure man made waterways look like a waterway even if no water is flowing, it is often best to eliminate the stretches of gradually sloped creek beds and instead make them up of a continuous string of small and even elongated rocky pools, each linked by a small cascade. This type of waterway appears very natural when water is running, and even when it is not, the only thing missing is the water running over each cascade from pool to pool. The waterway still appears full of water, and can go quite a period before evaporation will empty the pools. Even in extremely dry weather, a pump can be run for a short time each day, just to fill each pool in the chain, which is much more economical than running it continuously for effect.

This concept also assists fairway drainage, as pools of water facilitate the inclusion of outlets from fairway drainage pipes, which can be installed invisibly under the water level of the rock pools that make up the rocky creek.

Construction – Construction of these and any type of natural rock features such as waterfalls or dry rock walls is very much an art form in itself. It requires a skilled machine operator to accurately place each rock, as well as a skilled foreman to direct the operator and hand-select the rocks, which will make up each section of any rocky feature.

It is very time consuming work, but worth it, as much as for their beauty, as for the creation of very functional and low maintenance features.

Strategic Use Of Waterways – Rocky creeks such as those described here are one type of waterway that is possible to use more successfully to cross a play zone. Because of the abrupt nature of the edges of such features and the use of rocks to clearly demarcate their limits one can usually position them quite easily such that they can be readily seen and avoided. These type of narrow waterways give plenty of interesting strategic design opportunities, however one must be careful not to overdo it, and be mindful of not having the waterway cross the play zones too many times as this becomes a very tough playing proposition even for pro golfers.

With a pond, once you get past it, its gone, but a long, snaking creek which comes in and out of play for several holes is always lurking, waiting to gobble up a slightly wayward shot.

Possibly one of the best and most well known strategic uses of a creek is on the 13th hole at Augusta National, home of the U.S. Masters.

The hole is a par 5 that doglegs from right to left, with Rae's creek running along the whole left edge, defining the optimum line of play, all the way up to just short of the green where it crosses to the right, diagonally cutting across the line of play and separating the green from the fairway. Hitting close to the left side hazard on the tee shot with a slight draw and on the second shot for those that lay up, gives the best line to the green that is angled from front left to back right, with the creek along its right side edge. There is ample space out to the right side for those who do not wish to hit close to the creek, but from this side the approach to the green is not only longer, but the length of the approach shot must be more exact, because it must be hit more across the long axis of the green and the creek is directly in front.

The golf hole has been perfectly positioned to take advantage of the creek and its very naturally complimentary surroundings. The fairway naturally slopes down to the creek on the left, giving a helping hand to those balls shaped with a draw, by bouncing them closer to the optimum line of play, for the best angle and a shorter distance for the 2nd shot.

The green, on the far side of the creek also angles naturally toward the creek, affording good vision of the putting surface and a general awareness of the challenge, as well as providing very natural locations for the bunkers at the back left of the green. In designs such as these that work closely with nature, all elements simply belong, and the function could not be better.

7

Design Of On-Course Buildings

Detailed design of on-course buildings, such as clubhouse, maintenance facility, practice range shelter, and even half way houses, storm shelters and starter's huts, must of course be undertaken by specialist Building Architects. However, the Golf Course Architect should have a fairly major input in setting the design brief, based on the function of those buildings and their relationship with the golf course proper.

In the master-planning phase of a golf course design, the Golf Course Architect would have allocated spaces for all buildings. As the detailed design of all surrounding golf course elements come together, much of the building design brief will crystallise, at least in general terms in the mind of the Golf Course Architect.

The flow of patrons must be the basis for the design brief, or more specifically the initial space allocations or the conceptual "bubble diagrams" for the internal elements of most on-course buildings. More than most other buildings, the flow of patrons is severely affected by what goes on outside and around these buildings. Quite often, there are so many issues that need to be addressed, that quite innovative planning solutions are required for the architectural building layouts in order to simply come up with solutions that could be termed "reasonably functional".

Clubhouse Layout Design

In clubhouse design, one must usually position the car park, 1st & 10th tees, 9th and 18th greens, practice range, chipping and putting greens, swimming pool, tennis courts, and other possible club facilities all in easy access of the relevant public areas of the clubhouse building and preferably in close, easily visible and logical locations. As well as that, service access must be allowed for, preferably in a location unseen to patrons, as well as the specific golf related operations elements, such as storage & access to golf carts. All these elements invariably surround the clubhouse site and are usually positioned in ways that maximise their function without undue building cost or excessive earth movement. As well as that, they are invariably part of a large jigsaw puzzle that is the golf course proper. As such there is often not a lot of scope to simply move these golf course items in order to appease a premeditated architectural clubhouse concept.

That is why the general planning of almost any clubhouse must evolve along with the layout of the general area of the golf course which it is there to serve, according to the balance of the total layout and the overall site constraints, as well as the generalised wishes and priorities of the client.

In looking at the internal bubble diagram layout of a clubhouse, the first and possibly most important factor to consider is the facilitation of easy and logical flow of patrons. These patrons must be easily led to and through different areas of specific function and sufficient size, from the time of arrival to the time of departure. As well as that, additional peripheral requirements, such as the appropriate views and aspects from internal public spaces, must also be considered.

Of particular importance is the flow of patrons from the point of arrival, through to the first tee.

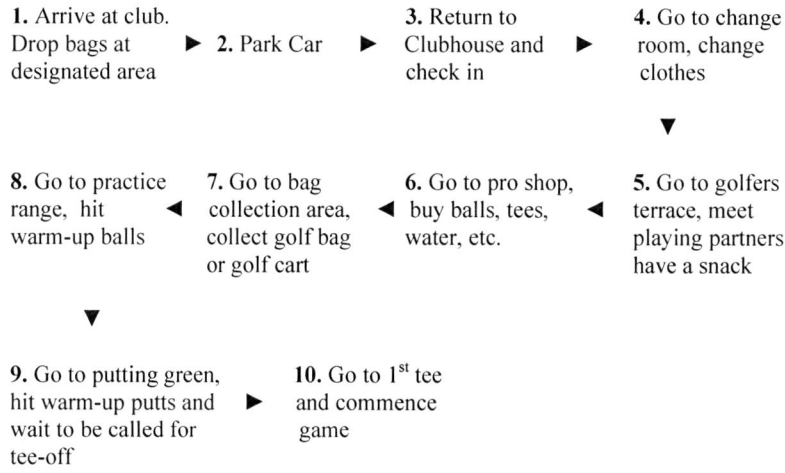

Diagram 37. Club House Layout Design,
10 Steps to Tee-Off

A major influence in the level of satisfaction that golfers will gain from a day of golf is determined by the mental state they find themselves in, by the time they arrive at the first tee. If one arrives at the first tee confused, rushed and flustered, a bad tee shot is more likely, which could well set the tone for a negative overall golfing experience. It is therefore imperative that all the things a golfer needs to do after arriving at the Golf Club and prior to arriving at the first tee are laid out in a logical, easy to find, step by step arrangement that makes for a minimum of confusion and a maximum amount of relaxation.

The 10 steps shown in the diagram are virtually the same set of requirements that golfers all over the world expect to able to undertake prior to the commencement of a game of golf. Therefore, in laying out a golf clubhouse, one must allow for the easy succession of events by all golfers, including those patrons that have never been to the golf course before. It is usually advisable to simplify the layout as much as possible, and semi-open plan layouts are often good as they enable golfers to see areas where different activities are happening, making it easier for them to choose in which order they wish to undertake which activity.

If this is not possible, then the design should be such that it is impossible to miss the next step after leaving the last.

Likewise, the time spent in the clubhouse after finishing the game and leaving the property should be considered in a logical manner. However it is generally not necessary to structure these activities so much, as time is usually not the critical factor that it is on arrival when golfers are rushing to make their tee times.

The importance of the clubhouse layout formation cannot be underestimated. Even a simple, low cost clubhouse, if well laid out can easily purvey a feeling of elegance and class by making golfers feel totally relaxed and at ease with their time spent there. If golfers can meet their friends without hassles or mix ups, sit on a terrace with a commanding view over the golf course and have their day go like clockwork, then this will have a positive effect which is almost, if not as great as playing golf on a good course.

A well-organised clubhouse also has the potential for making great long term savings on operations costs, as compared to a poorly laid out clubhouse. In a clubhouse where the approach in catering for the golfers needs is not obvious and practical, a lot more manpower and organisation of human resources will be required. Extra staff will be required to assist golfers to find what they want, and to bring items over long distances (such as food, golf carts, golf bags etc.) in poorly planned layouts.

152

This detracts from golfer satisfaction and costs more in staff and co-ordination. Indeed, good architectural design in public spaces like golf clubhouses, can make a lot of money through creating a comfortable ambience where people will be happy to frequent as well as spending money on Souvenirs, Food and Beverage. As well as that, good architectural design can save a lot of money, through in-built efficiencies, which sees a high level of job satisfaction for staff as well as long term savings in overall staffing requirements.

Design Of Maintenance facility Layouts

Although maintenance facilities deal only with internal staff and not golf course patrons, the flow of activities is no less important.

Golf maintenance facilities are traditionally the most neglected element of any golf course site and there has been a historical misconception that there is no point in investing time and money in an area that is for the most part, unseen by golfers.

Nowadays, of course we understand nothing could be further from the truth. Maintenance generally makes up the greatest proportion of Golf Club expenditure and as such, its efficiency is of very high priority. On the other side of the equation, the standard of golf course maintenance has a major influence on golfer satisfaction, which in turn greatly influences overall profitability of a Golf Club.

Efficiency of maintenance operations is therefore crucial in a) assisting in attracting paying patrons and b) assisting in keeping maintenance costs in check.

The first key element in achieving both of those goals is the layout and set-up of the golf course maintenance facility, of which the flow of activities, in this case the activities of the staff, are priority number one.

The general, ideal flow of a maintenance machine operator going about his daily duties might in simplified terms, look like the flowchart shown in diagram 38.

As can be seen from this flow chart, most maintenance workers must undertake quite a definite set of tasks, and if they can be done correctly, the maintenance facility will at least have the infrastructure in place to facilitate an efficient ongoing maintenance operation.

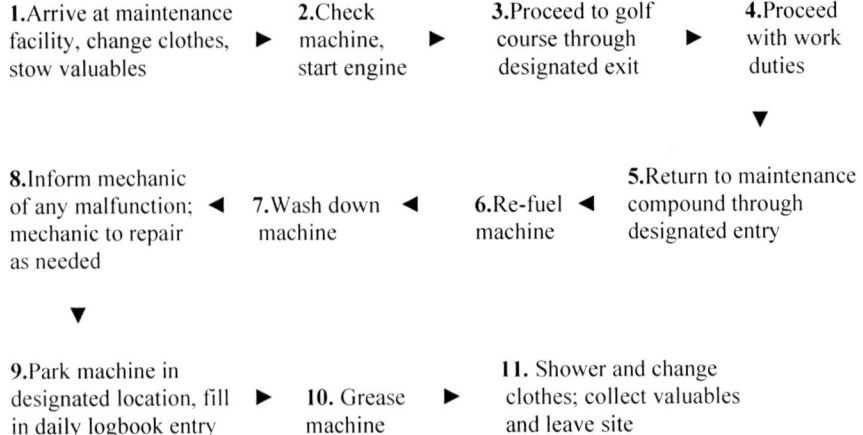

1.Arrive at maintenance facility, change clothes, stow valuables ▶ **2.**Check machine, start engine ▶ **3.**Proceed to golf course through designated exit ▶ **4.**Proceed with work duties ▼

8.Inform mechanic of any malfunction; mechanic to repair as needed ◀ **7.**Wash down machine ◀ **6.**Re-fuel machine ◀ **5.**Return to maintenance compound through designated entry

▼

9.Park machine in designated location, fill in daily logbook entry ▶ **10.** Grease machine ▶ **11.** Shower and change clothes; collect valuables and leave site

Diagram 38. Golf Course Maintenance Facility
machine operator's typical, ideal daily schedule

The actual methods of storage of machines, layout of mechanics areas, types of buildings and many other issues are subject to local labour, building, weather and security issues. The main constant in planning and design is to facilitate the easy and practical flow of workers and machinery that facilitates proper care and upkeep of machines and minimises worker down time.

Some other general points that should be observed in allocating space and generalised planning for maintenance facilities are as follows: -

- A maintenance compound should ideally be located in a reasonably central position on its golf course site to facilitate easy access by workers and machines to all parts of the golf course.
- Access of maintenance workers and deliveries of material and machinery to maintenance facilities should ideally be via a road not used by Golf Club patrons.
- Superintendent's office should afford easy access to mechanics, irrigation and machinery part store areas and machinery parking area for easy checking and security.
- Allowance for designated machinery exit and entry points to facilitate easy and orderly access to the golf course.
- Separate, well secured and well ventilated storage buildings for chemicals and fertilisers
- Large storage bins for specialist sands and gravels.
- Parking areas for staff and visitors.
- Adequate turning circle area for large delivery vehicles.

- Adequate facilities for worker safety and amenity, such as poisons wash down facilities, lunchrooms, toilets, lockers, etc.
- Allowance for environmentally sound disposal of oils, grease, and other hazardous waste materials.
- Lockable perimeter fence.

8

Drainage

We have spoken previously how drainage is considered as second nature in all design decisions and they are so intertwined one might go so far as to say quite often the design decisions are dictated by drainage.

In considering drainage, our initial design decisions made about any section of any golf hole are designed to do one of two things with regard to drainage, to either *concentrate* the flow of surface water to specified locations or *disperse* the flow of water over a wide area.

Where contours are positioned parallel to each other in a convex arrangement, this has the effect of dispersing water that falls on this area. Therefore, providing the areas in question are not too large, and the water does not have to travel too far to the nearest out flow point, sub-surface drainage can be minimised.

Where contours are positioned in a concave, gathering arrangement, surface flows are being concentrated in areas that must be serviced by sub-surface drainage, providing the turf and sub-surface soils cannot absorb all water channelled to these areas as they commonly do on links type courses.

These two basic types of storm water flow are illustrated in the following diagram 39. Areas of concentration exist around the drainage inlets (shown as small circles connected with double lines). Areas of dispersion are shown in the lower portion of the diagram, where flow arrows indicate water flowing off the sides of a large gentle mound, and into a pond.

Of all the parkland golf courses in existence, including new, well-constructed courses and those with relatively sandy soils, there are very few that have the capacity to absorb all water into their soil profile, including storm water and the requirements of artificial irrigation. And in tropical conditions, it is virtually impossible to prepare any type of soil such that the amount of water that falls on a site is dissipated solely by soaking into the soil.

156

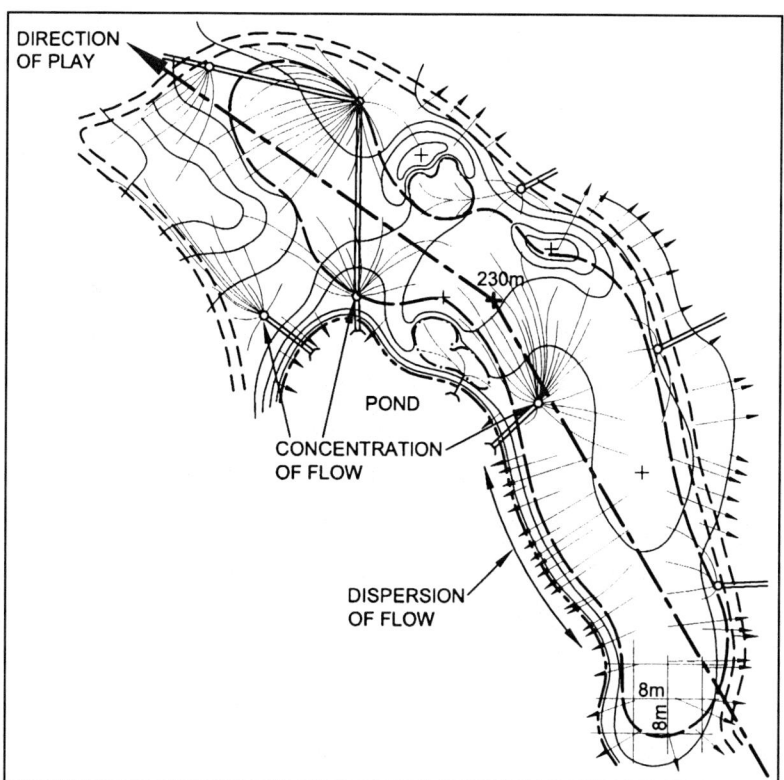

Diagram 39. Partial plan of a golf hole with arrows showing the flow of storm water from the intersection points of an 8 metre grid to their nearest points of egress.

We therefore generally promote surface run-off as the primary manner in which the water is dissipated. Our designs, whilst appearing naturally free-form in shape, are actually carefully designed to divide the golf course into small catchment areas, each one serviced by its own inlet, with a steel grate through which water passes from the fairway into a concrete sump. From there it flows through a pipe, and out to the nearest pond. Careful design ensures no area is overloaded with excessive amounts of run-off.

Although we are by design, limiting the amount of water that flows into each sump, the flow of water is concentrated somewhat at each inlet. The immediate surrounds of each inlet are therefore most prone to dampness, although most do not become damp at all.

In addition, minor inconsistencies in sub-surface soil types, the possible presence of natural springs, etc can cause dampness, and all these areas require a strategy to keep them dry in all conditions, hence the implementation of post construction, or herringbone drainage.

The herringbone drainage works in the following manner: -

Trenches are cut at regular intervals of 2-4 metres, depending on local conditions, into which a flexible, perforated pipe is bedded into clean gravel. A thin layer of sand is laid on top, and the turf is replaced after washing soil off it. This allows any surface water to soak through the turfgrass, sand, gravel and into the pipe, which carries it to the nearest sump. Sub-surface water is also free to seep into the system out of the walls and bases of the trenches. In this way, these trenches dry both the surface and the sub-surface, thereby eliminating soggy conditions.

The trenches are laid in a herringbone arrangement, meaning the pattern appears in plan like that of a fishbone, or herringbone. Water is captured in one of the off-shooting spurs of pipe and channelled back to the central spine pipe, which carries it to the nearby concrete sump. This type of drainage is also installed in a ring around each sump, for added effect.

Nowadays there are many variations of this sub-surface soakage or herringbone drainage, but they all serve the same basic function, in their own similar ways.

One may ask why this procedure often cannot be carried out as a part of the construction, before the grass is properly grown. The reason is twofold, as follows:

1) The full extent of the requirement for this type of drainage often cannot be ascertained until turf is established. That is, the presence of the turf actually changes the drainage properties and these changes are often impossible to foresee.

2) It is important that the materials used for this type of drainage remain clean and free of silt at all times, otherwise they will not function. It is virtually impossible to avoid silt contaminants during construction because the water must flow in these areas when it rains, and without grass cover, water will certainly carry some silt, thereby rendering this type of drainage less effective.

Excavations on completed work to install the "2nd stage" drainage system are designed to further enhance and facilitate high quality playing conditions of already well-finished fairways. When complete, the drainage is totally invisible, with the only difference being top class playing conditions in all weather.

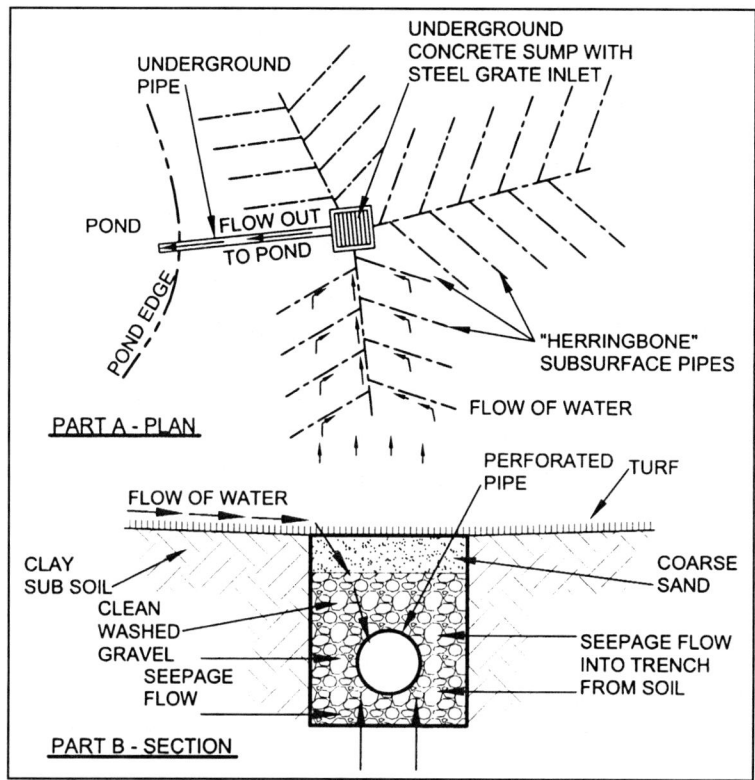

Diagram 40. Plan and section view of subsurface "herringbone" drainage

Sand Capping Of Play Zones

There appears to be a general misconception among a lot of people that simply applying a layer of sand on any area will automatically cure all drainage issues. In studying the natural, sand based links golf courses; one finds many large hollows with no drainpipe in the bottom. Indeed, it is amazing how quickly a large puddle can dissipate on some of these golf courses; in fact in most cases the rain has finished before a puddle of any sort has formed.

In areas like this it must be remembered that the consistency and depth of the sand, the climate, the frequency and intensity of the rain, the turf type and the style of maintenance all combine perfectly to allow such free drainage to occur. If one of these items is not quite right, drainage will become a problem.

Endeavouring to bring the virtues of free-draining sand to a golf course site where this type of drainage does not already happen naturally is fraught with danger, and the following pitfalls should be understood and allowed for.

Sand depth – The naturally free draining golf courses are usually built on very deep tracts of natural sand, usually tens, and even hundreds of feet deep. At a level somewhere below the lowest playing surface, the sand invariably becomes saturated with water, and the level at which this saturation point exists is known as the "water table". The drainage functions by allowing any surface water to gradually seep down through the profile to eventually join the body of water below.

The top level of this ground water (the water table) will usually change its level only very slowly and gradually over time and a storm here and there will usually not have a major short-term effect on its level. In fact even if its level does change somewhat, the sheer depth of sand will usually ensure the effects on the drainage of the golf course above are quite minimal.

In golf course construction we rarely have the opportunity to import 10 or 20 feet of free draining sand to cover a whole site in order to achieve this abovementioned, naturally occurring effect. A thickness of maybe 1 to 2 feet is usually about as much as most clients can practically supply.

However, simply blanketing a site with a foot or two of sand will invariably create as many drainage problems as it solves, according to the following sketch.

In the following diagram 41, part A) shows rain hitting a sand capped slope, and providing the rain is not too intense, almost all of the rain will penetrate the sandy slope were it falls. Any run-off will make its way down the slope to a flatter area, where its reduced velocity will allow it to soak into the surface. So far, so good.

Part B) shows the same slope a few minutes or hours later. The sand on the slope has done a good job in absorbing the storm water, all of which has now gone into the slope's sand surface. After that happens, the water has percolated vertically until it hits the impervious clay base, where it has nowhere to go except to follow the gradual incline of that base. The problem is the process of water percolating through sand is quite slow, and the water in the sand layer from up on the steeper sections of the slope (right side) has moved down faster than the lower areas are moving. The mid to lower sections of the slope therefore become saturated. This results in very wet conditions underfoot and in extreme cases water will actually seep *back out* of the slope and run down the outside surface.

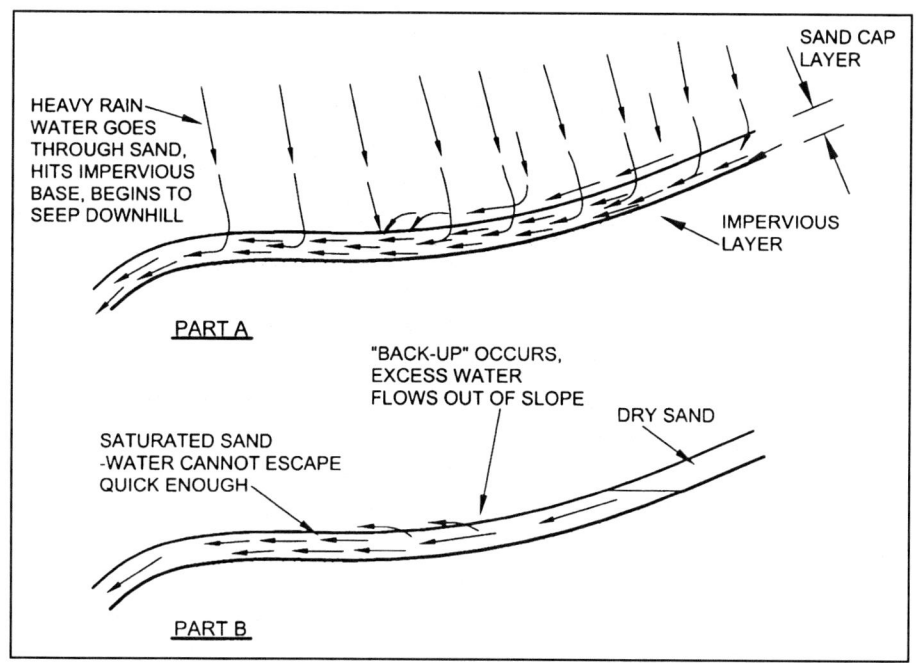

Diagram 41. Schematic section through a sand capped slope.

In this example the sand capping has actually impeded the flow of storm water, which if encouraged to exit the scene primarily by surface flow would be long gone. Waiting for sand to percolate all the way along a profile could take days or weeks and if the base has not been shaped to fall, it may never happen, resulting in continuously wet and stagnant conditions.

For this reason, if a sand layer is to be installed over an impervious base, sub-surface drainage like the herringbone type explained above must be installed first. As well as this, the normal sumps and pipes to collect run-off for heavy storms, must be included should the location be prone to experience these, as will any area of a tropical or sub tropical climate.

This in effect means all areas of the golf course will be constructed to a similar specification of the greens, most of which incorporate a free draining sand layer over a drainage layer of washed gravel and drainage trenches. Even with this in place, the results are often not great. Aside from assisting in alleviating the effects of a light shower of rain, the sand capping generally impedes the passage of water from the surface through to the subsurface or herringbone drainage, by providing another layer through which the water must first percolate.

Maintenance

If one does, however construct all play zones with a sand layer over herringbone, one is in effect building a golf course with a drainage strategy the same or similar to that of a green. It therefore follows the maintenance standards must also be similar to that of the greens.

The "perched water table" style of greens construction, utilising a relatively free draining sand layer, no doubt enables the production of high quality putting surfaces, but only when combined with an intensive level of expert maintenance. One of the important attributes that facilitate this level of maintenance is the amount of control that the maintenance superintendent can exert over the turf, due to the fact that the percolation rate of moisture through the soil profile is well known. The superintendent can be quite comfortable and exact with the controlled amounts of fertilisers, chemicals and irrigation water that is applied, as he knows these additives leach out of the system at a quite consistent rate across all the green surfaces. This rate of leaching in sand capped areas is generally quite fast compared to heavier soils, in terms of the time that soil additives will stay in the soil before washing through to the sub surface drainage system. This is very good for putting greens as it very much reduces the incidence of inconsistencies in the condition of the putting surfaces, because few residues are retained, as could be the case in less impervious soil.

The down side is that similarly to greens, a more intensive and costly maintenance regime is required. In particular, more fertilisers and irrigation are generally needed, as the porous nature of the soil allows these materials to exit the system relatively quickly. The maintenance team must also be on the lookout for a build up of thatch or any other conditions that might prevent the free vertical flow of water down through the sand profile, potentially rendering it ineffective.

The overall result of such a sand capping exercise is that it can be successful, provided the level of maintenance is similar to that of a green. Considering that care of greens already takes a reasonable proportion of the maintenance budget of most golf courses, maintaining an area something like 30 times the size of the area of all the greens is cost prohibitive to most golf courses.

My experience is in almost all cases I've come across, it's just not worth it, as the results do not justify the cost and hassle. Take for example the course shown in the design examples in the previous chapter. With over 3 metres (10 feet) of annual rainfall and extremely poor clay soil, one would think this would be a candidate for sand capping if ever there was one.

But even here, we have managed to create a result that plays just as well, and can be kept in just as good a condition as any artificially sand capped golf course that I've ever seen. A well thought out drainage design strategy, coupled with diligent construction techniques and careful selection of well adapted turf grasses has facilitated a great result saving many millions in construction and ongoing maintenance that would have resulted, had sand capping been undertaken.

Turf, Agronomy And Maintenance

This is perhaps a good time to lead into touching on these specialist areas, in which I am by no means an expert.

Every surface that a Golf Course Architect creates on a golf course has to be maintained, preferably to a high standard, without undue expense or problems.

The agronomy of a site, that is the condition and treatment of the planting medium (the top layer of soil) as well as the treatment of unsuitable soils found on site in preparation for growing turf, is probably the first set of considerations that need to be made with regard to turf growing and future maintenance.

To undertake this; to give input and feedback on selection of turf-grass species, as well as providing the specifications for green, tee and bunker sands and gravels, most Golf Course Architects employ specialist agronomists. These people must be expert not only in soils and maintenance, but also experienced and knowledgeable of the local site, labour and working conditions of the projects on which they have input.

The turf and agronomy business is a fast moving industry, with advances in breeding of turf species and improved maintenance strategies happening all the time, at an ever-quickening rate. Researchers based in the mature golf course markets make most of these improvements, particularly the U.S. In mature markets such as the U.S., new advances in agronomy and maintenance can be put to practical use fairly quickly after development. This is because the market is so big (the U.S. golf course market is several times larger than that found in any other country) and already quite technologically advanced. Economies of scale enable new products and services to be presented in the U.S. with the appropriate advice and backup service, which ensures most are successful.

Other mature markets that are no where near as big, such as Japan, Western Europe and Australia can still take advantage of many of the advancements in the turf and agronomy industry, however they often have to make their own allowances and amendments to suit their local conditions. In addition, if testing of a new product has only been done in far away locations with different climates and different sets of constraints, one can never be sure that similar results of an acceptable standard will be achievable in the location where one's latest golf course design is being realised.

This is a dilemma that constantly confronts Internationally active Golf Course Architects in their day to day business. As Golf Course Architects we are often, by definition working on the frontiers of the industry, in places where few -if any- golf courses exist, much less an established turf-grass industry with backup support and local testing facilities.

In terms of agronomy, many agronomists like to look at other products in the area to see what is working best, and use that as a starting point in working up a strategy for other new projects. If nothing exists to give any true local evidence of success or failure, many agronomists may be loath to recommend turf-grass types and techniques for their upkeep that are basically untested in the local environment.

In most cases it is up to the Golf Course Architect as the principle consultant and adviser to the client, to clearly put forth the available information and risks. Thereafter it is up to the client, who will hopefully take the crucial decisions that will facilitate progress in the field, for the long-term betterment of their golf course and the overall industry.

In any progressive industry there are always time lags between the time of the discovery of a new product or technique and the time that it will be able to be practically implemented in any given locality. As Golf Course Architects we must be very much conscious of the developments as they come to hand, as well as the lag period, and put all of this in the context of the local environment where each of our design products exist. We need to be able to allow new technologies to be applied to our products in the future, without causing undue cost and hardship for the present.

For example, in many new markets, labour is cheap and maintenance machinery is expensive. In most cases we still insist on constructing our designs in these areas such that they maximise the potential for mechanised maintenance. If other emerging markets are any example, sooner or later labour will become expensive and machinery will in relative terms become much more affordable.

If possible, we of course opt for the most modern and technologically advanced solution for all items that facilitate an ever-higher level of quality in the finished product. In emerging markets, however, one must be very careful to ensure the required standards of upkeep can be put in place to guarantee the new technology will function as it is supposed to, for the long term.

I personally know of many golf courses in developing areas that installed and paid for fully automated, computer controlled irrigation systems that have never functioned to anywhere near their full capacity.

Regardless of the level of diligence during installation, any number of small isolated incidents can easily render these hi-tec systems useless, such as an uninformed subcontractor digging in the wrong place, misuse, or unprotected lighting strikes. Above all it is the human element, more than anything that is most difficult to control. A sudden change in management might see some things at a Golf Club done differently for only a short time, but this could be enough to ruin a touchy and expensive hi-tec system.

For this reason, providing the desired level of quality can be attained and we are not creating problems for the future, we tend to employ the simplest and most fool proof systems that we can, in building and maintaining golf courses.

Construction Specifications

It is always advisable to adhere to a consistently high standard of construction in all areas, but especially in areas of high use and high maintenance such as greens, tees and bunkers. A consistent and high standard of construction in these key areas will generally assist all facets of maintenance and give a greater chance of achieving consistency and quality of playing surfaces across all golf holes at any facility.

Golf Course Architects must be careful to work closely with their Agronomists and Golf Course Construction Managers to tailor the specification such that it will not only achieve the desired environment that is conducive to a high standard of maintenance, but that also can be practically achieved onsite, with full consideration of the local resources and constraints.

As responsible Golf Course Architects, we must be careful in specifying materials and styles of construction that have been laid out by people and organisations in other countries and environments, as these may be both inapplicable for the local environment and in many cases impossible to implement.

The United States Golf Association Greens Section has its own specification for greens construction, which has become renowned worldwide and seems to serve as the basis for the specifications of the majority of new golf greens that are built in any location. This USGA specification as it is known, is relatively easy for those in the U.S. to adhere to, and no doubt gives very good, consistent results. This specification is frequently mentioned and is however, more often than not, misconstrued outside the United States.

In the Australian context, for example, it would be a fair statement to say that there would be very few, if any greens that truly conform to the USGA specification.

If this is the case in Australia, a country that is considered to be quite advanced in terms of the design and construction of golf courses, then how is this information to be construed and what of the rest of the world?

I personally do not take this to mean that everyone outside of the U.S. builds golf courses of an inferior quality. Granted, the average level of quality in the U.S. is probably highest in the world, due if nothing else, to the well-defined construction standards that are maintained and driven commercially by what is a huge market.

I contend that this wholesale non-adherence to what is obviously a good specification indicates that in most cases outside the U.S. it is either impossible or pointless (and quite often both) to adhere to a specification that cannot practically cater for all such cases.

Australia, for example is a very old continent, much older in geological terms than North America. Consequently, Australia has a large variation in the type of sands and soils that one can find for use in Golf Course construction. Many of these work very well for construction of greens, tees and bunkers, but not all of them fall within the set of constraints that would qualify them for use as a part of the USGA specification. So in most cases, there's no point in conforming, so long as the agronomist is sufficiently skilled in selecting and conditioning the available materials for the best results for the respective set of local environments and constraints.

In addition, the USGA specification for greens construction contains very specific directives with regards to mixing of sand and additives. In the U.S. this is done offsite by the supplier prior to delivery of the sand. In most places outside of the U.S. sand suppliers are not geared to provide such specific services, and amendments usually must be added to the sand onsite, after it is placed in the green base.

For these reasons, "USGA specification" when applied to greens in most places outside the U.S. is virtually unattainable and thus the term: "USGA specification" is generally mis-used. Most greens constructed nowadays could be best described as a *variation* of the USGA specification or as a form of a "perched water table" type green construction, specified to best suit the local conditions, using the best available materials.

9

Construction Managers And Key Construction Personnel

In chatting with a good many Golf Course Superintendents over the years; it appears that many harbour ambitions of becoming involved in golf course construction. After working his (or her) way up through the ranks as a part of a golf course maintenance team, doing the due formal training as a superintendent and finally being hired or promoted to head up a maintenance crew, many superintendents are looking toward the next challenge.

It is only natural to want to progress and improve as one goes through life. Nowadays it is not so easy to become a Superintendent, much less a Superintendent employed as he or she was trained to be, in charge of golf course maintenance. Once this often long and arduous climb has been completed, the newly qualified and appointed Superintendent is usually itching for the chance to make a difference on the golf course with which he or she has been entrusted. After all the years of learning, it is now finally time to put these things into practice without having any more senior employees looking over their shoulder, preventing them from doing things totally the way they'd prefer.

The new Superintendent is more often than not able to make a good initial positive impact. Aside from being well trained by modern day institutions that are in tune with the latest developments and techniques, the sheer vigour and enthusiasm that is usually apparent in a newly qualified superintendent given free reign is enough to make a big difference on many golf courses.

The unfortunate inevitability is that there is usually a limit to the amount of positive impact a superintendent can create, for a number of reasons.

There could be limitations to the resources a club can extend to their superintendent in order that he or she can continue to improve and elevate the condition of their golf course. The nature of the golf club structure, as opposed to a corporate structure also means that internal politics often come into play, making the decision-making processes a little longer and more arduous than they otherwise might be. The Golf Course might need some

167

major infrastructural changes to get rid of some inherent problem areas that are preventing the superintendent from bringing the golf course to top condition.

Over time the interesting and exciting processes of learning, discovery and experimentation tend to slow down. Whatever the case, there often comes a time when a golf course Superintendent feels they have given all they can to a club. Thereafter they need for the club to either undertake some major upgrading or remodelling to go to the next level, or for the Superintendent to find another, new challenge possibly outside their club.

In a quest to feel they are continuing to progress, learn and improve, similar to the enjoyable way they did as trainees and freshly qualified superintendents, many look to golf course construction as the next creative conquest.

Superintendents, in their studies, touch on a good many practically based techniques and theories that are related to golf course construction. The knowledge a good golf course Superintendent possesses is without doubt very useful in golf course construction. However, it is not necessarily a pre-requisite for good Golf Course Construction Managers to first be qualified as Superintendents.

It should not be assumed that the knowledge gained in studying to become a competent Superintendent automatically qualifies one to act as a competent Golf Course Construction Manager. Many of the theories and principles of construction learnt by a good Superintendent are related to golf course construction, however, these make up only a relatively small portion of the total set of skills required to competently oversee the construction of a golf course or part thereof.

Similarly to that of a Pro Golfer and a Golf Course Architect, the professions of Golf Course Superintendent and Golf Course Construction Manager are kind of parallel professions. They deal with the same product, but at different stages of its lifetime, and consequently, they require quite different modes of approach.

In today's specialised environment, the positions of Superintendent and Construction Manager are essentially very different professions. In addition there is also another parallel profession that fits, one could say, in between these two, that being the specialised profession of Grow-in Superintendent.

The Grow-in Superintendent, as the name suggests is the person who takes control of a golf course just after grass has been planted, and brings it to a playable level. This task, one can imagine has a very different set of requirements to that of the Superintendent's role, whose main responsibility is to maintain existing turf and associated facilities.

It is rather unfortunate that the three different professions seem to be held in a certain order of esteem, being Superintendent, Grow-in Superintendent and Construction Manager as the most revered.

In actual fact, each position has its own, very unique set of requirements, all of which are essential if any golf course project is to reach its full potential. I will note the important points of consideration for each profession from a Golf Course Architect's viewpoint.

The Superintendent

As far as Golf Course Architects go, Superintendents play a vital role. A Golf Course Architect is only as good as his previous works, and if the Superintendent caring for these works does not or cannot upkeep the golf course as it was intended, then everybody's reputation has the potential to become tarnished.

In addition, one must remember golf courses are living, evolving entities. They need to change, and evolve somewhat over time, in order to remain in a healthy state of growth and renewal. In order to be able to ensure that this constant renewal process is happening and continues to happen, the Superintendent must have an eye for detail and be continually questioning every facet of every daily chore that he and his workers undertake.

I do not mean the Superintendent should make change for the sake of change - far from it. But a Superintendent needs to be hungry for information, new techniques, products, changes in the way people play and use the golf course on which he works, as well as trends in the industry, etc. This should still be the case, even if the employer does not have the financial wherewithal to facilitate the Superintendent to make use of any but the cheapest of money saving innovations.

Any Superintendent who does his own research will, sooner or later get his opportunity to employ his knowledge, simply by being well informed, which enables one to see opportunities that are invisible to the less well informed. In any case it is my experience that just from a designer's viewpoint, there are multitudes of issues that can be considered on almost any golf course. If a Superintendent questions why everything is done and maintained the way it is, and makes sure he has a well considered answer for all of these questions, he will most probably be maintaining his course in the best way possible.

Much of this requires no extra cost beyond mind power. Items such as bunker and fairway profiling for example, can have a profound effect on the way one might play a golf hole. Changing a bunker profile by 6 inches in a few places, and a fairway profile by a few feet here and there can have a drastic effect on how a golf hole looks. This in turn has a drastic effect on how one feels about playing the hole, which in turn can have a drastic effect on the shot making decisions a golfer takes. These design related issues should not be underestimated, for in the end they are the difference between quality and mediocrity. But one needs to know why they might make a change in this regard, and in order to do that one requires knowledge, that can only be gained by constant, personal study and inquiry over a reasonable period of time.

Countless times I have visited an existing golf course and listened to grandiose plans of how to make the course better, when in actual fact the Superintendent is surrounded by design related opportunities that require little cost and would have just as big an impact.

Another important trait a Superintendent should strive for is a certain humbleness that best facilitates the discovery of new information. A common human misgiving is that of making one's own decision and then unwaveringly sticking to it and defending it, regardless of how wrong that decision might be or how inapplicable that decision may become over time. This especially seems to happen when somebody spends a lot of time and effort working on a particular concept. The further they progress with this concept, the more protest they are likely to put up if somebody suggests that maybe there's a better way.

We all need to be humble enough to acknowledge a good idea can came from anywhere and anybody. Quite often, a fresh unbiased opinion from somebody totally removed from the situation, regardless of his or her qualifications might give the best solution. If one is humble enough to take in such information when it arrives, and if one is already in possession of enough background information and knowledge to be able to adequately, accurately and practically consider such new information, one can either move to dispel the notion, or choose to take it on board, giving factual, practical and reasonable reasons for the decision. This benefits everyone as well as the golf course, and contrary to popular opinion, it makes the decision maker-in this case the superintendent- appear a bigger and more intelligent person, because of the ability to take on board and properly process an idea that was not his own.

I have on a several occasions had the experience of being engaged with a view to act as the design consultant for a golf club, and have arrived onsite to have a look at the golf course, usually with the superintendent as the tour guide.

On several occasions, the Superintendent has proceeded to show me all of the design related changes he has recently implemented on the golf course, many of which may have been done in the time since the club decided to obtain the services of a design consultant.

I assume this exercise is designed to show me (as the Golf Course Architect) how talented or suitable the Superintendent is, in the field of golf course design or construction. In actual fact this exercise illustrates to me that dealing with the Superintendent is quite possibly going to be the element that has the greatest chance of preventing us, together from creating a great product.

In situations like this, I would prefer that the Superintendent show me how, since the club decided to hire a design consultant, the superintendent has gone to great pains to save time and money by *not* making any changes to the course. It is quite impossible for anyone, regardless of how good they are in their field to forecast the design process, and implement changes that will act in sympathy with the future goals that will be brought forth over time by the Golf Course Architect, in consultation with a great many other stakeholders, as a part of a structured planning exercise.

For a Golf Course Architect to come to site and see a whole lot of recently completed work just makes it harder in most ways, for his actions to facilitate the creation of a great product. If the Architect advocates changing recently completed work, many people assume this is a vote of no confidence against those who did the work. If the Architect is forced to retain this work then the final result will probably be less than ideal. It is often a case of finding some middle ground, but even this does generally not do justice to both the club and the land, in the long term.

On a remodel project there is rarely space or funds to be continually re-doing work. As such, a good Superintendent will be aware of the limits of his field of expertise and will respect and welcome the Golf Course Architect's input. By the same token, a good Golf Course Architect should work hard to find common ground with the Superintendent, and involve him with the finer points of the design process. Golf course design and remodelling is not a "first in-best dressed" situation. A good Golf Course Architect will not simply dictate a design style without consulting the people whose responsibility it will be to upkeep it. The design process, or at least the final finishing, profiling and the like should be put in place with the whole hearted agreement of the Superintendent, who should also feel free to put forth his views on these matters that directly affect his area of expertise.

Knowledge and respect for the delineation of the areas of expertise cannot be overstated and should be respected by all involved, including Superintendents and Golf Course Architects. A good Golf Course Architect, regardless of natural ability, likely became competent though dealing full time for many years with a continuous stream of golf design issues. Likewise, a competent Superintendent became that way through dealing full time for many years on turf and maintenance related issues. Nowadays it is quite rare and difficult to be an expert in both. Indeed, I know of no top line Golf Course Architects who claim also to be turf and maintenance experts, and vice versa.

The Grow-in Superintendent

The Grow-in Superintendent is a specialist position that is usually required on new projects and major remodel projects. The Grow-in Superintendent, as the name suggests is responsible for grassing and establishing the new turf, and growing it to a full cover, invariably to a playable condition. In addition to that, the Grow-in Superintendent is often responsible for recruiting future maintenance staff, instigating short term grow-in as well as longer-term maintenance regimes, dealing with the teething problems of grow-in and training of new staff, as well as patch-up grassing, weeding, stabilising of newly formed bunker edges and the like, noting of construction defects, establishment and upkeep of landscape such as pest control and tree staking, ordering of machinery and materials, and set-up of maintenance facility.

As well as this he must generally be in control of maintenance of completed work, until such time as the maintenance Superintendent is employed onsite.

As can be seen, most of this work is of an extra-ordinary nature when compared to the normal maintenance duties of a Superintendent. This obviously poses a different and more changeable set of constraints. As well as that, the Grow-in Superintendent is required to act in a more subservient role than of a Superintendent who is for the most part, controller of his own work and maintenance regimes.

A Grow-in superintendent must act as a part of a team rather than the leader of it, and his actions with regard to grassing and grow-in are dictated by the contractor's work program as verified by the Construction Manager in conjunction with the Golf Course Architect.

It is necessary that the Grow-in Superintendent be well qualified and experienced as he rarely has time to waste and must think on his feet as he deals with ever-changing constraints and site conditions.

For a Superintendent used to the normal duties of maintenance, taking on this role can appear like a backward step. The hours are longer and more variable, there are an infinitely greater number of more variable problems to be solved (especially on sites prone to extremes of weather) and one does not get to be fully in charge of one's own time and schedule.

For these reasons we find that fairly young, well-organised and very energetic superintendents generally fit best in this role. It is also an excellent stepping-stone for those Superintendents who harbour ambitions of becoming Construction Managers. Whilst the Grow-in Superintendent is not generally directly involved in the construction, he is able to observe all facets of the construction including the practical methods of dealing with consultants, contractors, clients and unexpected construction related issues, all of which can only be truly learned by practical experience.

In grassing he is also often required to put in place, together with the Golf Course Architect and Construction Manager, much of the finishing touches that can only be properly implemented during and after grassing has been done.

All in all, the position of Grow-in Superintendent it is quite a task, and one that is often downplayed or even overlooked. Those who excel at it are those who have the greatest propensity to work hard, learn fast and be humble, and because of this I believe that most good Grow-in Superintendents have the greatest chance at becoming very successful at some time in their respective futures. Indeed, good Grow-in Superintendents are hard to find.

The Construction Manager

I prefer to call this position one of Construction Manager as apposed to Construction Superintendent because although the knowledge of a Superintendent is very much helpful, it is not necessarily a pre-requisite that one be a qualified golf course Superintendent.

In my experience of the best Construction Managers I have worked with, half have come from the Superintendent's line, and half from the shaping/earthworks line, a field that I will touch on later.

The important traits one requires to be successful as a Construction Manager are as follows: -

i) An appreciation of maintenance and grassing - Whilst I do not believe it is totally necessary to be qualified as a superintendent, one must have a reasonable appreciation of maintenance, especially which shapes are machine maintainable and which will require intensive hand maintenance. One must also be conscious of how the grassing process will be undertaken such that construction can be staged in order to achieve good success in grassing and grow-in.

This issue, in fact, extends to all aspects of the golf course, such as irrigation, landscape, bunkers, drainage, etc.

The bulk of this information can be obtained by being involved in the construction of golf courses for an extended period, in a lesser role. For example, an unqualified maintenance supervisor who is involved in overseeing a team of workers undertaking parts of the grow-in would be exposed as well as anybody to the effects of good and bad construction techniques. With diligence in carefully noting and learning from what he sees, and providing he has other practically based skills, he will have every chance of becoming a Construction Manager.

ii) An appreciation of earthworks and construction techniques, as well as timing and staging of construction works - It is not enough to have experience and be knowledgeable in matters pertaining to generalised earthworks and construction. This information is valuable, but if one cannot amend one's thinking on these matters such that they can be applied specifically to golf course construction, then this information is less than useless. This is because the application of "normal" earthworks and construction techniques on a golf course project often causes Managers to create shapes and features that, in aesthetic terms are not closer, but further away from the desired product than is the original or natural terrain.

If one is highly skilled and experienced in general earthworks and construction he must be even more humble and respectful of the notion that golf construction is a specialised discipline in itself. If one cannot make this distinction and "re-learn" what he knows to a certain extent then it is likely his future in golf course construction will be short.

iii) A technique for understanding and achieving shapes that have been proposed by others. - Contrary to popular belief, I contend there are few, if any people that can accurately, at a glance take in all the nuances of the contour design of a whole golf hole that has been compiled by another person.

It is a matter of gradually working oneself along the plan from one end to the other, storing data about levels and shapes as you go, ascertaining which

174

shapes and how much of them will be visible from which locations and then putting it all in the context of a raw piece of land, whilst making allowances for clearing, landscape and the like.

The Golf Course Architect might provide sketches of parts of the design from one or two key locations, but I contend that quite often it is near impossible for anyone other than the designer to achieve a full appreciation of a design from a bunch of squiggly lines on a piece of paper.

However, when a design of a golf hole or part thereof gets to a certain stage on site, part way through construction, Construction Managers, Supervisors and Shapers that have a good natural appreciation of shape will suddenly "get it". At this points the incessant descriptions and waving of hands by the Architect will cease to sound like gibberish and will start to hit emotional chords in the Construction Manager, or Shaper who usually responds with his own descriptions for verification. It really is happy times when this occurs as all begin to feel like a great product is about to be born.

The question is, how to go about bringing designs to this stage onsite, without wastage of time and re-doing of earthworks. A good Construction Manager will be able to quickly analyse an earthworks or shaping plan in order to be able to accurately estimate what it will take to get it to a stage onsite where the finer points of the design can be meaningfully discussed with the Architect and the Shapers. This will *not* give him a full appreciation of the design but gives a technical assessment of how to go about accurately achieving earthworks and rough shape.

It appears that every Construction Manager has his own personalised method of achieving this, which gives him the information in the best format for *him* to interpret and convey this information to his earthworks operators and rough shapers.

Some Managers apply survey pegs to mark high and low points and make hand signals and gestures to their machine operators. Some have the surveyor set out grid arrangement and begin placing and pushing earth according to that. It appears to depend on the background of the person, and it is amazing how well and quickly a construction supervisor gets results once he's refined his best personal technique.

For example, one of my most efficient Construction Managers has always been able to bring my designs very close to the plan on the ground in a very short timeframe, without much intervention from me as the designer. I always assumed it was due to my descriptions and discussions we always had whenever a new plan was passed to him, (as well as his creative interpretation of those plans) despite the fact we do not share the same first language. After working with him for a couple of successfully completed projects, I learnt through a mutual friend that in actual fact he did not understood a great deal about what I'd said about my designs and that he gained very little idea of the desired shapes from looking at my plans.

I was amazed and of course wondered how on earth he did what he did, considering his background was in road building and he had no formal training in golf or the turf grass industry, he did not play golf when he started, although he is now a very good golfer.

I discovered he was an unqualified surveyor, and very early on in his career he hit on a way of selectively pegging contour designs onsite from the plan, that gave him an extremely accurate and efficient way of achieving earthwards and rough shape. In addition, his process enabled him to forecast issues that might require design amendments, in most cases prior to them being constructed to completion.

His improved golf playing skills and natural feel for shape quite often enable him to take advantage of opportunities to improve my designs in ways that cannot be shown on the plans. This enabled us to achieve close to optimum results onsite, simply through my supervisor interpreting my hand signals as much as anything else and applying them to a product that he had been able to get very close, prior to my site visits.

iv) An appreciation of shape –This is obviously a generalised understanding of the principles of shape and proportion that were described in chapter 5, and in particular how they apply to each golf course situation.

I am a little undecided on the question of whether this appreciation can be taught and learnt, or whether it is a god given gift. There are some who once they see it once, they just "have it" from there on. There are others who show glimpses of it occasionally and for whom it can be brought out a little more with constant work and "practice" for want of a better term. And unfortunately there are those that just never get it, regardless of how hard they try.

It is always a pleasing experience when you find somebody who has that appreciation of shape. To be the most well prepared and hardest working of potential Construction Managers, however does not necessarily mean the magic ingredient will be present. Conversely there are many who obviously do have the appreciation and eye for shape, but do not have the other, equally important personal traits, making them equally unsuitable for a long-term future as a Construction Manager.

Indeed, when it all gets boiled down, out of all those who appear to covet such a vocation, there are very few who have sufficient amounts of the right personal and professional traits to facilitate their success.

In looking at successful Construction Managers, it is definitely apparent that each one has his own personal way of achieving the result, as nobody is equally as good at all of the necessary requirements. Although it is necessary to have a reasonable grip on all of them, everybody has their weaknesses, and in the successful proponents, their weaknesses are nullified and compensated to a certain extent by extra strengths in other areas.

A supervisor who is poor in team building might be able to obtain results through obtaining respect through personal strength, discipline and unquestionable knowledge. One whose appreciation of shape is not perfectly refined might obtain results through strength in team building, thereby maximising the qualities of the shapers and supervisors in order to create the desired initial shapes. Surveying and a natural feel for shape can overcome weaknesses in plan reading and interpersonal communication skills.

Everyone has his or her own way of achieving the result, and this can only be discovered by the individual, with honest feed back from a competent Designer.

v) Team building – Golf course construction is a very changeable type of work, which often requires work to be amended or re-done in order to obtain the optimum result. Workers can tend to get a little demoralised by this, unless the reasons for it are properly and skilfully communicated. Therefore, an ability to build a team is imperative if everyone is to enjoy their work and feel the creative sense of satisfaction despite having to occasionally re-do work that technically has no problem with it.

I always hate to change work that has been done, but on a site that is run by a good team-building supervisor, where the pride of work and the goals of 100% quality has been instilled in even the most basic of labourers, one senses they actually feel good when you make a change as it shows them that you, like them are prepared to leave no stone unturned in the pursuit of quality.

In this type of work environment everyone feels inspired and uplifted, and if the skills are present in the Golf Course Architect, the only result will be a great product.

vi) Work Ethic – The Construction Manager is in effect, the leader of the construction site. Many members of staff are involved and to a great extent, they are generally a product of their leader. Those whose style of work does not sit harmoniously with that of the leader will feel the urge to leave the site, whilst those that do appreciate the style of their leader will be motivated to stay on, and attract their like-minded friends and associates to the project.

It is therefore essential that the Construction Manager display a strong personal work ethic. Those who instruct their workers before sitting under a tree in full view of them to read the newspaper will breed a simmering resentment, if not a degree of laziness or lack of loyalty.

This work ethic goes hand in hand with the next important trait, namely:

vii) Perfectionism - or absolute pride in oneself and one's work.

Golf course construction is to a certain extent, a free-form type of work. As such it risks having its standards lowered unless the leader advocates an absolutely perfect finish to every element of the construction exercise, at every stage.

Also, in waiting for grass to grow, and regardless of the high standard of the work, some minor settlement, erosion and movement of soil cannot be avoided, and this must be repaired. If the initial finish was substandard, these irregularities cannot be easily detected, and the work required to bring the course to the optimum condition is much greater. This can quite easily signal a gradual downward slide of the condition of a golf course, from which it may never recover, unless a major upheaval is instigated in terms of changes to personnel as well as renovation and maintenance practices. The construction supervisor must exude perfection such that everyone is aware from the outset that anything less than absolute quality will not be tolerated.

viii) Detecting deviations from the design - Another element of the pursuit of absolute quality is being able to quickly detect when a deviation from the plan has occurred and either condone or reject such deviations. If a Construction Manager cannot detect when a contractor has made his own changes, it could well become difficult to stop such a contractor from taking too many liberties.

This type of plan reading is an exercise in logic and simple measurement. Counting contours and measuring them approximately onsite against one's own height to check the depth of a bunker or scaling distances off a plan and stepping out these distances between features, for example, enables one to quickly check the size and location of all onsite features.

This type of checking is borne out of suspicions that a Construction Manager will feel from time to time that maybe something is not quite right with a section of the work onsite. This is related to that fairly intangible trait, being the understanding of the design concept and the appreciation of shape.

ix) The ability to adhere closely to the plan – This is a trait that is obviously sought after and desired by any good Golf Course Architect. A competent Golf Course Architect works very hard to ensure the shape and location of every design contour and bunker edge has been positioned for a very specific reason. As such, any modifications to the design must also be made for a very specific reason and in direct consultation with the Architect.

I have found that many would-be construction supervisors, especially those from a maintenance superintendent's background, assume the position of construction supervisor is similar to that of maintenance superintendent, where he is the sole decision maker on whether on not to adhere to the plan at hand.

A competent Architect will not be happy at all to come to site and see his plans have not been followed, whether intentionally or not. Without doubt, changes often have to be made onsite from time to time, however the Architect is the one who will primarily be judged on the results and therefore he must be an integral part of the decision making process.

The best Construction Managers I have worked with are those who can get the designs quickly rough shaped quite close to the plan, such that there is quite a few partially completed areas for the Architect to inspect on his regular site visits. The Architect and the Construction Manager can then critique each section of the design very accurately and realistically, and *together*, agree on the best course of action, should changes need to be made. Two heads are better than one in any situation and it is healthy to get agreement from specialists in both fields before setting in place any permanent piece of work.

This will ensure the client and the land itself receive optimum value of the input of all the experts involved.

The commonly held misconception that the position of construction supervisor is one of ultimate freedom of creativity cannot be stressed enough. The first and most sought after quality that I, as a Golf Course Architect look for in a Construction Manager is the ability to build the designs according to the plan. There is plenty of scope for creativity in the finishing of the designs, where a good Construction Manager will see opportunities to add to the design by including subtleties that cannot be drawn on a plan. This creativity, however, must always be with the blessing of, and signed off by the Golf Course Architect.

As a Construction Manager gains more and more experience and builds a greater level of synergy with his Architect he will be able to add more and more value to the designs. I find with the less experienced Managers, it is usually a matter of trying to keep them focused on the primary job at hand - building according to the plan - which does not leave a lot of time and scope for proactive onsite creativity, on anyone's behalf.

With my more experienced Managers their creative input is very much valued, because they know when and how it can be best implemented. With these Managers, I try to involve them in the actual design process as well as the onsite adjustment because their input is so relevant. We often go over any design concepts or image based ideas that we both might have prior to the detailed design of each green. In the end, the final creative input on most of our designs is at least a joint effort and often a team effort, not simply one person imposing his will on all others and the land, which seems to be the common perception.

x) Paperwork – The typical snapshot of golf course construction would be that of the Architect, possibly holding his plan and pointing or making some kind of hand signal, with his Construction Manager, shapers and the client looking on and probably nodding or agreeing.

You can rarely figure out from these types of photographs what they might actually be talking about except that it seems important. This scene tends to project the image that golf course design and construction is more than anything, an onsite exercise, where issues are solved for the most part by talking and gesticulating onsite. This is, no doubt the most enjoyable aspect of the job, but unfortunately it is only a small part of the whole process. The onsite element makes up possibly 10-20% of the Architect's total project commitment, and possibly 60-80% of the Construction Manager's time, the rest of which is generally dominated by paperwork.

Paperwork unfortunately is a part of modern day design and construction supervision that cannot and should not be avoided, especially when dealing with formal construction contracts.

In today's litigation-inclined society it is in everyone's interest to keep detailed records of all happenings onsite as well as issuing written confirmation of all important site instructions relating to technically based issues. Paperwork is a matter of course for all Golf Course Architects, who are forever utilising the written word in design submissions and all manner of communications with clients and fellow consultants.

Many Construction Managers, especially the older ones try to avoid paperwork at all costs, but nowadays this can no longer be tolerated.

There are many stories of situations where construction has been supervised and built to high standards except for a few vital technical issues, the quality control of which was the responsibility of the Construction Manager. Later, when the problems surface, it is good to have signed documents which prevent the Construction Manager from being used as the scapegoat. The modern day Construction Manager should instigate such checking mechanisms, involving the keeping of detailed records and ensuring the contractors sign off on all aspects of their work. This practice will in the majority of cases actually prevent contractors from taking any short cuts, as they know they will surely be caught.

Shapers

Another key set of members of the construction team is the Shapers. Shapers might best be described as specialist machine operators responsible for putting the landforms and earth shapes together in accordance with the design plans and the Golf Course Architect's design intent.

The key ingredient of their set of qualities is a good appreciation of shape, as described in the above sections. The shapers' level of appreciation of shape is in most cases directly related to: a) How quickly they can create the desired results, and b) How many amendments need to be made after the general concept has been basically physically established onsite.

In other words, after the general concept of shape for a project has been communicated to the Shaper, (usually through trial and error in completing the first couple of golf holes on a project) a good shaper with a well refined appreciation of shape will be able see, to a great extent the opportunities to not change, but improve the design on the ground, without needing to be specifically directed by the Architect on every detail.

Of course, he will rarely get everything 100% optimised as he cannot read the Architect's mind, but it is more likely his first attempt will be quite close and will require relatively little further onsite amendment.

This basic appreciation of shape and the ability to "see" and imagine the concept in something close to its finished form is a great asset to the Shaper and to any project he is working on.

If he has a good understanding of the desired look and function of any respective section of the work, he will see opportunities of creating the desired shapes with the utmost of efficiency. For example, in simple terms, if the design requires the effect of a mound 2' (60cm) high in a certain location, a good Shaper will have such an understanding, that he might be able to cut in certain key adjacent locations by only 1' (30cm), and fill the mound area by only 1', thereby creating a 2' high mound with only half the work. In the meantime, the adjacent cut also gives a head start, or possibly completes the shaping of the adjacent areas. A Shaper who does not have such a refined appreciation of shape and the design concept, might call for 2' of fill to create such a mound, and then still have to do more work to shape this fill, as well as still having to shape the surrounding adjacent areas.

In this simple example, the better Shaper will likely be able to complete the task in half the time or less, without having to call for extra soil and machines to provide fill.

The level of expertise of the shapers is also the primary governing factor dictating the overall pace of construction of a golf course project, which of course can greatly affect the cost of construction. As in most forms of contracting, costs are dependent to a great extent on the time spent undertaking the works.

With almost every other element of golf course construction, the speed of the work can be slowed or quickened by simply subtracting or adding more resources. The same operators, however must do all of the fine shaping in order to achieve a consistent character over all of the golf holes on a golf course. The speed of shaping thereby becomes the critical factor governing how fast a project can proceed. It is for these reasons that good Shapers command high wages in comparison to other machine operators.

Following on from that, the factor that governs how fast a shaper can shape is his appreciation of shape, his understanding of the design concepts and his practical skill in achieving these shapes in the most efficient manner.

Contrary to popular belief, many years of general earthmoving experience and the ability to finish engineered features to small tolerances with big machines do not in themselves make a good shaper. In fact, I would go so far to say that in many cases these types of experiences trains one to think the opposite of that required to be a good Shaper, and thus is often more of a negative asset than no experience at all.

Likewise, previous experiences of creating free flowing shapes with no definite plan is probably not so bad, but it still does not give experience of that key quality of being able to understand the very specific design concepts put forth in plan and speech by the Golf Course Architect and the Construction

Manager. For these reasons, a Shaper's work requirements are very much specialised and should not be compared to other types of earth moving. Having said that, it is amazing how competent shapers emerge seemingly from nowhere, simply by observing the progress of work by other competent shapers.

As such, shapers most often reach a level of competence through first working on a golf course construction site in some other, lesser capacity.

I have seen basic bulldozer operators, involved in simply spreading earth as a part of a bulk earthworks organisation, begin to gain an appreciation of shape through observing how the competent Shapers were working and changing the ground levels after the bulk earthworks phases were completed. After a few golf holes of this, one can usually see which operators might be able to become shapers, simply by seeing where the earthworks began to take on a more accurately shaped look, conforming closer to the final plans.

I have seen a basic labourer, involved in hand finishing and digging drainage lines in green bases, become an expert skid steer loader driver in the space of a few months. I expect his motivation to do so was expedited by his ability to save his co-workers months of backbreaking work, as much as his sense of self-satisfaction at exercising his natural appreciation of shape.

The fact of the matter is, anybody with a reasonable amount of eye-hand co-ordination and patience can learn how to drive almost any earth moving machine in a matter of a couple of weeks. (Albeit without a great deal of finesse).

The key issue is not being able to operate a machine; *it is knowing what one is endeavouring to create*. Someone with a highly refined sense of shape and the design at hand, and barely more than a basic knowledge of machine operation can quickly give the appearance that a lot of earth has been moved onsite when in actual fact, he has simply been able to make use of the differential between small amounts of cut and fill.

Summary - Like the Golf Course Architect and Construction Manager, the best Shapers have advanced logical and mental spatial abilities, or the ability to at least partly imagine and see 3 dimensional shapes from a 2 dimensional plan, as well as the ability to foresee the most efficient manner of achieving them onsite.

In addition to these in-built spatial abilities, a humble nature and a solid work ethic are very much desirable qualities in a shaper. As the people who create the final appearance of the golf course, it is easy to assume the shapers are the ones most responsible for its creation.

Shapers are without doubt, a critical link in the chain of events; and they govern the speed of work onsite. However it should be remembered that for every project, many months and sometimes years of work has been undertaken by many other people to get a project to the point where the shaper can bury the blade of his machine in the onsite soil.

When the time comes to proceed with the work onsite it is generally a sign that the major part of the work of the Golf Course Architect (possibly 70%) is complete. The last 30% is by far the most enjoyable and rewarding as one gets to see the designs come to life and it makes all the previous months of hard work worthwhile.

A large part of this hard work in planning and design is spent in seeking out the most naturally harmonious and appropriate design solution that is felt will best suit the land. Thereafter, the Golf Course Architect must work persistently and diligently, through all the often-testing technical requirements to preserve and positively amend these design solutions through to the point of being able to proceed onsite. This is often a harrowing period, where all manner of technical reasons are put forth why the designs cannot be built according to the way they were envisaged. The Golf Course Architect and his staff must patiently and laboriously work through all of these issues, amending designs only where amendment will have technical and golf design benefits, and finding totally new solutions where golf design amendment is unacceptable.

Less talented, or inexperienced Golf Course Architects, who are not able to give fully informed reasons for persisting with original concepts when no better alternatives are available; or who are unable to come up with totally new and better design solutions when required, will at times see their designs destroyed somewhat, by the weight of technical argument.

A competent Golf Course Architect will never allow his designs to be destroyed and will work hard to find solutions that satisfy all constraints. Quite an amount of personal drive is often required on the part of the Golf Course Architect to see this process through. For the Architect, the motivation for this is an inherent sense of responsibility to the land that Golf Course Architects and all involved onsite in the construction of golf courses must possess.

It is not a God-given right to be the creators of golf courses. Rather, it is an honour and a privilege to be able to be involved in the reformation of the earth for the benefit of that earth and the plants, animals and people that frequent it. In return for this honour, all people involved on a creative and managerial level have a responsibility to do their best to achieve the most appropriate result.

One might say it doesn't matter, since the shapes and environments are ultimately man-made. One must remember that ultimately all things in the universe are connected and effect each other. Human beings are a product of that universe and as such, qualify as a part of nature, regardless of the fact they can make many of their own choices. All man made things including golf courses are therefore also a part of nature. The question here is quality and sustainability.

For most people working and living in modern day cities, it is difficult to know if what we do on a day-to-day basis is sustainable and ultimately adds value to the universe. Golf courses are unique pockets in this modern day environment, in that it is possible, relatively speaking, to observe them from prior to inception through to completion. We are therefore able to evaluate somewhat, their net level of quality and value at least to the local area in which they are built. We know from experience that natural land in its original pristine form, never goes out of style, and is a benefit to all the plants, animals and humans who utilise it. Those of us who work creatively on golf courses have an obligation to aspire to nature in creating human-use environments. We have a responsibility to leave no stone unturned in the quest for natural perfection. This is of course, unattainable as there is no such thing, but if we can come close, the level of quality and sustainability will be enhanced, which therefore contributes greater value to the universe.

This creative set of people, including the Golf Course Architect and all the key onsite personnel must therefore cultivate the optimum mindset in order to function as the most efficient conduit between natural creativity (from any source) and the site with which they are involved.

If they have information to enable better results they must give it, but they also must be attuned to pick up and receive information, which can come in many formats. Their demeanour should ideally be multifaceted. If a good idea is present, it should be put forth in a clear, forthright manner, even forcefully if important.

At other times they should be eager and receptive to the gathering of further information and ideas from wherever they may come; something best achieved by an open, friendly and somewhat humble approach. All the while they must be keen to exercise their skills and learn from their results, requiring a very strong work ethic.

If all involved take on these traits, one finds that despite the hard work, the design office and construction site are most enjoyable and uplifting places to be. The final results are therefore easily produced to a satisfyingly high level of quality, not to mention the lasting friendships that are cemented through working together as a team.

10

The Relationship of Hardscape and Engineered Features to the Natural Terrain and their Influences on Modern Day Golf Course Design

We speak continuously about the virtues of naturally appearing shapes and features in golf course design, however many of the most traditional and revered examples of great golf course design have man-made, hardscape features positioned quite prominently as key design elements.

Not only is there in most cases, no attempt to disguise these features, which appear quite obviously as man-made items, but many of the most famous holes in golf would be considered incomplete without their very distinctive hardscape elements.

What would be a picture of the 12th at Augusta without the bridge that crosses Rae's Creek? And what of the links courses? Many are littered with bridges, roads, and walls, none more famously than the 17th hole at St. Andrews, aptly named the Road Hole.

Here, one must aim one's tee shot over an old railway shed, whizzing one's ball closely past the windows of a multi storey hotel to obtain the best line to a green seemingly squeezed on the right side by a paved road and a stone wall, both of which are in play and have many times had a big say in deciding who will be the British Open Champion.

This hole is recognised around the world as a golfing treasure and yet, should a modern day Golf Course Architect design anything similar to it, he would no doubt be ridiculed for producing an extremely unsafe and dangerous golf hole.

So what is it that enables such features to be embraced to the point of being considered as natural as the sand and grass that surrounds them, but only in specific locations on specific golf courses?

To my way of thinking, there are a couple of reasons that make this happen, and they are as follows: -

1) *A sense of history* – A hard feature, such as a wall, path, bridge or building, if left in place for more than 50 or so years can become a valued symbol of the past. This can appeal to the feeling of comfort most people gain when they can label and compartmentalise an item.

   A hard item gives people confidence that it must have existed in pretty much the same format at the time that possibly some great thing happened or in the very least when people's habits and customs were different. The fact that most hard-scape items built 50 or more years ago are of an earthy nature, such as stone, also fits well with the sense of timelessness that well defined, naturally appearing landforms evoke.

2) *The element of chance* – The element of chance that exists in the location of most of these hard-scape items adds certain "quaintness" to their existence that is somewhat comforting to those who experience them. There is no doubt that when most of these hard-scape elements were built, their purpose was primarily practical and often had little to do with the playing of golf or the beauty of the golf course.

Fences contained sheep and roads traversed the wastelands that were the links. That some of these elements could by chance be placed in locations that facilitated the future formation of some of the most distinctive and functional golf hole strategies simply adds to the mystique.

Beyond locating features on many old courses, this element of chance has also paved the way for the use of hard-scape in modern day golf course design.

The story goes that discarded timber railway ties were left on the adjacent golf course land at Prestwick Golf Course, an old links course on the west coast of Scotland that has staged the British Open some 30 or so times. Rather than removing them offsite, many of these timbers were used to shore up some steep slopes, thus confirming railway ties and rough sawn timber as an acceptable retaining medium along with the stone as used in the many fences or "dykes" that go around and through the courses of Scotland.

Like stone, the railway timbers give an aged, weathered look that fits well with the sand and course-leafed rough grasses of the links lands.

One will note that nowadays, where a soil-retaining medium is required on a golf course, coarse stone walls or rough sawn timber seem to be the materials of choice.

We find it is usually beneficial to keep in mind the origins of the use of these materials in golf as we plan for their use in modern day applications. Long stretches of shored up earth can appear contrived and premeditated, whilst short sections in key locations can add focus and promote the original intent of the use of the respective materials. - To shore up and prevent failing of the landforms that were already more or less in place, in order to create the optimum, stable conditions on which to create a teeing ground, green or key fairway landing area.

This can then have the effect of creating that quaint, almost historical effect inherent in old, practically based hard-scape. In the old days when working for the most part with hand labour, one would only create such highly labour intensive features in the minimum quantities in areas they were most needed, which would be close to the high wear and key areas that are strategic to the way the golf holes are played.

On occasion, in design, one might find ruins of an old building or feature on a site that fits the criteria of interest that will make its vicinity unique. These are opportunities for the designer to add something extra to the memorability factor of the adjacent golf holes and generally, opportunities to work such unique elements into the fabric of the design should not be missed if at all possible.

Indeed, it seems there is an acceptance of man made, hard structures in golf course design, in formats that are specifically earthy in nature, so as to give the impression they actually pre-date the golf course, if not the game of golf itself. This indicates that for most people, many man made items that are created by past generations are seen as being just as valuable as the non man-made landforms. Whether this is because people relate these items to their own predecessors, or whether it is because most people really do see humans as a part of nature, is hard to say, but for whatever reason, these romantic connotations have been responsible in part for building the traditional values of the game of golf.

In addition to the inclusion of such hard surfaces there seems also to be a modern day acceptance of engineered shapes, particularly square and rectangular tees. Even though it is possible to create new free-form shapes, the square-ness of tees is a way of acknowledging the past traditions and formal nature of the gentlemanly game. In addition, the square-ness of tees, especially on the edge closest to the target assists those golfers who may otherwise tend to misalign their tee shots.

This idea can be readily incorporated where a golf course has some kind of connection to the past times when these types of engineered shapes were embraced on a widespread basis on golf courses. This might occur when upgrading an old course whose roots are from another earlier era.

This type of square or straight-line concept might also be used on some new courses, where the owner wishes to portray such traditional values. In this case, however, the designer might wish to ensure all other aspects of design similarly adhere to these traditional values through portraying images similar to those of a past era. Like the example of our retaining structures above, the general design approach might be a little more minimalist than it otherwise could be.

In essence, the straight-line concepts in golf course design as used in modern day applications are incorporated in recognition of the design principles and standards of yesteryear. Following on from this, one might like to question how such straight lines came to be accepted on golf courses in the first place.

There is probably no definitive answer for this, but based on my own design experiences in various developing golf markets, I believe the reason is as follows:

When the first golf courses were founded, they would have been very much natural in their presentation. At that time, hundreds of years ago, the proponents of golf probably had no need to change the natural landforms, for the game at that time would not have yet matured to a point where any one type of landform would have been deemed much better or more appropriate than another. This is lucky, because at that time, there would have been little chance of mustering the workforce required to make changes on an area as large as a golf course. Indeed, it would have seemed like an outrageous extravagance to allocate such scarce resources for the betterment of a game played in one's spare time.

Bear in mind that at the time, few people were worried about what to do in their spare time. Most were preoccupied with finding enough to eat on a daily basis, trying not to be accused of witchcraft (for fear of being burned at the stake) and hoping one did not contract any of the many terminal diseases that were prevalent. Questions like what to do in retirement were not relevant, as most were simply happy to live past the age of 40.

At this time in the UK, the aims and goals of the human race were very different to the present. People were collectively trying to improve and prolong their lifestyles, struggling to tame the inconsistencies and ravages of nature. There were few examples representing how this could be done, but those examples were glorious. Great Cathedrals that are awesome even by today's standards, showed what man was capable of.

Such creations took hundreds of years to complete and the contrast between their quality and workmanship to what was at that time situated on the lands around them must have been quite extreme. One can imagine that bearing witness to this contrast would have been both uplifting and demoralising. Those few great buildings illustrated what was achievable by man, whilst continuously reminding the bulk of the population that the quality of their lives was poor and what they could hope to achieve in their lifetimes was relatively little.

Although many well-designed structures were built prior to the industrial revolution, I can only assume there must have been very few design opportunities for most people with design flair living in those times. Even for those designers who got the chance to see their designs realised, the pace of development must have in most cases been painfully slow. As a designer, I can only imagine feeling frustrated that virtually all of my theories and design ideas would never have been able to be built. Even today, I find myself wishing I had a huge pair of powerful hands with which I could simply and quickly build my designs like a child building sandcastles at the beach.

Gradually as the centuries passed, bit by bit, and piece by piece, the evolution of the human species reached a point where the struggle against nature was won, at least to a point where day to day survival for a great many of the population was no longer in question.

This process produced two definite shifts in human perception. The first came as nature was being "conquered". As each new machine, tool, or innovation was produced; people were obviously keen to exercise them to their full potential, as if to make up for all the generations of frustration at not being able to make changes where they were obviously desired. In terms of golf course design and construction this did not happen until the advent of the bulldozer, which was not prevalent in the golf industry until the mid 20th century.

Prior to this, from the late 19th century onwards, man did however use golf courses, among other things, to display their rising ascendancy over nature and the earth. A great many golf courses established during this period were done so with quite a definite man made, even engineered look to them. One can imagine up until that time people generally would have for the most part experienced only very natural landforms, be they very flat or undulating. At first, a distinctly engineered look, with square tees and the like, would have been difficult to create, and no doubt would have created quite a lot of interest. It would have been kind of a golfing celebration of human progress, in that it would have illustrated the marvels of the technical expertise available at the time.

One can still see examples of this style on many old golf courses in the UK as well as in the various former colonial outposts of the British Empire. At the time these courses were being built, particularly in the colonies, their engineered, distinctly unnatural look would have served as one of the many symbols of colonial supremacy. As well as that, it would have, by that time, been relatively easy to create such engineered looking golf courses, as one does not need to disturb nearly as much earth as is required to create naturally appearing shapes, especially on relatively flat country. And so these engineered golf courses had their place in history.

Gradually, however humanity became aware that not only had the battle against nature been won, in terms of the effects on the natural environment, the battle had been carried much too far. Far from being unusual, engineered structures and landforms had virtually surrounded humanity, and thus, according to the simple law of supply and demand, among other factors, the popularity for all things natural and naturally appearing, had begun to grow.

It has only been in the past few decades since this awareness of the natural environment (and environments that are sympathetic to them) reached the masses of the Western World. This has given rise to things like eco-tourism and widespread conservation efforts. It is interesting to note on that basis, the original golf course design "naturalists" such as Alistair McKenzie (who were often ridiculed in their time), were perhaps 50 years ahead of the mass perceptions of the Western World. And regarding some issues, I don't yet think we can say how far ahead of their time they were.

And so we are now somewhere near to coming full circle, with regard to this issue. The Quest for naturally sympathetic and sustainable design solutions in golf as well as virtually all other fields is growing deeper and stronger. It has in some areas even reached such a point of sophistication that we now have the ability to look back on the somewhat crudely engineered shapes of the past, with feelings of nostalgia.

People know deep down that in today's world, we must make ever increasing efforts to create all new things in a sustainable, naturally sympathetic, or at least easily recyclable manner. The potential for great creations in the future is immensely exciting, and in any case, the survival of the human race on Earth depends on it. It seems, however that the nostalgic tendencies of human nature regularly pull our minds back to the perceived safety of the past, when life was simpler.

The evolutionary theory described above took place over some 400 or so years, however mini versions of this have taken place in compressed timeframes in areas where golf is a relatively new and developing industry.

192

The decade of the 1990's saw similar evolutionary changes take place in many areas of South East Asia within the space of 10 or so years. The early 1990's saw changes to the economic and political scenery in much of South East Asia, facilitating a wave of development. This development saw the mass exodus of much of the population from their simple rural lifestyles to the fast city life. After years of feeling second best in comparison to the highly developed Western World, it was South East Asia's turn show it too could engineer, build and develop.

As a Golf Course Architect working in the midst of this, struggling to create naturally sympathetic designs that would stand the test of time, one quite often felt like the odd man out. Many developers were new to the field and were living their dreams, proceeding to create their own monuments to human endeavour, mostly using civil engineering, and all in their own "back yards".

Developers managed to find beauty in features such as massive engineered slopes, and landscapes that had been altered beyond all recognition compared to their original natural form. Golf courses seemed to be a mandatory ingredient of every real estate development scheme, but in many cases, the concept of naturally appearing golf was of little or no priority. In fact for many developers, it seemed the uglier, or more contrived, the better.

For a few years, these developers were vindicated. The market was hungry for real estate product and any product would do. Those developers who hit the market on its way up cashed in. In terms of golf, product didn't matter much at that time, because few people knew the differences between a good golf course and a bad one, and in any case, most golf courses were only there to raise premiums on adjacent real estate allotments.

Eventually the real estate market softened, new buyers were spoiled for choice, and those who had moved into their new golf development schemes were actually beginning to play golf and were demanding the golf courses be up-kept according to the original sales pitch.

The wheel had turned. High speed air travel and the Internet left a high proportion of golfers, the new middle class, well informed about the virtues of a world class product in both golf and real estate, and almost overnight the market became much more discerning.

Nowadays in South East Asia, widespread and blatantly engineered solutions on golf courses are largely frowned upon, and developers of golf courses are much more careful not to underestimate the specialised nature of the construction, as well as the long-term maintenance requirements. This realisation has occurred over the length of one Real Estate boom-bust cycle, or about 10 years.

"Quirky" golf holes

The issues of use of man-made items, and departures from the naturally appearing shapes and features in modern day design are tending towards the somewhat quirky, in a quest for elements that will give each golf hole and each golf course its own very distinctive character. In actual fact it is very easy to make a golf hole or a whole golf course very distinctive by the inclusion of unorthodox features. The challenge is to have it play well and to make it acceptable and treasured according to the quite definite but at the same time rather intangible guidelines of design.

It is a little easier to do this in some markets as opposed to others, or more specifically, the unwritten guidelines tend to change a little depending on which course one is designing and in what country or area it is situated.

I witnessed an example of this recently. Watching a professional tour event on television, played on a fairly old parkland course, a player hit his shot to a one shot, or par 3 green. On landing, the ball kicked off the edge of the green, rolled and bounced across an uneven gravel golfer access path and kicked, as if at least half by chance, into a bunker. The commentators busily extolled the virtues of the hole, hailing it as a 'classic" par 3 and a "gem". I found myself wondering why a gravel access path was positioned so close to the line of play that golfers would need to consider it, strategically as they play the hole.

Not more than a week or two later, while watching a professional tour event on another continent, this time on a brand new and very well groomed course, I witnessed another par 3 where a player hit his ball to the back left of a 3-lobed green. The pin was positioned on the front left, but because of the shape of the green surface, the player's approach putt finished on the front right of the green on a lower level at least as far away from the pin as he was for his previous shot. The commentators raised the issue of a possible design fault in the green, seemingly running on the assumption that if one's ball finishes on the green one should have an unhindered line to roll one's ball to the cup, although this idea to my knowledge is not written in the rules of golf. Another line of thought is that despite hitting the green, maybe the golfer played an inappropriate shot to that green on that day; as inappropriate as would be hitting a ball into water. Alternatively, maybe he should have considered chipping the ball, instead of playing an approach putt that was doomed to failure.

In both instances we have examples of design situations that, whilst they do not break any rules of golf, are seen as a little bit odd, or somewhat quirky by certain sections of the golf fraternity.

Right or wrong, Golf Course Architects must be careful and skilled at perceiving how far they can push such design issues, according to the culture and perceptions of the client, the local golfer population and of course, the views of the broader golfer community.

Having said that, it is impossible to satisfy everyone, and if one tried, surely somebody would (probably rightly) accuse one's designs of being boring or very similar to several other designs. This would be a very much unacceptable comment to any designer aspiring to greatness. Golf Course Architects therefore must tread a thin line, encompassing a respect of the past, an acknowledgment of the present and a brightness of the future.

Golf Course Architects as products of their environments

The above-mentioned issues are a function of experience. People can only comment and act relative to their own reality, which is to a large extent influenced by their personal experiences and environments. This is very much evident in many ways. For example, golfers whose home golf course has narrow tree lined fairways will tend to be more accurate players than those whose home course is wide open with few hazards.

This is why a Golf Course Architect, in remodelling an existing golf course can make such a large impact in the minds of the members. With a new course, there is no real comparison in the minds of golfers with what the site was like before the Architect's design was realised. As such, one will often receive all manner of contrasting opinions about a new course, based on the individual and respective experiences and realities of all the golfers who thereafter play such a new golf course.

But on a remodel project, the members generally have a much narrower range of comparative experiences and therefore have more similar perceptions about the game of golf, based primarily around the golf course and its state of play prior to remodelling. The Golf Course Architect can therefore, in general terms virtually achieve any type of response he may wish by manipulating the design such that the comparisons between the old and the new are favourable. In addition, many people don't quite believe what is possible until they actually witness first hand such a transformation.
This phenomena also extends beyond the golfers themselves and I believe that a similar force is in play on many, if not all Golf Course Architects, to varying degrees.

Competent Golf Course Architects go to great pains to travel and experience as many varied golf course designs as is possible, in order to negate the effects of conditioning. However one can never have a first hand experience of all facets of all types of golf course design and construction in all climates and cultures. Likewise, one can never re-experience something for the first time, and as such, I believe an Architect's first experiences of quality golf courses and their formats have a good chance of remaining indelibly etched in their subconscious.

For this reason, like a golfer under pressure, at the end of a tournament, there is always a tendency to revert to what one knows best. For a golfer, he will play his natural shot shapes under pressure. For a Golf Course Architect, there is the tendency to revert to a set of styles or techniques that he knows well, that he likes, and that he knows will work.

Nowadays these traditional and localised influences are becoming more and more diluted through the cross pollination of cultures and working alliances, facilitated by high speed air travel, electronic communications techniques and a general, progressive relaxing of national borders, in terms of business.

In the past, however and probably up until the last 10 or so years, I believe it was possible to isolate and sort some of the basic golf course design traits according to international and particularly inter-continental influences.

British And Irish Influences

As the home of golf, there was quite an amount of progress and diversity in design, which took place in this region long before golf was ever exported to other parts of the world.

This obviously began with Links Golf and a long list of golfing luminaries who each had varying roles to play in the formation and various amendments to virtually all of the great Links courses. This took place over hundreds of years, over which period of time many theories of design and playing strategy evolved and were implemented, rarely on a new course where they could be tested over 18 holes, but more so in amendments or extensions to existing courses.

Eventually, inland golf courses were established at a time when any real kind of design standards were yet to be established, and long before equipment and playing techniques approached anything similar to the modern day levels. The early inland courses were obviously laid out with their only predecessor being the links courses. With little scope for mechanised construction techniques and heavy soils, drainage and shaping was minimal, with features simply

196

constructed (in comparison to later efforts) in order to create what was required for play to proceed.

Due to many factors, most of which contributed to fairly substandard playing conditions in comparison to the free draining links courses, inland golf was not seriously considered for a long time. In spite of that, by early in the 20th century many examples of inland golf were in existence, few of which possessed naturalised man made shapes or integrated drainage solutions.

It was at about this time that demand for golf courses around the world began to rise. Up until then, the colonial masters had introduced the game in many of the outposts of the British Empire, and it had taken quite some time for these outposts to mature to the point where golf could be pursued as a pastime by enough people to warrant the widespread construction of new golf courses.

The United States of America and Australia were two notable outposts that had grown into prosperous countries and so, on the matter of golf development they looked to the U.K., to the origins of the game in order to find the right people to help them shape their golfing futures.

The U.K. by this time was an old golfing land. The game there had already survived hundreds of years. There existed a huge cross-section of examples of design ideas and styles. Several golf course architects of the day had made their own inquiries into the past and had thereby devised their own strategies and theories as to how they could assist in the evolution of golf and the design of its courses.

It is worth noting that over the course of its history the game of golf had been, at times, somewhat of a "political football". Its administration had been subjected to all manner of conditions depending on the political leanings of the day. Its playing had been banned for certain periods and different restrictions had been imposed on it and its playing fields for many and various reasons over its history.

Because of this long, varied, and quite political history, I venture to say that no tried and tested approach to design had gained widespread approval, and there was definitely no recognised approach for the successful implementation of fully integrated and functional parkland golf, although no doubt, some Architects had achieved good results in fairly isolated cases. There were, however just as many detractors as supporters of these new styles, and it must have been particularly difficult to make any types of accurate comparisons between different design approaches. All solutions at the time no doubt still appeared a little poor in comparison to the links courses due not in the least part to a lack of technological know how to facilitate drainage and turf grass propagation in heavy soils.

For any aspiring local Golf Course Architect, a study exercise of the golf courses of Scotland and England was and probably still is to a degree, quite a varied and often confusing and conflicting exercise.

As a result, I contend that the model for golf course design, especially inland parkland golf, remained in the U.K. decidedly nondescript for a long time. Man-made parkland golf features tended to borrow, quite literally in many cases from some of the features that were employed very successfully on links land, but which were often less effective in heavier soil, with broader natural shapes as their backdrop.

In links land, roughly formed ridges, humps and hollows and steep faced, small bunkers can be implemented in most cases without disturbing a large surrounding area and without the boundaries of such work being ultimately perceptible. In a broad scale parkland setting such shapes look decidedly man made and quite often create more drainage problems than they fix. Such shapes can tend to concentrate sections of an otherwise broad scale, sheet-flow natural drainage system, which can be a disaster without artificial sub-surface drainage solutions. Even if the designers had the idea of creating more bold, naturally sympathetic shapes, the technical wherewithal of the time to do so would have been at best, questionable and under a hail of protest from the Links golf traditionalists, it no doubt would have been near impossible to get such projects off the ground.

I am therefore inclined to believe the best available models for styles of golf other than pure links was, at the birth of the 20th century, limited to - for the most part - collections of a relatively small number of concepts and features that could be readily borrowed and amended somewhat in order to function in environments other than links land.

While this has changed over time, even today I know of few people who have gone on a trip to Scotland to specifically look at parkland golf courses, whilst millions do the same annually with regard to links golf. Many also do the same to experience the great parkland courses of the U.S., Australia and other countries, which tends to indicate the design and construction of parkland golf in Britain and Ireland has only very recently began to reach the heights comparable to links golf in the same countries.

Influences of the United States of America

Golf in the United States is today a massive industry, much bigger than any other golf markets in the world.

It grew on the back of the first, mostly parkland golf courses. The creation of most of which were designed and overseen by a number of British expatriate architects who, in the U.S. chose a fresh new canvas on which to test their sometimes-radical design ideologies.

The design philosophies that were no doubt considered very different at the time have since transformed themselves into what could be considered the mainstay of modern day golf course architecture.

As vastly experienced and well-respected design experts from foreign lands, the opinions and ideals of these designers were not, for the must part questioned or challenged in the new land. As such they were able to realise their designs more fully, to the benefit of their clients and I daresay to the benefit of themselves, through obtaining realistic and accurate feedback on their efforts.

Golfers and developers in the U.S.A were, in their typical frontier spirit, keen to push the boundaries of existing design and construction techniques. As such, advances in turfgrass know-how and construction techniques facilitated great steps forward in golf course design and construction, in ways that could only occur in such a vibrant young land.

Such must have been the rewarding experiences that these early designers achieved, that many of them never went back to the U.K, preferring to stay in the U.S. to be a part of what was obviously the cutting edge of the fledgling golf course design and construction industry.

Many great names from these early years are indelibly etched into the history books of American Golf. McKenzie, Ross, and Tillinghast, to name a few. Although all of these and more, together had a major influence in the development of golf in the U.S., I would like to focus here on the influence of Donald Ross, who without doubt is seen by many Americans as the father of the Architecture of the game of golf in the U.S.

Donald Ross was a Scotsman who emigrated to the U.S. and designed many of the country's most renowned golf courses. He was a founding member and president of the United States Golf Course Architects official organisation and his input is treasured in the U.S. Among other great courses, he designed Pinehurst No.2, which is often rated as the best golf course in the U.S. and his designs are, I believe the epitome of the way golf has for a long time been played and approached in the U.S.

The U.S. Masters is of course, played at Augusta National, which was designed by Alistair McKenzie, another great Scottish Architect. While it is indeed a dream for many to win the Masters on this famous layout, there is no substitute for the nationalistic pride of place that the U.S. Open holds in the hearts of the American Professional golfers. If the greatness of the Masters is due at least partly McKenzie's, then much of the prestige, and stylistic ingredients of the U.S. open must surely be attributed to Donald Ross, a great many of whose strategic designs have played major roles in U.S. open history.

The designs of Donald Ross were without doubt, highly strategic, and using Pinehurst No. 2 as prime example, Ross for the most part, employed risk-reward strategies that are accentuated by raised, sloping green surfaces with strategically placed run-off areas. These run-off areas are positioned such that a ball that is slightly misdirected or which hits a green from a non-preferred angle is likely to trickle off the edge of the green to a closely mown collection area requiring a rather deft chip back to the green surface.

Bunkers and other hazards are strategically placed such that in many cases it is necessary to aim one's shot close to them in order to achieve the best line and angle to the target.

The whole concept puts an absolute premium on ball position, with dire consequences quite often in store for those who do not make the right choices and achieve the preferred position. The strategies could not generally be termed penal, but they can definitely make life difficult for those who are somewhat off their game. For the unaware, the "trickle factor" of these run-off areas can make a reasonably good shot look quite poor. I would go so far as to say this type of design has played a major role in the evolution of today's golfers especially on the US tour to be extremely long hitters and very accurate wedge and approach iron players. This type of play enables golfers to hit high approach shots to greens, which somewhat negates the effects of the sloping greens and "trickle factor".

Under the right conditions this style of golf course design makes for very interesting golf with strategic plays equal to that of a game of chess.

Ross' style of shape was typically quite bold and natural, carefully observing the existing land features and making them a part of the strategy where possible.

Bunkers appeared in harmony with this, utilising elegant, but for the most part quite simple shapes, promoting a very bold, - what you see is what you get - image (in distinct contrast to Links Golf) without a whole lot of hidden areas or stylised bunker edgings.

Compared to the often blind, extremely variable and somewhat unknown nature of links golf this style would no doubt have been a breath of fresh air and very fitting for a vibrant new market as was the U.S.

Other, typically American variations of this very big bold style also came into being. A notable example is the "crumpled" edged bunker style where the sand edge of the bunkers tends not to follow the shape of the earth bunker face, but rather meanders its way up and down the bunker faces, creating sand faces here, grass faces there, and half situations in other areas, in a seemingly random creative arrangement.

It generally takes quite large bunkers to house such random shapes in a scale that is readily maintainable and this bunker style seems, even today to be virtually the sole preserve of North America.

Australian Influences

Although the Australian golf market is many times smaller than that of the U.S. its major golf course design influences are quite relevant for a number of reasons. The major lasting influences occurred in quite a short period of time and were focused on a very small number of participants.

The results however are quite incredible. Today Australia is a rather small nation of about one fifteenth the population of the USA, but it boasts a disproportionately high number of very mature, world-class golf courses. In addition, Australia has produced a disproportionately high number of champion golfers as well as respected golf course architects. Both sets of professionals continue to successfully ply their trades in markets around the world. Australian golfers currently make up the largest contingent of non-American players belonging to any one nationality on the U.S. professional tour, which is generally regarded as the premier professional tour in world.

This all tends to indicate a reasonably healthy state of the game at the grass roots level, where bright young golf playing prospects are motivated to pursue the game at least in conjunction with, if not in preference to other popular sports.

Granted, Australians are spoilt for choice in terms of good cheap leisure opportunities and an abundance of time to pursue them when compared to most other countries. But even in this environment, the model that even the most basic of golf courses aspires to, must be one that is interesting enough to encourage repeated use by a great many potential champions.

Likewise, this successful model must have been ingrained well enough into the ideologies of Australia's set of Golf Course Architects to see them become so well respected and sought after as design consultants in many parts of the world.

Like the U.S.A. the major golf course design influences came from overseas and similarly the foreign Architects were able to achieve their design ideals on the ground. In 1927 the Scottish Golf Course Architect, Dr Alister MacKenzie embarked on his world tour. Several Golf Clubs that sought to build or upgrade their facilities banded together and secured his services for various periods during his stay in South Eastern Australia. Their committees had done much research to find the best candidate and as such they were well read and very much prepared to take full advantage of his expertise when he arrived.

According to his writings he only stayed in Australia some 6 or so weeks but in that time he had a hand in the creation of Royal Melbourne, Victoria Golf Club, Royal Adelaide, Royal Queensland, Royal Sydney, NSW golf club at La Perouse, as well as design and bunkering input at Metropolitan and Kingston Heath. All of these courses are rated inside the top 15 in Australia with Royal Melbourne regularly rated in the top 6 to 10 in the world.

It seems incredible that one man could achieve so much in such a short space of time, and in actual fact McKenzie was able to utilise the skills of some very able local people. Most notably Mick Morcom, who was able to build natural shapes better than anyone McKenzie had ever seen, as well as Alex Russell, who as MacKenzie's design assistant quickly learned the essence of good design. These people were some of the first to spread the McKenzie legacy in Australia and many others obviously took up the cause after them.

The McKenzie design style as represented today in Australia is generally a fairly encouraging form of risk-reward golf in a framework of bold and very naturally shaped settings. The design puts a high premium on ball position and in addition there is a wide range of play options available to all standards of players.

The short hitters, the old or the young are encouraged, or at least given the option to play the running ball on most golf holes and one is under no pressure to take big risks if he does not so desire.

Although several of the tracts of land on which MacKenzie laid out these courses were some of the best pieces of land one might find for golf in the whole of Australia, each golf course portrays the intricacies of its respective site in ways that truly make the golf courses appear as if they simply grew out of the site of their own accord.

Fairways, where possible are very wide and there is a notable absence of anything thicker than light rough close to the play zones. These attributes do not make the courses play easier for the good players, because if one's ball is in the rough or on the wrong side of a wide fairway it usually means that one will be in no position to attack the pin. These attributes do a great service, however to the lesser players, who find it much easier to play recovery shots and keep the ball in play.

Bunkers are very distinctive, large with sharply defined edges and numerous turf grass tongues sweeping to their bases, aiding golfer access and creating hidden pockets for strategic effect. Each course has its own distinctive but similar bunker flavour according to the localised site conditions, with possibly the most dramatic to be found at Royal Melbourne, which is also arguably the most receptive site McKenzie worked on whilst in Australia.

The bunkering is possibly the most memorable image of the Australian McKenzie courses and more specifically, the Melbourne "Sand Belt" courses. Numerous attempts have been made to export this spectacular bunker style with varying levels of success, and one can see moderated versions of it all over Australia and on many courses elsewhere designed by Australian architects. Sharply defined bunker edges and turf grass tongues of varying sizes, styles and dimensions have tended to be utilised by the Australians more so than by designers from other backgrounds.

Through analysing some of these key elements, it is possible, I believe to see how some of these influences have somewhat affected the design tendencies of a great number of designers from the different regions of the world. These influences are more likely to be on a subconscious level, without always knowing to whom or what they owe a reasonable amount of their design decision-making tendencies.

As stated previously, the ever-accelerating cross-pollination process is breaking down stereotypes at an ever-increasing rate, but up until recently one could observe the affects of these influences in golf course development.

During the 1990's South East Asia went through a golf development boom. Many Golf Courses sprung up, quite often in close proximity to each other, mostly attached to real estate developments. In this climate of rapid and widespread development it was interesting and easy to see what different designers from different backgrounds were doing, and how they went about achieving their results, according to the following observations:-

There was a distinct absence of architects from a British design background. I have no real idea why this is so, but can only guess this to be due to the local climate, which, being tropical makes it virtually impossible for elements of a links influenced design to be made to function, particularly in terms of drainage.

The North American and Australian influences as described above tend to be more receptive to drainage in tropical conditions and designers from these two regions seemed to be dominant in the region at that time, at least in the areas I personally visited.

Of the Australian and American designers it was notable that the Americans generally went for very bold shapes and big bunkers and as such the shaping work was generally undertaken by machines no smaller than a bull dozer of D4 equivalent.

The Australian designers tended to include more small-scale shapes, particularly in and around bunkers and where these bunkers interfaced with green sites. This is consistent with the Australian model of including more turf tongues and noses around bunkers. Bulldozers, similarly to the Americans, finished the wider expanses of the fairways and roughs, whilst smaller machines were favoured for finishing green and bunker complexes.

I must stress this observation was a kind of snapshot in time, simply to illustrate how the happenings of long ago, in this case 70 to 100 years before, still had an effect, at least on a subconscious level on the design tendencies on the cross-section of a group of international designers.

That "snap shot" however was some 8 years ago, at the time of writing and was only indicative of a small section of the market even at that time. It would be difficult to generalise in this way about the current situation as the market is much more fragmented, without the "hotspots" of development that seemed to be prevalent previously. As well as this, most modern day Golf course Architects now recognise the need to continually progress, if not periodically re-invent themselves and their design styles in order to stay at the forefront of the industry.

As such, the industry is becoming over more professional, ever less stereotyped and Architects are working harder than ever to come up with progressively more innovative and ever-better design solutions.

11

The Changing Game

We have briefly touched on the various issues associated with the accelerating rate of change in the game of golf. While there is nothing wrong with change in itself, there are two questions I believe must be answered before we take on the major issue of whether there should be intervention to slow or alter the course of change.

Question 1

Do we wish to retain an obvious connection between the type of game pro golfers play and the type of game the average amateur plays?

Question 2

Which aspects of the game should we regard as the most valuable and do we wish to ensure they remain, or will what replaces them be better?

We should perhaps look briefly to the origin of golf's place as a game or sport, in order to build the context for exploration of such questions.

Games have been in existence for thousands of years, and initially their role was not so much for competition but for relaxation and to help hone survival skills.

For many thousands of years before the sudden technological advances of the past thousand or so years, humans were conditioned to undertake certain quite stereotyped roles in their quest for personal survival and survival of their families and the species as a whole. The men of most of the "tribes" were usually the designated hunters. They would go out each morning in search of a kill in order to sustain themselves and their family. The women were responsible for the young and for gathering edible flora.

Hundreds of thousands of years of this behaviour ingrained these traits into humans such that they became instinctive, and as much as we might hate to admit it, the remnants of these basic hunting and gathering instincts still exist to some degree in most of us.

When society evolved to a point where suddenly there was no need for all of us to go out everyday undertake these basic survival duties, other activities arose to fulfil the instinctive desires, which could not simply be switched off overnight. Bear in mind that although this evolution occurred gradually over the last thousand or so years, this is quite sudden in evolutionary terms. As such, today's humans are stuck in somewhat of a time lag, where modern day social requirements are not always in-sync with our instinctive desires. For many, modern day work challenges satisfy some of the elements of these ingrained tendencies, but quite often, the physical side also needs to be satisfied.

Enter the concept of sports, as opposed to games. Games were designed for relaxation when people weren't out fighting for their survival, whereas sports are the more involved and more competitive versions of games and pastimes that are designed to fulfil the inherent desires to compete and excel in a physical sense. For those of us who cannot ourselves physically compete, the next best thing is often to be a spectator or a supporter, pinning one's hopes and dreams (to a certain extent) on that of a selected team or individual.

This is the basic reason sports nowadays command such great attention and top sportsmen are admired and held in such high esteem. As the world becomes more affluent and automated, people have progressively less and less need to compete or undertake physical labour on a daily basis just to survive. It therefore stands to reason that this adulation for, and desire to be great sports people will for the more physically competitive among us continue to rise and increase, at least for a few thousand years until our species evolve to the next level.

One will note most of the biggest sports fanatics and late-night sports-watching couch-potato types are male. These are the people with the most amounts of pent-up, hunter-type tendencies that need to find an outlet.

So how does golf fit into this concept? Golf has for the most part existed as quite a subdued version of physical competition, especially when compared to the modern day versions of pack-hunting games such as football, etc. But golf has always held respect as a worthy game, even among the most intense of physical athletes, many of whom quite often play golf when they can, but more so as a game for relaxation and to help settle and mentally prepare them for their own sport. Perhaps this respect is due to the marksman type attributes a golfer must posses. The ability to gauge distance, evaluate and hit targets are attributes all hunters need. This may also be why golf seems to be the game of choice for businesspeople. It is a relaxing way of sharpening the mental skills of patience, persistence and control required in business.

For a long time golf was still considered a game, as opposed to a sport, but those days are now gone. In years gone by one would quite often see overweight or physically unfit golfers at the top or near the top of the sport (or game). Nowadays, nothing is left to chance and everyone is striving for that last little edge they might be able to capture in order to maximise their competitiveness.

In yesteryear, such obsessive competitiveness, if present was quite often scorned upon to some extent, as it was not seen as fitting in "the gentleman's game" as was golf.

So nowadays we have a situation that sees new products being put out at an ever-increasing rate, all designed to give better levels of performance. Every aspect and element of the game is being broken down in greater and greater detail, enabling golfers to understand more and more about what it takes to become more competitive.

The fact is, however that only the die-hard amateurs and pro-golfers have the time and motivation to take advantage of most of this technology, and this sees that group of golfers hitting the ball further and more accurate than ever before.

The average golfer is, however still for the most part, in "game" mode. Sure he tries hard to win money off his friends but golf to him is much more of a social relaxation game. As such, the average golfer gains some advantage through equipment technology, but most of the potential benefits of new training regimes, fitness, mental strengthening and repetitive swing training drills, are for the most part, lost on the average player. He just wants to go out, play and have fun, and feel like a champion on the relatively rare occasions when he hits a good shot or has a good round.

Because of this, top line amateur and professional golf is becoming further and further more removed from the style of golf that an average club golfer can employ. This trend is not uncommon, in fact it is common in modern day society that one must be increasingly specialised and committed to become good at anything (relative to the competition). This is indicative of progress and for the most part, progress should be embraced as it facilitates the bringing of the human race to an ever-higher level of existence, with progressively better living conditions for everyone into the future.

The question is, do we want golf to be a part of that future and if so, in what format? To put it another way, will the effects of leaving technology unchecked in golf give us a game that is more valuable to society? Or should we look to change the rules "to put the brakes on," or possible more appropriately -change the direction of the technological advances- in order to preserve some of the present day attributes or revive some of the past attributes that helped to give the game the widespread appeal it commands today.

In considering such a question, one might wish to keep the following points in mind.

Technology in Isolation – Technology when applied without restraints to golf equipment particularly, will most likely have effects similar to its ongoing application to most other fields of human life. Technology has a habit of radically changing our lifestyles, and rendering certain elements of our lives obsolete. In most areas the effect on our general quality of life is positive, however the essence of sports is not usually quality of life. A popular sport is made that way by the interest and excitement generated through human endeavour.

It has therefore been seen as necessary in many sports to somewhat moderate the effects of technology, in order to ensure the essence of such sports remains intact. Some examples of where sporting bodies have taken steps to apply rules intended to control or redirect the application of technology are as follows:

- In primarily physical sports, such as football, rugby, athletics etc, technology is limited mostly with regard to drug use, which artificially alters player's performance. This is not to say the problem is fixed, but at least regulations are in place

- In car racing it is necessary to continually re-evaluate the rules in order to ensure technology remains the facilitator of the human endeavour and not the endeavour itself. In the beginnings of this sport, it was a showcase for technology that required intensive and creative human input under stressful and often dangerous conditions to make the machines function for the length of a race.

  Nowadays, if it weren't for the rules, teams probably would not need to have a driver on board, as technology has the means to overcome most, if not all of the driver's on-board input.

What makes the sport and particularly the Formula 1 version of it so popular is the spectacle of watching young men in a very fast and dangerous pursuit to be the best. Or in other words, it is the human element of skilled warriors (or hunters) cheating death as they test their skills. Organisers have had to make some very unorthodox rule changes in recent times to ensure this popular formula is retained, in the form of moderations to the direction of technical advances. Nobody except a scientist wants to watch one machine compete against another without the human factor.

- In tennis, there has been limitations placed on racquet head size and dimensions, and importantly, ongoing monitoring of the type and characteristics of playing surfaces and tennis balls. Governing bodies are careful to try to keep as many different player types in the game at the highest level, and therefore promote widespread interest by endeavouring to disallow technology to give undue advantage to players of certain type or specification.

Unlike most other sports, the technology factor in golf has greater ramifications than just the equipment used, as there are also the golf courses to consider. Some of the issues pertinent to both of these elements are as follows:

Golf Equipment

The most notable advances in golf club technology have perhaps been the cavity back club heads which give a better shot consistency even for off-centre hits, as well as light weight shafts and enlarged driver heads. These items have afforded your average club golfer a lot more scope to keep the ball in play and thereby enjoy their golf a lot more.

The other important element of the equipment set is of course the ball, and it is here that possibly the biggest game-changing advances have and continue to be made.

Up until recently, say 10 to 15 years ago, there were two distinct types of golf balls, which could be labelled hard balls and soft balls.

Hard balls flew further off the club head giving maximum distance, but one could not impart any substantial spin, either side-spin or backspin. These balls were therefore good for amateur players who are generally looking for more length, and since this set of players are not adept at using spin to any great advantage; these balls' lack of spin generally had no major negative impact.

Soft balls, on the other hand were able to accept a lot of spin, making them more receptive to the "shaping" of shots through the air and for the imparting of backspin which helps to bring the ball to a controlled stop on the greens. The trade-off was these balls did not fly as far off the club head, but pro golfers tended to use these softer ball varieties anyway, because the control factor that the soft balls gave them positively outweighed the potential benefits of distance that a hard ball could give them.

Under this scenario club golfers using a hard ball could hit distances that were fairly close to that of many of the pro golfers with their soft balls, most of whom could in addition play all manner of shaped shots, as was needed to score well in tournament conditions. As such the perceived gap between pro golfers and good amateurs was not so great (at least in the eyes of the amateurs) as many were able to play shots that appeared similar to those of the pros, albeit without the control.

Modern day ball technology has, in effect taken the best attributes from the old hard and soft balls, and put them together. Where one used to have to trade distance for control, now the good players can have both. The new balls fly high and long with a lot of backspin for those who have the skills to impart it. The balls do not take as much sidespin as some of the earlier softer balls, meaning they generally fly straighter and are not so easy with which to hit shaped shots. This however, becomes less of a factor when the distance is there. Take for example an average par 5 of 470 metres. With an old soft ball, a pro might hit his tee shot to maybe 240 metres, leaving a long second shot to the green. He would have to play a 3 wood or 1 or 2 iron, and if he shaped the ball well, it might take advantage of the terrain and kick on to a location near the green for a regulation chip, or if the second shot is played perfectly, maybe even roll onto the green.

Nowadays, many pro golfers will be able to hit their tee shot 280 – 300 metres, leaving a mid to short iron second shot. There is generally no real need to impart sideways shape to such a shot, especially when it can be hit so high and with so much backspin.

What this means is that in effect, general long iron play from the fairway is now virtually obsolete in the pro game. Most pro golfers don't even carry a 1 iron any more and they only usually hit their 2 irons off the tee in situations where they are afraid their woods might go too far!

With such a situation already in place, how does this affect the relationship between the pro game and the club golfer's game? Whilst the equipment improvements have no doubt benefited the average player, talent and skill is required to get full benefit from the advances in equipment. This means there is a widening gap between the games of the average club players and that of the pro golfers. Where an average club golfer used to hit his ball 180 metres, now maybe he can hit it 200. Where an average pro used to hit it 230, now maybe he can hit it 280, meaning that for good or bad, the distance gap has perhaps widened from 50 metres to 80 metres.

In addition, the relatively inaccurate general play of most club golfers means that what benefits are gained in extra distance are quite often ill directed. If a golfer is inaccurate, extra distance will simply mean that in most cases he will be simply hitting his ball further into the rough, for a negative net result.

The Rate of Change

One might be wondering where this will all end, and is this wave of recent equipment improvements close to reaching a point where there is nothing left to improve?

If history and evolution is any indicator, the rate of technological change in most fields can occur in fits and spurts, but generally occurs in an exponential manner, and there is a reasonable amount of evidence to suggest that this is happening with golf equipment. This can be seen in that, looking to the past it seemed that although there have been many improvements to equipment; none have been as influential as those which have taken place in the past 10-15 years.

While this appears like a recent "wave" of improvements, perhaps it is more like the compounding effect of progressively improving those new innovations originally mooted 20 or more years ago. Viewed graphically, this might appear like the curve shown in diagram 42.

If this theory is correct, the first section of the graph signifies the history of golf, with a very gradually rising rate of change in equipment. In the mid section of the graph, the rate of change begins to curve more dramatically upward and it is quite possibly somewhere in this section that the evolution of the game is now situated.

If this is true then the future will see a rapidly and ever-increasing rate of change, which will have more far reaching ramifications than what has happened to date. So far, we have seen long iron play become virtually extinct and one can speculate what might happen next.

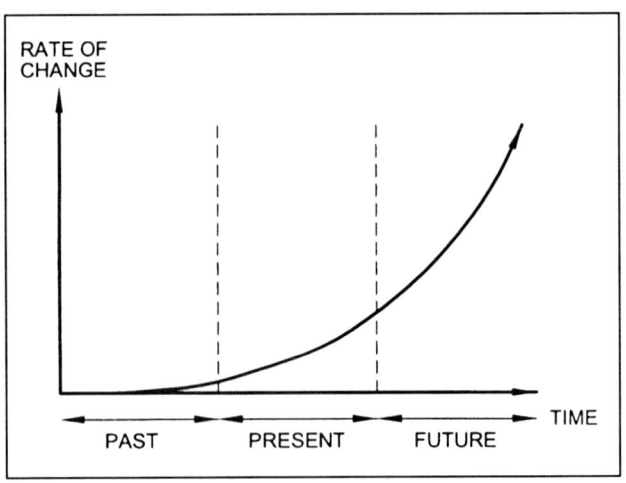

RATE OF
CHANGE

TIME

PAST   PRESENT   FUTURE

Diagram 42. Accelerating rate of change.

For example, if the average pro has gained, over the last 10 years, 50 metres of distance off the tee, in the next 10-15 years he will likely gain another 100 or so metres. This means that quite soon many par 5's and virtually all par 4's will become one-shot holes.

It stands to reason that aside from hitting off the tee, pro golfers will need no other clubs than a sand wedge and a putter. Distance, once the treasured commodity coveted by all, is fast becoming easily attainable. And this is only one facet of the game. With all other elements combined, God only knows what will become of the game.

I seriously doubt the pro game can survive if it comes to that, and if it does, it will have transformed itself into another game, because it will have little relationship to the game of golf, as we now know it.

Golf Courses – In sports such as tennis and football, which are played on well defined playing fields of exact measurements, it is perhaps a little easier to pinpoint the effects of technology and make changes to ensure its effects have a positive impact on the spectacle of the game in question.

Golf on the other hand, takes place on very natural playing fields, where the effects of technology are quite often a little more difficult to define.

This natural, living, evolving nature of golf courses fools many people into thinking they are somehow immune from the major effects of technology. Others believe all the effects of technology will simply be able to be

212

overcome by making small adjustments and amendments to the design of the golf holes, within the context of the overall original site plan.

I believe that presently the latter is true, but should the advances in technology proceed at the same flat rate, (never mind a possible exponential rate), within 15 to 20 years a major proportion of all existing golf courses will become obsolete and/or too dangerous for regular use.

The obsolescence will come from, -among other things- the length scenario described above. The danger factor will come from magnifying effect that length has on errant balls.

For example, consider a ball that is hit 10 metres off line for a shot 180 metres in length. If the same error in shot making is made by the same player who now has the capacity to hit the ball 260 metres, the ball will be 15 metres off line, or 1.5 times as inaccurate. This is not an unrealistic assessment of the changing capabilities of an average player, and is in fact based on the personal experience of yours truly, over a 15-year time period, all things considered. Admittedly this is a rough, one off indication, but assuming it is somewhere close to reality it means designers should have, over the past 15 years, increased the width of all buffer zones between golf holes and especially between golf holes and site boundaries, by 1.5 times.

Accordingly, a fifty-metre width between a golf hole centre line and an adjacent boundary in 1988 should have become a 75-metre width in 2003. In theory this adds over 7.5 hectares of land (18.5 acres) in boundary safety buffers to a 60 hectare, 18-hole core-style layout, without even considering the internal buffers, or extra length desired of most golf holes.

In an age where land is becoming ever more scarce, it might quickly become unfeasible to allocate an extra 7 to 15 odd hectares for a golf course. And consider the existing, residential-bound golf courses. If this trend of unchecked length continues, they will no doubt be forced to continually remodel their layouts, knocking a few strokes off their par each time until they eventually become totally unusable.

Do We Need A Change?

Referring back to our exponential "Rate of Change" graph, it is fairly obvious that some kind of intervention will be required to prevent changes to the way the game is played from spiralling into an ever-quickening flurry of golf playing anomalies.

John Daly has proven that "Grip it and Rip it" can work and can win major championships. While John Daly is an amazing talent, he definitely is not in the traditional golfer mould, and his unorthodox use of modern day equipment and conditions gives testament to the already changing face of the game.

His British Open win at St. Andrews in 1995 gave insight into how the game can be turned on its head, and St. Andrews was the perfect place for John Daly to do it. The Old Course at St. Andrews is laid out such that out of bounds is on the right side of most holes. Normally this is not such a major factor at St. Andrews as the rough on the left side of most holes is usually almost, if not just as penal as the out of bounds. 1995 was a fairly bad growing season and as such the rough was not quite as thick as usual. This suited Daly's style as what fairways he missed, he tended to miss on the left side. With his superior length, he was always within wedge or short iron distance and was usually able to attack the pin, even if playing from the rough. Coupled with his fantastic touch around the greens he was able to win the British Open in a way that was never before achieved.

I am not for a minute insinuating that John Daly was not a worthy winner of that British Open Championship. On the contrary, his win was well-deserved, fantastic to watch and a great positive influence on the popularity of the game at that time.

My point is John Daly was able to take a large portion of the hazards of St. Andrews out of play, not through throttling back, but through the application of more length and power. Back then, in 1995 and to a lesser extent in the present day, that practice is prone to come unstuck as often as it will work. But the new breed of young players is showing with increasing regularity that length and accuracy can be successfully combined with consistently good results, thereby simplifying the way the game is played. This tendency also negates the need for intelligent golf course design. It is pointless to design shapes for the purpose of the running ball, if most balls are flown over them and land softly, negating much of the effect of the design contours.

In response to this, some of the world's most revered golf clubs have taken steps to significantly lengthen their layouts. Augusta National and the St. Andrews Old Course, most significantly. I am of the opinion that while this may match the effects of technology in the short to mid term, ultimately we will be back to the same or similar issues. This is due to the fact that whilst the capacity for technology to produce longer golf shots is infinite, technology has get to come up with a method of magically creating more land for the lengthening of existing golf holes!

Even by today's standards of pro golf, in order for golf holes to play like they did 20 years ago, all par 5's would need to be over 600 metres (660 yards) in length, a large proportion of par 4's would be 450 to 500 metres and at least one par 3 might be 250 or so metres long.

A "super course" of this type of length would be basically unplayable for all but the pros, and it would give the result of creating in effect, a separate game that is exclusively for pro golfers only, thereby completely removing one of the last methods of identifying with the pro game that average club golfers still have.

In addition, it is fairly difficult for on-course spectators to see what is going on when players hit the ball so far; they are often literally hitting the ball out of sight. (When one considers distance and the natural undulations of a golf course, which tend to hide the results of long modern day golf shots.) Quite regularly on TV one will see the on-course spectators clap and cheer a tee shot that sails straight into the rough, without anyone standing on or near the tee being quite sure of whether the result is good or bad.

The effects of extreme length combined with unprecedented ball control by the top players also makes it extremely difficult to set up golf courses for the optimum level of challenge for major tournaments.

Major tournaments such as some of the national open events of the major golf playing countries of the world are renowned for being set up as the toughest tests of golf, and there is an expectation that the winning scores will be not quite as low as they are in other tour events.

The modern day professional game is played in such as way that renders all but the toughest of nearly unplayable conditions open to a barrage of sub-par play. In an effort to defend par, those who prepare the golf courses for such tournaments have an ever-smaller window within which to work to achieve their goals, with virtually no available margin of error. The modern day style of play means that the "toughening" of tournament courses can only be achieved in a couple of ways, such as narrowing of fairways, growing of roughs and making playing surfaces very hard and fast. Narrow fairways and thick rough only work for inaccurate shots, however this "slickening" of playing surfaces reduces the degree to which the players can control the ball. In other words, it directly hinders the playing of good shots.

This definitely makes golf courses tougher to play, but whether or not it is healthy for the game is a matter of great conjecture. In addition, it is a dangerous practice, which requires perfect control and weather conditions, lest the situation can easily get out of hand.

In a recent Australian Open, a severe drought coupled with a few other issues caused one of Melbourne's finest traditional golf courses to become almost unplayable, to the point where the most prestigious tournament in Australia was reduced to only 3 rounds. And just recently, the 2004 US Open saw good scoring on the first 2 days, before a drying, but not overly strong wind came in, making the greens progressively harder and quicker. On Saturday the golf course was extremely difficult. On Sunday, no player broke par, and the average score was almost 9 over par. Had it not been for the outrageously good 1-over par rounds of the two leading players, it might have all began to look a little farcical, which would have put the integrity of the event severely at risk.

Whichever way I look at it, with all these unprecedented issues cropping up, it seems that a major decision will be forced upon the rule makers of the game in the not-too-distant future, and the signs are already there to suggest in many places that future is quite close.

Already some government planning bodies are drafting legislation that in some areas may see future integrated golf and residential development outlawed.

If some of these pertinent and mounting issues are not addressed, we could see a massive stifling of the golf industry, with the potential to virtually stop golf course development in its tracks.

It seems crazy to expose the development of the game to these kind of risks, and to continue to re-plan and redevelop thousands of golf courses on the basis of length alone, when the issues could very simply be solved by using equipment specifications to direct the development of the game in a way that will serve everyone's needs.

I believe some firm guidelines and directives need to be laid down by the governing bodies of the sport in order to give some structure to the future progression of the game. This would give some comfort to those concerned with safety issues and enable Golf Course Architects to realistically plan for a safe and happy golfing future.

Possible Solutions

In formulating what could or should be done to safeguard the future of the game we might wish to re-cap on some of the virtues of the game that helped make it great. Thereafter, any measures can be cross-checked to ensure they assist in achieving those goals.

Retaining the human factor

When a pro golfer tees off, the crowds do not cheer for the ball, the Titanium headed driver or the graphite shaft, they cheer for the player. Professional sport is the celebration of high human achievement. Unbridled admiration for the best proponents in their respective fields is a tendency that is designed to prolong the human species. It would not matter if Tiger Woods used a stick off a tree to hit his ball, as long as he is the best at such an endeavour, which requires high degrees of *human* skill, people will watch and cheer.

Retaining an element of chance; good luck and bad luck

One of the keys to the appeal of golf has been the very natural and highly variable nature of its playing fields, which require application of the very human traits of estimation of conditions, much like a hunter in a wild or natural environment. These types of conditions should be retained and their effects heightened, as they add an extra dimension to the drama of the execution of well-honed human skills. Elements that remove the need for such human estimation kill off part of the human factor of any sport. This might not be so bad if they are replaced with another element of greater interest and variety, but if they are not, such technological elements should be moderated or excluded.

Encourage the use of a wide variety of skills

It is a commonly held principle that a good test of golf is one in which a golfer is required to use every club in his bag. This fits with the idea of the game showcasing a wide array of human skills. The future of the game should be directed such that not only are pro-golfers required to use every club in their bag, but preferably in widely varying and different ways. The requirement to hit low balls, high balls and ball flight patterns of very different shapes is an element of the game that should be reinstated, as it better showcases the skills of the players than does the consistently high, straight shots of the modern day game.

Narrow the perceived gap between the professionals and the amateur club golfers

Continuing efforts to reduce differences between pro golfers and amateurs in the way the game is played gives lesser golfers a shot of confidence, thereby motivating them to play the game. If people find it hard to personally relate to what they see played out in pro tournaments on TV there will be a lesser tendency to play the game and its popularity at the grass roots level will suffer.

Equipment

At the club level, new age balls and clubs that make it easier for club golfers to keep the ball in play are no doubt good and a positive addition to the sport, as they encourage the involvement of lesser players who are most prone to become discouraged and then give up, if they cannot attain a basic level of achievement.

Pro golfers in tournament situations don't need such encouragement. Items which simplify the skills needed by them to win actually detract from the game by preventing these great players from exhibiting all manner of the substantial skills their years of practice, hard work and god-given talent has bestowed upon them. Nowadays, a high proportion of what we see is driving, wedge and putter play.

I therefore contend that rather than concentrating on "holding back" the progress of time, the issue should be looked at as an opportunity to further and perfectly showcase the full range of skills of today's golfers, who are more dedicated and more highly skilled than any set of golfers before them. That we do not get to witness their full range of skills in action is a travesty of justice for all golf fans.

The first stop towards this is to moderate the distance that the golf ball can fly. This appears negative, but I contend that it would only be so for the ball manufactures and even for them, only for a short period until a new set of goals are set in motion with regard to the ideal set of properties that golf balls should posses.

Distance has become a cheap commodity and the focus needs to be taken from it as the primary factor in the production of golf equipment. The best place to start must be at the showcase level of the game, the professional tournaments.

Looking to create the ideal spectacle for a mythical pro tournament, and standard par 72 course, the following scenario might apply.

- Of the four par 5's, two would be out of reach in two shots for all players, and two would be reachable for those who play two exceptional shots, which use the angle of play, the terrain and its interaction with the shape of the ball flight on landing, to direct the ball into the preferred areas.
- Of the par 3's, one and sometimes two of them would require the use of a long iron or wood for the bulk of the players in most conditions.
- At least two par 4's on each nine (four in total) would require long iron (2 or 3 iron) approaches for the players in most conditions.
- The tournament should be played on a course of reasonable championship length – say 7,000 yards – 6,300 metres which is a length that is playable by a reasonable cross section of club golfers, and is

therefore a course that amateur club golfers would be able to identify with.
- The winner will need to employ the running ball on occasions in order to obtain optimum length and best ball position to shoot low scores.

In order to create such a set of scenarios, the golf ball would be one that would not fly any further than 230-240 metres. Rather than stepping back in time and selecting a ball that conforms to such a specification, new technology can be used to produce balls that give unprecedented control and options for an unprecedented variety of ball flight types, while disallowing the longest tour players of today to fly the ball more than 230-240 metres.

Adding the potential for ever-greater shot variation will encourage golfers to become ever more skilled at a wider variety of shots, and this would then become the main focus of advances in the game.

Such a scenario would then encourage Golf Course Architects to come up with ever more variable designs, which encourage the use of, and exploration for newer, different types and shapes of golf shots. With modern day turf growing techniques, the possibilities for exploiting the value of the running and bouncing ball in design could open up a whole new and very exciting phase in golf course design history.

There would still be long hitters and short hitters but the longest of hitters might not necessarily be the players with the strongest physical attributes to create the quickest club head speed. The longest hitters might then be those who possess the best skills to create the most optimum shot shapes, coupled with the ability to accurately hit the most receptive slopes and landforms. The quest to play good golf would become a more expansive, creative endeavour, as opposed to the progressively more focused set of skills that has encapsulated the top level of the sport in recent times.

Administering such a system could be done in a number of different ways. Tournament organisers could simply adopt a "tournament ball" and issue the balls that are to be used exclusively for their tournament similar to how it is done in tennis.

There might be a list of "approved tournament balls" golfers can choose from. Alternatively, all the different golf balls produced by each manufacturer might be given a grading. Some particular grades of ball might be disallowed for use at tournaments, and the approved grades of balls could vary between different tournaments depending on the length and other playing conditions of the particular courses in question. This would encourage pro golfers to learn how to play with more than one ball type, or alternatively, only play in events that allow the type of balls they like to use.

Not only would this add another element to the pro game, but it would also give new meaning to the Order Of Merit and money list winners of each tour, as true, all around champions.

Such systems might also be applied to golf clubs and their components, however to start with the ball in the professional game will make the biggest and best impact. Once such a strategy is employed at pro level, one will find that the effects will slowly but surely filter back to the amateur, grass roots level. Aspiring young golfers will want to practice with "pro balls" and so on, meaning that the way the game is viewed will change from that of a power game to that of a new-age, thinker's game of a highly controlled, but extremely variable nature, of which power is but one important element.

I believe such a strategy will not even have a major effect on which golfers become the most successful, aside from the fact that more shorter hitters will be encouraged to participate at the highest level.

In the 2003 Formula 1 season, radical rule changes helped create the most closely contested and popular season in recent years, but the same driver, and undisputed champion, Michael Schumacher won the championship for a record 6th time. At the end of the day, the rules do not make a champion, the champion emerges through his ability to take the best decisions and make the best plays at the crucial, high pressure times when the championships are up for grabs.

In this way, golf will assist more in the positive evolution of the *people* that play the game, rather than the evolution of the *equipment* used to play the game.

In golf, Tiger Woods is undisputedly the best player of the present era. He has won an unprecedented number of major tournaments compared to any other player at the same stage of their careers and has broken many other records.

While he is a long hitter, this alone has not been the secret of his success. A good many of his best victories have been very close encounters where he, like all true champions made crucial decisions that when it came down to it, had little to do with length off the tee. Indeed, like Jack Nicklaus before him, he seems to have an ability to take the right decisions and to make crucial putts drop into the hole with sheer will.

I venture to say that he, like any great champion would not shy away from any new challenge as a way to further test and prove his true champion status.

12

Professional Golfers and their Role in Golf Course Design

As a part of the introduction to this book I painted an image of the pro golfer-designer that could be seen as somewhat negative. In light of the bulk of my design ideals, which have been for the most part laid out in the body of the book, I would like to further clarify and put these initial images in a better perspective.

Modern day golf course design, as can be seen even by the contents of this book, is a very involved and multifaceted discipline. It requires much experience and years of dedicated single-minded pursuit in order that one may be able to reach a minimum standard expected in the design of every new modern day golf course.

Today's industry is, I contend, far removed from the days of old, when a Golf Course Architect would often "peg out" a golf course layout onsite over the course of a few days, before giving verbal instruction to those that might be involved in the formation of the golf holes. Thereafter he would leave the site to return the next year for the golf course opening.

Like everything, modern technological advances are occurring at an ever-quickening rate and one must be increasingly diligent and committed to whatever one's chosen profession might be, just to keep up with the progress of change, let alone be a leader in one's field.

In days of old, the frequent users of almost any product would usually have quite a good level of knowledge about how that product worked, and even how to create and modify the products they utilised.

For example, up until 20 or so years ago, a car racing enthusiast could fairly readily access and comprehend virtually all parts and the treatment of all of the parts that went together to make up what was considered a very high performance race car.

It was quite common for people to do virtually all the work on their own cars. With mechanical knowledge generated by interest, as well as the inherent knowledge and feel of the way their car drives and performs garnered through frequent usage, many car owners were able to be the best mechanic their car might ever have. A professional mechanic who takes a customer's car for a one-off drive has no way of knowing if the car felt slightly different from yesterday or last week because that feel, obtainable only by frequent usage is not present. Consequently, mechanics often have difficulty picking up on small performance related changes or problems with your car's workings. Therefore, if one had the capacity, it was often better to fix one's car by oneself.

I think most people will agree those days have basically passed. Logical thought and basic mechanical knowledge will rarely help to figure out what is going on with a new 2004 model car if one pops the bonnet after experiencing a power failure.

Automotive engineering has evolved to such a point that I doubt there is any one man who knows the full operations of every part of any new, modern day car. This has, in a high degree of cases rendered the back-yard mechanic obsolete, save for the simple tasks such as changing the engine oil. One can readily see the changes to the industry by taking a look in most mechanic shops, where one will find instruments and machines that up until a few years ago would have looked more at home in a hospital I.C. unit. Indeed, today's mechanic is more likely to pull out a laptop computer than an oily rag when he goes to check the performance of a car.

This type of phenomena can be seen in almost every facet of human life. 70 years ago when my grandfather started having kids, he extended his house all by himself, with the help of his brothers and the materials they produced by themselves on their farm.

Nobody would argue nowadays that because you live in a house and drive a car, you are automatically qualified to design or build either one of these items, no matter how interested you are in houses, or how well you can drive a car.

This, I contend, is very much consistent with modern day golf course design and just as applicable to the business of professional golf itself. It should be stressed that playing golf at the highest level and golf course design are their own separate fields; each requiring years of diligent and focused training in order to attain any kind of success.

At one time, back in the romantic pages of the past, the two were no doubt intertwined, but a few facts about each of their modern day equivalents will easily enable one to see they are now definitely their own separate fields, and becoming more so every day.

Let's compare the modern day golf pro with his equivalent of 30-40 years ago. Back then, health, nutrition, physical fitness, sustained training and practice regimes were virtually unheard of. Playing success was virtually a function of natural talent, with the most successful being those endowed with the best physical features and the natural mental capacity to make the most of them on the course. There was no such thing as physical trainers, sports psychologists and even the job of swing analysis was mostly undertaken by fellow players, who would usually be happy to give their opinion if asked.

Also, at that time, playing schedules were nowhere near as full as they are nowadays, and although a top professional golfer could make a good living from the game, the prize money and endorsements were a speck in the ocean compared to modern day standards.

This allowed time and in many cases, a need for many professional golfers to pursue other streams of interest and income away from the golf playing scene. For some, golf course design would have been a very good choice, as it would at that time have been very complimentary to the lifestyle of the pro golfer, when taken into account the golf design profession was at that time also nowhere near as consuming as it is now.

One of the first and most glaring examples of somebody who changed this approach to playing and training was the South African, Gary Player. His holistic approach to playing, physical training, nutrition and the like were at the time, seen as obsessive and quite ridiculous to most people. The results however, became obvious for all to see and nowadays there are few pro golfers on the major tours that do not observe health and fitness regimes to somewhere near the standard of Gary Player.

Add to this the full playing schedules, commitments to sponsors, constant travel, and the unprecedented amount of competition just to obtain a place on a pro-golf tour, let alone win events, and one can see success can no longer be attained if one's focus is split between more than one field of expertise.

I also contend that the game of golf and its playing has for the most part, become more focused or standardised in nature, a fact which I believe also creates an increasingly wide distance between the psyches of the personalities that are likely to succeed in each respective field.

In the past one would see all manner of styles of golf swings at any pro tournament. Players were more a product of their own trial and error and as such there was more variation of styles. There was also much more varying imagination and creativity employed by the golfers and their often unorthodox swings, as they used whatever methods and techniques they could to get the most out of their respective, naturally evolved golf games. The swings of most successful present day pro golfers, have by comparison been put together by qualified teachers and then refined from early childhood.

In the past, more tournaments were won by players who executed a couple of freak shots from bad positions, and this was often what separated the winner from the rest of the field on that particular day.

Who could ever forget Seve Ballesteros' recovery shot from the car park to win the British Open?

Nowadays, the competition is so intense and the golf swings on tour are so pure and orthodox you are unlikely to be in contention to win it you are hitting it into the car park. Golfers are taught intense focus and posses grooved swings that consistently hit the ball long, high and very straight. Too much tinkering and playing around with one's golf swing will not win tournaments nowadays.

Whilst golfers are taught how to get out of trouble and play varying shots according to the conditions, this must be done only within the confines of one's own specific game plan. Too much lateral thought destroys focus and is detrimental to playing success.

I contend the modern day thought processes required to be employed by successful pro golfers are becoming more and more different to that required by successful modern day Golf Course Architects .

The modern day pro golfer's view of the game and each course is by design, very insular and inward looking. Today's pro golfers need to focus on their own game and block out all peripheral issues that do not concern the way they play golf. A Golf Course Architect, on the other hand has to take a very outward looking or expansive view as he considers all standards of golfers and all possible playing scenarios that might occur on one of his designs.

This phenomena was plainly illustrated to me one day when I got a chance to chat with a pro golfer who had recently played reasonably well in a tournament staged on a course designed by my organisation.

I asked him what he thought of the course and his reply was it was okay, but it had a few design issues we may wish to rectify in the future. Obviously eager to hear what these issues might be, I prompted him further. He explained that in most cases, the locations to where he wanted to hit his ball had a hazard near or in it. This made him drastically change his game plan, obviously making it more difficult for him to play his natural game, and hindering his chances of winning the tournament.

I was very happy to hear this as it showed to me we were able, in our design to challenge the pro golfers on a golf course that incidentally, is extremely popular and therefore enjoyable for the average amateur golfer.

It does however, also illustrate the exclusive nature of the intense focus of the modern day pro golfers, which prevented this particular golfer from even being aware that extensively thought out risk-reward strategies were at play, and not design oversights as per his view of things.

So where and how do Pro Golfers fit into the industry of modern day Golf Course Design?

In considering many of the successful modern day career designers, that is, those that were not previously successful golf professionals, one will see many have some kind of connection to professional golf. Several designers I personally know were in their youth, aspiring professionals who, fairly early on in their careers realised they were never going to cut it as a pro and refocussed their energies on another facet of the golf industry.

Others, such as Tom Fazio, The American Master designer was groomed to take care of the design business started by his uncle George Fazio, a successful pro golfer of the time.

In the present day context I would suggest most new golf architects enter the field in a similar way that I did, as a junior in an established firm that was likely formed years before according to one of the above mentioned scenarios.

There still is the occasional pro golfer, mostly not from the set of top flight pro golfers who are changing their focus and personally attempting to become proficient at design.

With regard to the top flight pro golfers, meaning those who have won major championships or at least managed to remain competitive over many years, one will note many of these players have golf course design companies that bear their famous names.

It has long been a contentious issue as to how much involvement these top line golfers actually do have in the design of the projects that bear their names. Whilst I cannot speak for all the companies that fit into this bracket, my own personal experience and knowledge borne from my occasional contact with them suggests in most cases, the real design input of the pro is quite minor.

Knowing what it takes to become proficient at design, and knowing that nowadays golf course design is its own, distinct profession, quite separate from the profession of golf playing, it is difficult to see how any active, modern day pro golfer would have the time to seriously learn it. Sure, one can read about it, visit sites and obviously play lots of great golf courses, but one must "live it" to a certain degree; that is be immersed in design for an extended period of years to truly become proficient. This immersion needs, ideally to start at the ground level and work up. I cannot image a top line golf pro quitting the tour and putting himself in the position of office junior in a company he owns, for the sake of truly learning the craft.

As previously mentioned, I believe the thought processes largely employed by modern day pro golfers is to a certain extent at loggerheads with those required to be a competent golf course designer. One often hears a golf pro's game is a bit off due to "off course or outside business interests."

Maybe this is a sign of an attempt by some pro golfers to get to know more about their outside interests, including design, but I doubt that it can ultimately by very good for their core business, which is playing golf.

The true value that can be brought to golf course design by most top line pro golfers is I believe not necessarily in personally designing courses, but more so in openly assisting or facilitating the design and construction of top class golf courses. And this, I believe, is naturally tending to occur more and more often as time goes by.

Look back to the mid 1990's, for example, when golf development in south-east Asia was booming. At this time, the young golf markets of Asia were crying out for "signature" golf courses, designed by famous golfers, or their companies as it was thought this would, through marketing guarantee long-term popularity and success. With money as no object, lavish signature courses were built, with many designers going to the extent of imparting pre meditated design styles seen most distinctly in bunkering, as a way of accentuating their distinctive "signatures".

When the Asian economic downturn occurred in 1997, the prohibitively high cost to maintain such unnatural features in an unwelcoming tropical

226

environment saw many of these type of courses become some of the first to succumb to severe cost cutting, thereby negatively affecting playing conditions. And so began for many clubs, a downward spiral. Poor playing conditions mean fewer golfers, which means less income, which means another round of cost cutting and so on.

Many clubs were forced to make large-scale design changes just to survive and I believe that although it was a tough period, it was a good thing to happen as it quickly facilitated the maturation of a young industry as it then was in Asia.

Nowadays we see a very much more discerning and practically oriented approach to most golf developments in the Asian region. We see more co-operation between pro golfers and career golf architects, as we see pro golfers providing endorsements of architects' work and in some cases design collaborations are formed. There is no doubt the name of a pro golfer will help kick start a project, but clients are now aware this is a short lived effect unless the course itself can stand the test of time. A career designer, who is only as good as his last project has virtually no choice but to ensure this will be the case, so depending on the project, it can often be a prudent move to employ both a pro golfer and a career architect.

One can look to the past for confirmation of this, at the home of possibly the most famous and sought after tournament in the world, the U.S. Masters.

Possibly the most famous design collaboration of all time took place when Bobby Jones facilitated the formation of Augusta National including his famous collaboration with Dr. Alister MacKenzie, the Scottish doctor of medicine and career Golf Course Architect.

The measure of credit given to each of these shining lights by the other, indicates a high level of design synergy existed between them, with the result being one of the all time great master pieces of golf course design, left now for future generations to remark upon and aspire to.

That is obvious the way to true greatness in golf course design. High Quality people, the leaders in their field acting together without personal gain as their prime motivation, in the best interests of the game of golf.

13

The Future of Golf Course Design and Development

The preceding chapters detail a view of the where the industry has come, and the choices it might make in its future. With this in mind, one might be given to wonder what is being produced in terms of new golf course developments, in light of these issues.

As a Golf Course Architect, I cannot speak for the whole industry because we do not operate in an even spread across all of it. In fact the industry is now so large, we can only realistically operate in relatively small pockets of it. As such we cannot generalise about future projects on behalf of all. However an inkling to the current trends might be gained from studying the projects presently under way in our design organisation, and considering them in light of some of the issues already raised.

The first example refers to a project I consider to be the modern day equivalent of the Asian Golf/Real Estate projects alluded to in chapter 10, however this example is a highly evolved version of a formula that even in its raw form had great commercial success.

The project consists of a 1400-acre development on previously clear-felled land about 50 kilometres from a city centre. The land sits close to a major river junction approximately 1 kilometre from the ocean outlet and consists of low river flats as well as a large section of quite interesting hilly country. In days gone by, such a development would in most cases dictate a maximum frontage golf course/real estate product mix, with the obligatory school, town centre, etc.

This project employs a rather advanced development strategy based on the concept of emphasising the natural beauty of all elements of the site. In keeping with this, real estate premiums will be achieved based on improvement and rehabilitation of the *whole* of a reasonably degraded site, rather than simply cramming as many developments as possible into each phase of the project. In following with that, the development of the site will take place in a manner that will support the lifestyles and values of the existing villagers of the site and promote specific local cultures and ways of life, as tourist attractions.

The project is consequently a very much more long-term proposition than most developers are willing to be involved in. However, the beauty of the site and the relatively fast rate of change of the attitudes of purchasers (in developmental terms) will no doubt see healthy premiums on land sales achieved as the environmental rehabilitation efforts take effect and begin to mature.

The golf course element of the project fits in line with this. The golf course will not be a linear single fairway profile arrangement as may have been employed on such a project in the past, in order to maximise residential frontage to it. Instead, it will be relatively mixed in nature, consisting of some areas of core golf and some areas of single and dual fairway profiles, to cater for those who desire direct golf course frontage.

The golf courses - there are 36 holes planned for this development - will be of rather contrasting character, based on the two basically different landforms styles that make up the site. The flat land 18 holes will be for the most part a core golf layout, accentuating the serene elements of the adjacent river. There will be large expanses of water in the form of ponds and quietly trickling waterways incorporated into the planning of the golf course. In addition, an extremely eco-friendly strategy will be put in place to drain, irrigate and upkeep the turf grasses free of weeds, whilst encouraging native plants in out-of-play areas, seeking a balance that is very close to nature.

The hilly 18 holes will be more drawn out in nature, taking advantage of the light, airy and breezy conditions that will prevail closer to the hilltops. The golf holes will be laid out with more single and dual profile arrangements, in order to take in as many different aspects of the site as possible. The golf holes will be spectacular in nature, climbing gradually higher to exposed peaks before plunging deep into the narrow valleys, which will be bound by thick tropical forest plants.

In considering our basic Golf Course design ideals, of using and accentuating the existing virtues of each and every site, one can see evidence of these ideals in *all* aspects of this development, rather than just the Golf Course elements. By considering the development land at a grass roots level, first and foremost, the developer has been able to implement a development strategy, which is very inclusive of the needs of all stakeholders.

Normally, in the early stages of a real estate/resort development, indigenous people and farmers are simply relocated. In this instance, their potential is maximised as an initial source of cash flow for the development, from sales of their produce. As well as that, their production methods are showcased as a tourist attraction.

In the initial stages of the development, the primary production element will consist of perhaps 70 to 80 percent of the works onsite. Over time, according to demand, the balance will change. However the developers will be well advised to retain elements of these activities for the long term, as they will no doubt grow into being ever more rare examples of the traditional ways of life, who's value as a tourist attraction will only grow.

This, therefore is an example of how modern day Real Estate development can be intelligently undertaken for the best interests of all stakeholders and the land.

The second example represents a type of golf course development, which has been quite noticeably rare and even absent from many markets over the past several years, but which appears to be making somewhat of a comeback.

We are referring to Golf Course Development driven solely by demand for playing of the game. In large, developed markets such as the United States, and Japan there has always been a reasonable proportion of Golf Courses that have been developed under this pretence, since the game of golf was first introduced to these areas. In other developed golf markets, these types of developments tend to come in waves, according to the cyclical nature of the development of the sport.

Australia for example has in recent years seen the demand for good golf courses severely outstrip supply in many of the major cities. In spite of this, most new golf course developments in these areas have been combined with Real Estate or other forms of land development. The reason for this is that in most cases, regardless of the potential returns achievable from the sale of golf club memberships, the returns are not as great as those achievable from other forms of development, such as residential, on any given piece of land. In addition, the cost of a piece of developable land big enough to house a golf course *by itself* usually makes a golf course development unfeasible, unless it is combined with other forms of development which have the potential to attract greater financial returns.

Put simply, in comparison to most other forms of land development, golf courses usually do not make enough profit to see them developed in isolation.

Thankfully, however, an increasing number of the authorities who govern land development around the world are now conscious of the need to restrict the urban sprawl that has already eaten up some of the most fertile, unique and naturally precious areas on our small planet.

This has given rise to the inclusion of designated "green" areas of open space as a part of many long-term government zoning and planning schemes. These land areas are often located reasonably close to population centres, and because they cannot be built-up, their monetary value stays quite low, comparative to many of their locations.

This scenario has the effect of producing a set of conditions that are conducive to the implementation of golf course developments, by effectively removing or lessening the otherwise prohibitive land cost issue. In fact, golf courses as a part of designated open space are quite often an excellent economic solution to the upkeep of this open space. Almost every city dweller likes to have more, rather than less public open space near to their homes and workplaces, however such large tracts of land can quite easily become a negative impact on society, if not properly managed.

Regardless of their social value, large parklands can have large costs attached to their maintenance and upkeep, which are very difficult to recoup. In addition, parklands quite often require extensive security measures to prevent them becoming known as havens for muggers and other small time criminals, which obviously destroys their social value.

For this reason, golf courses often act as good promoters of a healthy use for public land, in terms of social influences as well as acting in the capacity of custodians of the natural features of a site. In addition they also give the landowners a means by which to pay for the maintenance, upkeep and policing of the activities that take place on that land.

This is not to say such land needs to be totally devoted to Golf, which in the eyes of many is seen as somewhat of an elitist activity. On the contrary, a golf course and its associated club might exist primarily as the base management structure around and through which, other activities can more easily be facilitated.

Golf courses are one of the few man-made, naturally sympathetic elements that have the capacity to tap into a ready-made market of reasonably well to do patrons, who do not mind paying good money or travelling long distances to utilise well designed facilities.

With this in mind a well designed golf course can have the effect of elevating the potential income of an area that would otherwise have no attraction to paying customers of any description. In addition, golf courses can be planned to incorporate various other adjoining parks, lakes, tracks for walking, jogging or biking, whilst thereby utilising the management and maintenance structures that would in any case need to be put in place for a golf course.

The project referred to in this example is the proposed development of a golf course project on university land that was designated for golf course development by the planners of a new university campus.

Like most modern day universities, this particular facility will rely somewhat on the income of foreign, paying students for its upkeep and progression, and so must do what it can to promote itself in what is an increasingly lucrative and competitive sector of the education market.

The land slated for the development of the University and golf course is supplied by the government, and as such, the land cost issue is alleviated as per the above explanation. The university, not being expert in the field of golf course development, have thereafter called for developers to design, build and manage a golf course on a turnkey arrangement.

In light of this, the inclusion of a golf course in the planning of the University is, I believe a very shrewd decision, for the following reasons:

a) The university can, through tendering the development of a facility, take advantage of the benefits of a world-class golf course without incurring any costs or liabilities.
b) The inclusion of a world-class golf course will raise the profile of the University in an area of the market it would otherwise not directly reach. Well paying foreign golfers will be more likely to send their children to study there if their first impressions of the University are through a game of golf on a very high standard golf course.
c) The development of a golf course without the land cost constraints will assist in ensuring the viability of the golf course.
d) In an area with a distinct shortage of golf courses in terms of local demand, the golf course will without doubt be well frequented by local golfers, ensuring cash flow and assisting in the social integration of the University with the local community.
e) The structure of the arrangement means the golf course can be developed with the emphasis on absolute maximisation of the design and golfer experience elements of the project. This will facilitate a mostly, if not all "core" style layout, which can only assist in matters of maintenance, upkeep and playability.

The current 27-hole layout has the clubhouse located centrally; accessible just off the main road, which is also the university's loop road, circumnavigating the campus. The golf course will sit comfortably adjacent to the main campus, on low-lying, gently undulating land next to an existing river tributary. The golf course will create a very pleasant green image at the entry to the campus, as well as providing spectacular long views from many areas of the campus, which is somewhat elevated in comparison to the golf course land.

The golf course will be very complimentary to the Campus, socially, visually as well as economically.

The 3rd example deals with the category of Resort Golf, and concepts which endeavour to bring a higher level of excellence to such types of golf courses. In days gone by, the question of whether a golf course was considered great, by world standards depended on the natural site attributes and whether they were conducive to the production of particular playing properties that are desired and are generally present on any great golf course.

Nowadays, with modern construction technology, the features required of a great golf course can be artificially created. This does not mean every new golf course can automatically be considered as great, as there are many other vital ingredients that must be included in order to attain a degree of greatness in the finished product. In the past, most great courses only existed in places like The United Kingdom, Ireland, California and Southern Australia where the weather and natural landscapes easily lent themselves to the creation of great golf, created at that time with limited available resources, both human and machine.

Nowadays, the distribution of great golf courses is much less concentrated and golf courses with an element of greatness exist in several wide and varied locations around the world. This is good for the game of golf, in that it gives a taste of quality to more people in more places. It does, however create somewhat of a dilemma when planning an international golfing vacation.

Golfers do not mind travelling long distances to play good, high quality golf courses, however golfers rarely travel long distances or internationally to play *just one* great golf course. The challenge is to find golfing destinations where golfers can play a different and equally great golf course every day of their vacation, for 3 days, 5 days or even for a whole week. Ideally these golf courses should be in close proximity to each other and a central accommodation facility, to eliminate or at least cut down on the need to waste one's time on transfers, once a holiday destination has been reached.

Ideally such areas should also have nearby facilities for families and especially children. This enables golfers to bring their families along on a golfing vacation and be sure that everyone will enjoy it.

With an allowance for a different golf course for every day of a weeklong vacation, and other associated facilities, those golfers with families can play golf comfortable in the knowledge their families have a multitude of ways to enjoy themselves. Golfers may for example play early mornings in order to spend the afternoons with their families at some of the other facilities, preferably without the hassles of traffic and transport to confuse and slow the transition between activities.

If the relationship between golf and all other facilities enables complete optimisation of precious vacation time, whilst providing a vast array of recreational choices for all members of a family or group, then one would without doubt be in a very sought after destination.

What we are describing here is possibly the ultimate in golfing destinations, being a place where the families of golfers would be just as keen and happy to visit and stay, as would be the golfers themselves.

This could be described as somewhat of a "super-resort", to which the concept of a holiday, or beach resort is a fairly distant relation. A normal beach resort is essentially a place to relax, to unwind. As a part of that process, patrons undertake various activities, such as golf, tennis, swimming, etc, usually on a fairly casual basis. This is quite different to a specific golfing vacation, where total relaxation is not necessarily the aim.

Golfing vacations combine the enjoyment of the structured challenge, competition and discovery of several games of golf, with the after-golf activities that are preferably as unique as possible, in order to make the whole experience more memorable and enjoyable. These are vacations for people who like to have plenty to do and see when they're away from home, with the option to withdraw and relax for certain periods, as desired.

Purely golf-orientated facilities are beginning to appear in various remote locations, especially in the U.S. These are golf courses built on unique sites, regardless of their accessibility. They are frequented by the rich, who are prepared to pay for exclusivity, in order to for example, have a whole golf course to themselves for the few days they are visiting, as well as the chartered flights required just get to some of these places. Such golf destinations could be described as boutique facilities, and are likely to cater to a more exclusive, rather than inclusive spread of patrons, as they are not the type of places one would bring an extended family group or conduct a company trip.

This however could be seen as an indicator of the future of Golf Course Development, not necessarily in terms of exclusivity, but more in terms of the growing amounts of disposable incomes that more and more people are able to allocate to their recreational activities.

Indeed, more and more people recognise that quality comes with a price, and more and more people are becoming more and more tired with mediocrity in an age when an unprecedented amount of people have the wherewithal to actually purchase quality. Without doubt, there is a growing trend towards the pursuit of excellence, and this is especially apparent in leisure activities.

People want the perfect holiday. They want to see pristine examples of nature, not degraded ones. They want exciting activities, not boring ones. They want great golf courses, without hassles and headaches.

Early versions of these "super golf resorts" have began to appear, which have one golf course for each day of a vacation, however none that I am aware of have yet been structured to provide the ultimate, and perfectly integrated golf vacation.

Certain organisations have discovered that like fast-food outlets, the more golf courses there are in one locality, the more business they all generally attract.

This has the effect of generating high levels of use of a golf facility; however it does not in itself give golf vacationers the experience of seemingly endless amounts of absolutely pristine golf. Nor does it package such experiences in a fully integrated structure that caters to the every need of each golfer *as well as* their families.

In terms of golf, there has been a huge amount of recent innovations in the areas of water conditioning, as well as turf breeding and management. Because of this, it is now physically possible, by my reckoning to create such a golf facility whose pristine condition has barely, if at all been conceived in the minds of any developers, let alone golfers. I am led to believe that similar opportunities exist in the evolution of other complimentary family based activities.

What's more, the costs, in both monetary and environmental terms are rapidly decreasing, whilst the demand for such excellence continues to rapidly increase.

On that basis we can conclude that quite soon, somewhere on earth, golf course developments will appear which possess mind-blowing proportions in terms of design, construction, maintenance, service, naturally harmonious aesthetics, environmental stewardship, and integration to other forms of nature and leisure activities.

Golf still has a long way to go in terms of evolution and change, and whilst the future is exciting and hopefully very bright, we must endeavour to remember, through all of this excitement, what brought us to this point, and where we would like to go with it in the future.

It is up to us, as Golf Course Architects, Developers, Clubs, Golfers and lovers of such a great and wonderful pastime, sport and game, to assist in ensuring all development and change occurs in the best interests of golf and the well-being of the people who play golf, as well as the land that is borrowed for the playing of golf.

REFERENCES

Pease, Allan and Barbara
"Why men don't listen and women can't read maps"
Sydney, Pease International, 2003

Chopra, Deepak
"Golf for enlightenment"
London, Random House, 2003

Printed in the United Kingdom
by Lightning Source UK Ltd.
127261UK00001B/56/A